The Supreme Court and American Constitutionalism

The Ashbrook Series on Constitutional Politics

Sponsored by the John M. Ashbrook Center for Public Affairs at Ashland University

General Editors: Peter W. Schramm and Bradford P. Wilson

American Political Parties and Constitutional Politics

Separation of Powers and Good Government

The Supreme Court and American Constitutionalism

The Supreme Court and American Constitutionalism

Edited by

Bradford P. Wilson
and Ken Masugi

ROWMAN & LITTLEFIELD PUBLISHERS, INC.
Lanham • Boulder • New York • Oxford

ROWMAN & LITTLEFIELD PUBLISHERS, INC.

Published in the United States of America
by Rowman & Littlefield Publishers, Inc.
4720 Boston Way, Lanham, Maryland 20706

12 Hid's Copse Road
Cummor Hill, Oxford OX2 9JJ, England

British Library Cataloguing in Publication Information Available

Library of Congress Cataloging-in-Publication Data

The Supreme Court and American constitutionalism / [edited by]
  Bradford P. Wilson and Ken Masugi.
      p.   cm.—(Ashbrook series on constitutional politics)
  Includes bibliographical referencesd and index.
    ISBN 0-8476-8658-2 (cloth : alk. paper).—ISBN 0-8476-8659-0
(pbk. : alk. paper)
    1. Judicial power—United States.   2. Constitutional law—United
States.   3. United States. Supreme Court.   I. Wilson, Bradford P.,
1951—   .   II. Masugi, Ken.   III. Series.
KF5130.S87   1997
347.73'262—dc21   97-30588
                                                           CIP

ISBN 0-8476-8658-2 (cloth : alk. paper)
ISBN 0-8476-8659-0 (pbk. : alk. paper)

Printed in the United States of America

∞ ™ The paper used in this publication meets the minimum requirements
of American National Standard for Information Sciences—Permanence of
Paper for Printed Library Materials, ANSI Z39.48—1984.

CONTENTS

PREFACE

THIS VOLUME COMPLETES a trilogy of books on American constitutionalism conceived for Rowman & Littlefield's Ashbrook Series on Constitutional Politics. It therefore takes its place alongside *American Political Parties & Constitutional Politics* (1993) and *Separation of Powers and Good Government* (1994).

Each of the three volumes addresses a distinct set of institutions and themes. What was said in the preface to the second volume is true of the trilogy as a whole: "It represents no school of thought, no consensus of opinion. As there are different authors, so there are different views and scholarly interests represented." Behind this diversity, however, lies a common intention. Each of the volumes brings together American political scientists and legal scholars who have established reputations for taking the Constitution seriously as the architectonic law of the United States. Through their contributions to the Ashbrook Series, these scholars have helped to reintroduce students of politics to a distinctively constitutional analysis of American political institutions.

This mode of analysis is at once recognizable to those familiar with the political discourse of the 18th and 19th centuries. For most of this century, however, constitutionally informed analysis has operated in the shadows of a political science that prefers to see the Constitution as only marginally relevant to the ideas and activities of political actors. The new political science has been accompanied by the rise of a political rhetoric silent about the Constitution, a phenomenon lamented by Walter Berns in this volume. A properly constitutional analysis, on the other hand, approaches the study of political institutions and activities in terms not only of their efficacy in satisfying the infinite variety of human wants, but also of their relation to the forms and ends of republican constitutionalism.

The American Constitution was written neither to create work for lawyers nor to provide an object of contemplation, free of practical concern, for scholars and their students. According to our founding documents, it was written to form a more perfect union, one in which Americans could better secure their rights and pursue their private and public happiness. In explaining the purpose of constitutional government in these terms, the Founders provided a standard of political health by which their work could and should be judged.

vii

In effect, they compel any who desire to understand American politics to consider the soundness of the constitutional design in light of its ambition to frame a democratic way of life more competent, more decent, and more free than any other polity in human history.

This book takes as its subject that part of the constitutional structure that wields the judicial power of the United States, with a necessary emphasis on the Supreme Court. A cursory reading of the debate over the ratification of the Constitution reveals that the federal judiciary, with its powers and its jurisdiction, was an object of both fear and favor. To some, like Alexander Hamilton, the federal judiciary was to be the guardian of the higher law of the Constitution. The reason of the Framers embodied in the Constitution would be championed by experienced and learned judges whose independence from ordinary politics would make possible their dependence on the law of the Constitution. To others, the powers and independence of the federal judiciary posed the greatest of threats to constitutional government. In their view, judges would be empowered, in the words of an Anti-Federalist, "to mould the government into almost any shape they pleased."

We offer these essays as a contemporary effort to understand the role the Supreme Court was meant to play, the role it has in fact played, and the role it ought to play in our republic as we enter the third century of the Constitution's abiding presence among us. This volume grows out of a conference held at Ashland University in April 1996 and sponsored by the John M. Ashbrook Center for Public Affairs.

Bradford P. Wilson
Princeton, NJ

Ken Masugi
Colorado Springs, CO

Part I

THE SUPREME COURT AS REPUBLICAN SCHOOLMASTER

THE SUPREME COURT AS REPUBLICAN SCHOOLMASTER: CONSTITUTIONAL INTERPRETATION AND THE "GENIUS OF THE PEOPLE"

Walter Berns

THE FRAMERS OF THE Constitution believed, or, at least, would have us believe, that they had solved the political problem facing the nation in 1787 by devising a structure that provided a "republican remedy for the diseases most incident to republican government." Had they been more candid, they would have said the diseases most incident to *democratic* government, for, although they insisted that the government was "wholly popular," by which they meant it was not a "mixed" regime, there was no denying the fact that it was not a democracy, certainly not a direct democracy.[1]

Plainly the Framers—or to be more precise, Publius—made no effort to conceal this fact during the ratification debates. On the contrary, they praised the Constitution for putting some distance between the people and the organs of government. For example, they said that the Constitution would exclude "*the people in their collective capacity*" from any share in the government.[2] Accordingly, their Constitution provided a president to be chosen not by the people but by electors who, having made their choice, would immediately disband; it provided a Senate chosen not by the people but by the state legisla-

[1] Alexander Hamilton, James Madison, and John Jay, *The Federalist*, ed. Jacob E. Cooke (Middletown, CT: Wesleyan University Press, 1961), nos. 10 and 14.
[2] *Federalist* no. 63, 428.

tures, each state, regardless of the size of its population, being entitled to choose two; it provided a House of Representatives chosen not
by a majority of the whole people ("*the people in their collective capacity*") but by majorities or pluralities within each of the districts into
which each state would be divided; and it provided a Supreme Court
with the power to veto popular legislation and with members who
would, in effect, serve for life.

They also said that "the accumulation of all powers, legislative,
executive, and judiciary, in the same hands, whether of one, a few, or
many, and whether hereditary, self-appointed, or *elective*, may justly
be pronounced the very definition of tyranny."[3] Accordingly, the
Constitution provided a system of divided power and checks and balances, and it was understood that what was most in need of being
checked were popular majorities. Popular majorities too readily become factious majorities, and it was for them especially that the Framers proposed a "remedy."[4]

Not everyone was confident that their remedy would prove to be
sufficient. The Framers might well insist that, in the absence of "better motives," safety could be had by dividing and balancing powers.[5]
But the Anti-Federalists were not persuaded; they would depend on
those better motives, on the good sense of the people at large. They
held that a "republican, or free government, can only exist where the
body of the people are virtuous, and where property is pretty equally
divided."[6] Nor were the Anti-Federalists the only ones to have doubts
about the viability of what has come to be called the "procedural
state." At the close of the Constitutional Convention the venerable
Benjamin Franklin was asked by a Mrs. Powell of Philadelphia: "Well,
doctor, what have we got, a republic or a monarchy?" Franklin replied, "A republic, if you can keep it." Which is to say, the Framers
had done what they were asked to do and whether they had done well
would henceforth depend on the people. The people had ratified
the Constitution, but would they continue to abide by its rules and
restrictions? Or, as Ralph Lerner puts the question (in the first essay
to speak of the Supreme Court as republican schoolmaster), "would
the system 'wholly popular' survive, even thrive, on talents wholly
popular?" It was surely not something to be taken for granted.

Lerner says "it was axiomatic," for thinking revolutionaries,

[3] *Federalist* no. 47, 324. Emphasis supplied.
[4] *Federalist* no. 10, 65.
[5] *Federalist* no. 51, 349.
[6] Centinel (Samuel Bryan?), in *The Complete Anti-Federalist*, ed. Herbert J. Storing
(Chicago and London: University of Chicago Press, 1981), 2:139.

"that securing the republic depended on first forming a certain kind of citizenry," and that "every organ of the new republican government could be expected to do its part in this project, each in the mode most becoming to it."[7] Legislator, executive, and judge alike, but each in his own way, were expected to provide the people with an education in republicanism.

Their ability to do this would seem to depend on their enjoying the confidence of the people, and, at the same time, on being somewhat removed from them. For this reason, probably less could be expected of the legislature, and particularly the more popular House of Representatives, which would be directly dependent on the people. Publius says that "the people commonly *intend* the PUBLIC GOOD," but they are sometimes mistaken about the means of promoting it. When that happens, when the "interests of the people are at variance with their inclinations, it is the duty of the persons whom they have appointed to be the guardians of those interests, to withstand the temporary delusions, in order to give them time and opportunity for more cool and sedate reflection." But Publius has to acknowledge the possibility of "parasites and sycophants" who, when seeking the people's suffrage, will "flatter their prejudices [in order] to betray their interests."[8] Even at best, legislators will be more likely to see themselves as servants of the people rather than their teachers or exemplars.

More might be expected of the executive, especially of a George Washington. During his eight years in office, Washington delivered eleven addresses, ten of them to the Congress and one, on a special occasion, directly to his "Friends, and Fellow Citizens." This, his Farewell Address, is nothing so much as a lecture on American republicanism: the patriot's duty to serve his country (and then to retire to private life); the pride associated with being an American citizen; the common interest binding the regions (and the dangers which may disturb the union, including the dangerous spirit of party); the connection between the Constitution and liberty; the need to avoid involvement in Europe's quarrels, to the end of "remain[ing] one people"; and, of course, the dependence of political prosperity on religion and morality.

Upon taking office, John Adams followed Washington's example by emphasizing the virtues of the republican Constitution: "What

[7] Ralph Lerner, *The Thinking Revolutionary: Principle and Practice in the New Republic* (Chicago and London: Cornell University Press, 1987), 91. This essay was originally published in the 1967 issue of *The Supreme Court Review*, 127–180.

[8] *Federalist* no. 71, 482–83.

other form of government, indeed, can so well deserve our esteem and love?" Thomas Jefferson continued the practice in his First Inaugural: "We are all Republicans, we are all Federalists," and all are obliged "to bear in mind this sacred principle, that though the will of the majority is in all cases to prevail, that will to be rightful must be reasonable; that the minority possesses their equal rights, which equal law must protect, and to violate would be oppression."

In 1825, John Quincy Adams devoted the major part of his Inaugural Address to the Constitution and, in the process, provided the people with an understanding of what a president, when he takes the oath of office, swears to preserve, protect, and defend, and why that Constitution deserves to be preserved, protected, and defended. "We now receive it," he said by way of summary, "as a precious inheritance from those to whom we are indebted for its establishment, doubly bound by the examples which they have left us and by the blessings which we have enjoyed as the fruits of their labors to transmit the same unimpaired to the succeeding generation."

These early presidents set an example for those who were to follow them, at least until the turn of the century. Only Lincoln and Grant, each in his Second Inaugural, failed specifically to refer to or speak of the Constitution. But after William McKinley, references to it became the exception rather than the rule. Theodore Roosevelt made no mention of it; William Howard Taft had something to say about the three post-Civil War amendments, but Woodrow Wilson (who elsewhere suggested that it be scrapped) did not utter the word "Constitution" in either of his Inaugural Addresses, nor did Warren Harding or Herbert Hoover. Calvin Coolidge acknowledged it in passing, but Franklin Roosevelt, after a perfunctory reference to it in his Third Inaugural, spoke of it only in his Fourth, and then only to complain of its alleged imperfections. Harry Truman ignored it altogether, as did Dwight D. Eisenhower, John F. Kennedy, and Lyndon Johnson. Richard Nixon mentioned that he had taken an oath to uphold and defend it; and, as one might expect, considering the conditions under which he assumed the office, Gerald Ford referred to it in 1974; but from Jimmy Carter came not a word about the Constitution. Instead, he appealed to the Bible, quoting this passage in Micah 6:8: "He hath shown thee, O man, what is good. . . . [A]nd what doth the Lord require of thee, but to do justly, and to love mercy, and to walk humbly with thy God." That said, Mr. Carter proceeded to walk proudly down Pennsylvania Avenue with his wife in hand. Sounding a note that has, alas, echoed among Republicans ever since, Ronald Reagan said that "in this present crisis, government is not the solution to our problem; government is the problem." George Bush mentioned that he had taken the same oath taken by George Washington; and, finally, Bill Clinton, uttering not a word about the Constitution, called upon us to "give this capital back to the people to whom it belongs," then handed the microphone over to Maya Angelou who recited a poem about a rock, a river, and a tree.

So much, then, for the possibility that presidents might serve as republican schoolmasters, reminding the people of the excellence of the Constitution and their duties under it. Over the years, the office has been democratized, so that presidents, like the typical legislator, see themselves as servants rather than as teachers of the people. Or if, like the first Roosevelt, they view the office as a "bully pulpit," it is only because it allows them to preach partisan sermons. No one objects, or no one except political scientist Jeffrey Tulis who points out that the Framers saw the office as above partisan politics and that, as late as 1840, a president was censured for delivering partisan speeches.[9]

Jimmy Carter epitomized the new understanding of the office, indeed, of constitutional government, when he spoke of a "government as good as the people." That might stand as a measure of the distance we have come since 1787, except that a President Ross Perot would take us further still. Campaigning for the office in 1992, he promised, if elected, to institute an "electronic town hall," or a government by call-in show. The people, under no obligation to think before they talk, would tell him what they wanted, and he promised to oblige them. He further promised to resign if he failed to oblige them. Under his care, the Framers' "wholly popular" government would become a government incapable to doing anything unpopular.

What of the judiciary? Lerner begins his account by acknowledging the obvious: that judges are empowered to decide certain cases and controversies, not to serve as a "propagandist, haranguer, or part-time philosopher." And yet, he goes on, "a thoughtful judge, reflecting on the close connection between judicial power and public opinion, might have reason to wonder whether the judge's task narrowly conceived is adequately conceived."[10] Narrowly conceived, his task is to decide cases and controversies and, in the process, to "guard the Constitution and the rights of individuals from the effects of those ill humors, which the arts of designing men, or the influence of particular conjunctures, sometimes disseminate among the people themselves."[11] The thoughtful judge, however, knowing that his deci-

[9] Jeffrey K. Tulis, *The Rhetorical Presidency* (Princeton, N.J.: Princeton University Press, 1987), 75.

[10] Lerner, *The Thinking Revolutionary*, 91.

[11] *Federalist* no. 78, 527.

sions might be politically unpopular, will go on to wonder what he might do to make them acceptable to a democratic people.

He might, of course, craft persuasive opinions in support of his judgments and, like the great Chief Justice John Marshall, see to it that he speaks for a unanimous court. Marshall's predecessors did more than that, or, in the event, did other than that. Required by a parsimonious Congress to go on circuit—in effect, to leave the capital and conduct their business among the people—they chose to speak directly to the people through the medium of the grand jury charge. In Lerner's words, the early justices (John Jay, Oliver Ellsworth, James Iredell, James Wilson) "were quick to see and seize the opportunity to proselytize for the new government and to inculcate habits and teachings most necessary in their view for the maintenance of self-government": that there is a connection between self-restraint and true liberty, that genuine liberty depends on law-abidingness, that it is the individual's interest to submit to decisions made by constitutional majorities, etc. In a word, they instructed the people in republicanism, and what is striking is that they did so not with appeals to their authority but, rather, to a common interest, an interest shared by judge and people alike: "It cannot be too strongly impressed on the minds of us all," Jay said, "how greatly our individual prosperity depends on our national prosperity, and how greatly our national prosperity depends on a well-organized, vigorous government."[12]

It was probably inevitable that this use of the grand jury charge would be abused, that admonishments to be good republicans would become admonishments to be good Federalists, or, in the case of Justice Samuel Chase, would become partisan harangues. For this he was impeached (but not convicted) and, more to the point here, his abuse of the practice led to its disuse. From that time to the present, if the justices were to serve as teachers of republicanism, it would have to be in the ordinary course of deciding cases and controversies.

That they were able to do this is largely the work of John Marshall, the greatest of the Supreme Court's republican schoolmasters. Asked, in the celebrated case of *Marbury v. Madison*, whether the Court might issue a writ of mandamus, Marshall reversed the usual and logical order of procedure, deliberately postponing the answer to that question to the last, so that he might deliver a lecture on the virtues of constitutional government. In the course of that lecture, he declared that the executive must obey the law, that the laws, to be valid, must conform to the Constitution, and (this by way of suggesting rather than declaring) that the Court has, as it is now generally

---

[12] Lerner, *The Thinking Revolutionary*, 99, 100, and passim.

acknowledged to have, the final word in determining the constitutionality of acts of Congress.

Constitutional government is first of all government by due or formal process, and that process, that *formal* process is prescribed in the Constitution. The problem, anticipated by the Framers and later elaborated by Alexis de Tocqueville, arises from the fact that "men living in democratic ages do not readily comprehend the utility of forms." Forms serve as restraints, but, Tocqueville points out, this is precisely what "renders [them] so useful to freedom; for their chief merit is to serve as a barrier between the strong and the weak."[13] That, over the course of the years, we Americans have been willing to be governed "formally," rather than expeditiously, is largely Marshall's doing. He taught us to venerate the Constitution and its Founders. He did this by initiating the process of determining the validity of legislation by its compatibility with the Constitution, which has the consequence of identifying constitutionality not only with legitimacy but with wisdom, the wisdom of the Founders who, as Marshall would have it, could do no wrong.

Justice Felix Frankfurter complained of this in his dissent in the 1943 flag salute case. "The tendency of focusing attention on constitutionality is to make [it] synonymous with wisdom, to regard a law as all right if it is constitutional." Such an attitude, he said, "is a great enemy of liberalism."[14] Well, not entirely. Certainly wisdom is not *synonymous* with constitutionality, or foolishness with unconstitutionality, but it is not foolish—at least, it is not simply foolish—to confuse them. In each case, a connection of some sort exists, and constitutionalism requires the people to recognize it, to believe that constitutionality and wisdom and unconstitutionality and foolishness are somehow related.

James Madison was concerned about this even before the Constitution was ratified. It was this concern that led him to take public issue with his friend and colleague Thomas Jefferson who, in his draft of a constitution for the state of Virginia, had suggested that questions of constitutionality be turned over to the people themselves. Madison acknowledged that the plan was consistent with republican principle, that, as constitutions derive from the people, it is appropriate that the people determine whether their terms have been violated. Nevertheless, and despite the great authority attached to the

[13] Alexis de Tocqueville, *Democracy in America*, vol. 2, book 4, ch. 7 ("Continuation of the Preceding Chapters").

[14] *West Virginia State Board of Education v. Barnette*, 319 U.S. 624, 670 (1943). Dissenting opinion.

name of its author, Madison felt obliged to state his objections—his
"insuperable objections"—to the plan. It was both impracticable, he
said, and dangerous, and dangerous because, among other reasons,
it would undermine the stability of government. "As every appeal to
the people would carry an implication of some defect in the government," he wrote in *Federalist* 49, "frequent appeals would, in great
measure, deprive the government of that veneration that time be-
stows on every thing, and without which perhaps the wisest and freest
governments would not possess the requisite stability."[15]

Ever the republican schoolmaster, Madison would have the people identify the Constitution with wisdom, to respect it and its Framers, for only then would they be willing to be guided by it when
decisions, made in its name, are otherwise unpopular among them.

It would seem to be obvious that, of the various organs of the new
government, the Framers expected the judiciary to be best situated to
do its part in the "forming [of] a certain kind of citizenry." Strangely,
they said nothing of the states, nothing to suggest that the states
might be, as the Anti-Federalists insisted they were, schools for citizenship where "the education of youth, both public and private, is attended to, their industrious and economical habits maintained,
[and] their moral character and that assemblage of virtues supported, which is necessary for the happiness of individuals and of
nations."[16]

The Framers were familiar with the argument—they read it in
the press and heard it from the lips of Patrick Henry when the Constitution was being debated in Virginia—and Madison was not alone
in holding it to be a chimerical idea "to suppose that any form of
government will secure liberty or happiness without any virtue in the
people," but, as I say, they made no mention of the states in this
context. Instead, they relied on the organs of the national government, and especially the judiciary, to form the character of citizens,
or as Marshall put it in his biography of Washington, they expected
the Constitution to influence the "habits of thinking and acting."
Perhaps they took it for granted that the states would do what the
national government was unable, even forbidden, to do: support religion, sustain the family, provide a moral education in its public
schools, and, not least, by being closer to the people, make it more

[15]*Federalist* no. 49, 340. This and the preceding paragraph are taken from my
book, *Taking the Constitution Seriously* (New York: Simon and Schuster, 1987), 189–
190.
[16]Mercy Warren, *History of the Rise, Progress and Termination of the American Revolution*, in *The Complete Anti-Federalist*, 1:21.

likely that they will learn the arts of self-government. All this the states did (more or less) until, in the *Gitlow* case in 1925, the Supreme Court began the process of incorporating the restrictions on the national government set down in the Bill of Rights into the Fourteenth Amendment, thereby making them applicable to the states.[17] As a consequence, a number of the laws, institutions, and practices that the states saw as essential to responsible self-government have been subjected to judicial scrutiny and been found wanting. The Court has done many good and necessary things with this new power—new because, prior to incorporation, it lacked jurisdiction in these matters—but, in the process, it has neglected its old role as republican schoolmaster.

Indeed, Oliver Wendell Holmes, Jr., next to Marshall probably the most celebrated of Supreme Court justices, denied that the Court had such a role. As he put it, "If my fellow citizens want to go to Hell I will help them. It's my job."[18] It is not clear where he picked up that idea, but it could not have been from anything written by the Framers. Their view was that the justices were to be "faithful guardians of the Constitution [even] where legislative invasions of it had been instigated by the major voice of the community."[19] In a word, the power to invalidate legislation on constitutional grounds (judicial review, as the practice came to be called), is an essential feature of republican government.

Holmes was willing to exercise the power, especially with respect to state legislation, but not because he thought his job was to defend republican government. On the contrary, like Senator Stephen A. Douglas who, as the champion of "popular sovereignty," did not care whether the people of the territories voted slavery up or down, Holmes, in his *Gitlow* dissent, said, "if, in the long run, the beliefs expressed in proletarian dictatorship are destined to be accepted by the dominant forces of the community, the only meaning of free speech is that they should be given their chance and have their way."[20] Or, as he had put it in the *Abrams* case six years earlier, the truth or validity of an idea is determined in the marketplace.[21]

[17] *Gitlow* v. *New York*, 268 U.S. 652 (1925). I shall say nothing in this essay about the effect of the centralization of power on self-government at the state and local level.

[18] Holmes to Harold Laski, March 4, 1920. *Holmes-Laski Letters*, ed. Mark de Wolfe Howe, abridged by Alger Hiss (New York: Atheneum, 1963), 1:194.

[19] *Federalist* no. 78, 528.

[20] *Gitlow*, 268 U.S. at 673. Dissenting opinion.

[21] "But when men have realized that time has upset many fighting faiths, they may come to believe even more than they believe the very foundations of their own conduct that the ultimate good desired is better reached by free trade in

With Holmes came the idea that now governs much of our public life, that republicanism, as the Founders understood it, is just one of those "isms," or "ideologies," or—Holmes's term—"fighting faiths," all of them equal insofar as none of them is true. And from this came the constitutional right of anyone to run for public office, regardless of the cause he espouses;[22] and the right of all to speak regardless of what they have to say;[23] and the right to burn the American flag, the symbol of our republic.[24] Originally understood as protection of the right to participate in government, freedom of speech is now seen as protection of the right not to be governed.

Generally speaking, the Court's power to review state legislation under the new or augmented Fourteenth Amendment has led to an expansion of private rights and a corresponding contraction of public authority, with little or no thought of the public consequences. Citizens have rights, and all persons "born or naturalized in the United States and subject to the jurisdiction thereof, are citizens," but they are not born good citizens. George Will had this in mind when he said, "human beings are biological facts, but citizens suited to self-government are social artifacts."[25] Knowing this, the states have long understood that they bear the responsibility for the education of children to the end of fostering the qualities required for republican citizenship: self-restraint, respect for others, civility, public spiritedness. Children are born self-interested, but these other qualities have to be acquired.

For this purpose, states encouraged the recitation of prayers, or the reading of Bible verses, at the beginning of the public school day; authorized a period of silence in public schools for meditation or voluntary prayer; allowed a clergyman to deliver a non-sectarian prayer at a graduate ceremony. Also for this purpose, the states prohibited the use of foul language in public places; expelled students for distributing newspapers filled with such language; removed "anti-American, anti-Christian, anti-Semitic, and just plain filthy" books from public school libraries. But, because children also have rights,

ideas,—that the best test of truth is the power of the thought to get itself accepted in the competition of the market. . . . That, at any rate, is the theory of our Constitution." *Abrams v. United States,* 250 U.S. 616, 630 (1919). Dissenting opinion.

[22] *Communist Party of Indiana v. Whitcomb,* 414 U.S. 441 (1974).

[23] *Nationalist Socialist Party v. Village of Skokie,* 432 U.S. 43 (1977); 434 U.S. 1327 (1977).

[24] *Texas v. Johnson,* 491 U.S. 397 (1989); *United States v. Eichman,* 496 U.S. 310 (1990).

[25] George Will, "The Cultural Contradictions of Conservatism," *The Public Interest,* no. 123, (spring 1996): 45.

each of these practices was declared unconstitutional.[26] As for the schools themselves, they've gotten the word. Today they are more likely to teach self-esteem than self-restraint, and as likely to teach multiculturalism as Americanism.

The censorship cases deserve another word because, in the process of deciding them, the Court has served as schoolmaster, or a sort of schoolmaster. It has taught us to despise the very idea of censorship. By putting its imprimatur on the principles advanced assiduously by the American Civil Liberties Union, it has made it impossible for even public spirited persons to favor censorship: Mary Elizabeth (Tipper) Gore, for example, who mounted a campaign against the recording industry and its sexually explicit rock lyrics and called upon Congress to do something, but said she "detested" censorship; and Senator Robert Dole who denounced Hollywood executives, charging that their films and music, with their "messages of casual violence and even more casual sex [have a corrupting effect on] our children," but went on to emphasize that he was not calling for censorship. Even jury members refuse to censor, finding nothing objectionable in Robert Mapplethorpe's photographs or 2 Live Crew's lyrics. Censorship is thought to be un-democratic and un-American.

Liberals and conservatives alike now agree that any governmental regulation of what we are allowed to read, see, or hear is simply out of the question. The law may properly be concerned with physical health—and we expect the president to set a good example by jogging around the ellipse every morning, and the government puts warnings on cigarette packages—but not with moral health; moral health or moral education is the concern of parents, not of the government. "Governments don't raise children, parents do." For this insight we are indebted to President Clinton himself. Like "Tipper" Gore and Senator Dole, he wants parents to serve as censors.

In his 1996 State of the Union Address, he called upon parents to "take more responsibility for their children's education and turn off the TV." Sound advice, that, but he apparently doubted that parents would follow it, because he went on to say that he intended to invite—and subsequently did invite—the television and film producers to the White House and persuade them to clean up their acts. But he must have had his doubts about this, too, because he subsequently

---

[26] *Engel v. Vitale*, 370 U.S. 421 (1963); *School District of Abington v. Schempp*, 374 U.S. 203 (1963); *Wallace v. Jaffree*, 472 U.S. 38 (1985); *Lee v. Weisman*, 505 U.S. 577 (1992); *Cohen v. California*, 403 U.S. 15 (1971); *Papish v. Board of Curators*, 410 U.S. 667 (1973); *Board of Education v. Pico*, 457 U.S. 853 (1982).

asked Congress for a law requiring television producers to rate their programs, and television sets to be equipped with devices, the so-called V-chips, allowing parents to block out the programs they regard as undesirable, preventing them from being seen by their children. But what gives him confidence that parents will be able to make these decisions or, more to the point, having made them, be able to enforce them? How can parents control their children's moral education at a time when no one else is seriously concerned with it?

Parents could more readily do this in the past because they had help from the law, mostly state laws that marked the distinction between the licit and illicit, the legitimate and the illegitimate, and, by so doing, served to reinforce the moral judgments made by parents. But the Supreme Court put an end to these laws when, some thirty years ago, it put the censors out to pasture. As a result, our public figures are reduced to delivering sermons.

Hillary Rodham Clinton, for example, recently advised the young—or was it only young girls? It doesn't matter because if the girls were to follow her advice, the boys would follow it of necessity—advised them to wait until they are 21 before they have sex. But in a culture saturated by sex—sexual films, sexual books, sexual magazines, sexual advertisements, sexual heroes and heroines, even sexual rights—there is little chance that her advice will be followed.

Does it matter? Here is a passage from a 1795 essay by Noah Webster on the education of citizens:

> [The influence of women] in controlling the manners of the nation is another reason [for paying attention to their education]. Women, once abandoned, may be instrumental in corrupting society, but such is the delicacy of the sex and such the restraints which custom imposes on them that they are generally the last to be corrupted. . . . A fondness for the company and conversations of ladies of character may be considered as a young man's best security against the attractiveness of a dissipated life. For this reason, society requires that females should be well educated and extend their influence as far as possible over the other sex.[27]

Not the Supreme Court but women as republican schoolmasters! How quaint this would sound to our actresses and rock stars. Yet Tocqueville provided a thematic treatment of the subject in the second volume of his masterpiece, *Democracy in America*, the best book ever

[27] Noah Webster, "On the Education of Youth in America," in *Essays on Education in the Early Republic*, ed. Frederick Rudolph (Cambridge: Harvard University Press, 1965), 68–69.

written about us. A decent popular government, he argued, depends on sound mores—*moeurs,* in the French, meaning morals/manners—and, he said, "women shape mores."[28]

Was he right? Or, can we learn to live with all the sex and violence to which we, particularly the young, are now subjected? Or, as Noah Webster and the other Founders of this country would have put the question, can people be trusted to govern others if, by acting on every impulse, sexual or otherwise, they prove to be incapable of governing themselves? Some of us might live long enough to learn the answer.

[28] Tocqueville, *Democracy in America,* vol. 1, ch. 17 ("Principal Causes Which Tend to Maintain the Democratic Republic in the United States") and vol. 2, book. 3, ch. 9 ("Education of Young Women in the United States"). Tocqueville also had much to say about the importance of the Constitution, as well as the importance of lawyers, lawyers as republican schoolmasters; but much has happened to the legal profession since his day. Our lawyers are trained in the schools where the talk is of a "living Constitution." Under a living constitution, judges ask not what the Constitution permits but, rather, what the times require. Robert Bork was denied a seat on the Supreme Court because he disagreed with this; he was said to be out of the "mainstream."

The Supreme Court as Teacher: Lessons from the Second Reconstruction

Randall Kennedy

IN THE SUPREME COURT'S race relations law jurisprudence there are all too few admirable opinions. The array of candidates is limited, of course, by the fact that for most of the history of the United States the Court, like all of the other branches of the federal government, championed white supremacy, producing such egregious decisions as *Dred Scott v. Sanford*,[1] *Ableman v. Booth*,[2] *Pace v. Alabama*,[3] *Plessy v. Ferguson*,[4] and *Giles v. Harris*.[5] During the Second Reconstruction (1954–1970), one might think that the Court's landmark opinions would warrant enthusiastic applause. After all, during those years the Court invalidated *de jure* segregation,[6] rejected efforts to nullify court-ordered desegregation,[7] shielded the civil rights movement from state-sponsored efforts to strangle it,[8] and upheld federal civil rights legislation such as the Civil Rights Act of 1964[9] and the Voting Rights Act of 1965.[10]

[1] 60 U.S. 393 (1856) (holding among other things that blacks were not and could not become citizens of the United States).

[2] 62 U.S. 506 (1858) (upholding constitutionality of the Fugitive Slave Act).

[3] 106 U.S. 583 (1883) (upholding law that penalized inter-racial fornication more harshly than intra-racial fornication).

[4] 163 U.S. 437 (1896) (upholding *de jure* racial segregation on intra-state railroad).

[5] 189 U.S. 475 (1903) (ruling that Court can offer no appropriate remedy even if state had violated the Fifteenth Amendment of federal Constitution).

[6] See, e.g., *Brown v. Board of Education*, 347 U.S. 483 (1954).

[7] See, e .g, *Cooper v. Aaron*, 358 U.S. 1 (1958).

[8] See, e.g., *NAACP v. Alabama*, 357 U.S. 449 (1958); *Gibson v. Florida Legislative Investigation Committee*, 372 U.S. 539 (1963).

[9] See *Heart of Atlanta Motel v. United States*, 379 U.S. 241 (1964).

[10] See *South Carolina v. Katzenbach*, 383 U.S. 301 (1966).

Why, then, do I offer only qualified applause? Am I simply being churlish? I hope not. The reason I do not look upon the Supreme Court's race relations law opinions of the Second Reconstruction with unequivocal admiration is that, typically, they fail in important respects to teach clearly and comprehensively the lessons that were most in need of dissemination during that trying period. If one wanted to educate a class of students about racial injustice in the United States at mid-century by assigning such decisions as *Brown v. Board of Education*,[11] *Gayle v. Browder*,[12] *South Carolina v. Katzenbach*[13] and *Loving v. Virginia*,[14] one would be well advised to supplement the opinions heavily with other materials. That is because the opinions for the Court that announce these decisions are either obfuscatory or misleading in significant ways.

Consider the most famous Supreme Court decision of the twentieth century, *Brown v. Board of Education*. That case invalidated state laws which directed or authorized local officials to assign white and colored children to equal but separate public schools. This decision represented, of course, a tremendous step forward in the moral and legal condition of the nation. Chief Justice Warren's opinion for the Court, however, is infamously unclear in stating the basis for invalidating *de jure* segregation in public schooling. The closest it comes to identifying a harm is stating that "[t]o separate [black children] from others of similar age and qualifications solely because of their race generates feelings of inferiority as to their status in the community that may affect their hearts and minds in a way unlikely ever to be undone."[15] The opinion makes no mention of segregationists' deliberate efforts to oppress blacks. Nor does it mention the racist beliefs that prompted politicians to mandate the separation of school children on a racial basis. Nor does it mention that, almost always, facilities set aside for blacks were not only separate from but obviously inferior to those set aside for whites. Nor does it mention the circumstances under which one racial subdivision of the polity—whites—monopolized power in such a way as to impose terms by fiat on the other racial subdivision of the polity—colored people. In sum, the *Brown* opinion fails to convey that the clear "social meaning of segregation [was] the putting of the Negro in a position of walled-off inferiority."[16] Instead the Court pretended that its decision was vitally

[11] 347 U.S. 483 (1954).
[12] 352 U.S. 903 (1956).
[13] 383 U.S. 301 (1966).
[14] 388 U.S. 1 (1967).
[15] 347 U.S. at 494.
[16] Charles Black, "The Lawfulness of the Segregation Decisions," *Yale Law Journal* 69 (1960): 421.

related to the increased importance of education in American society and increased knowledge about social psychology.

Brown is often spoken of as the case that reversed *Plessy v. Ferguson*, the 1896 decision in which the Court upheld *de jure* segregation in intra-state transportation. That is inaccurate. In *Brown* the Court hinted rather broadly that in its view *Plessy* was no longer good constitutional law. But it did not say so expressly. Moreover, insofar as *Brown* involved education, and indeed emphasized that specific aspect of the decision, it left plenty of room to distinguish between public schooling and other forums of public life. That is why in the late 1950s black communities throughout the South found themselves compelled to mobilize expensive, time-consuming campaigns to extend the Court's disapproval of *de jure* segregation in public education to other areas of society. The case in which the Supreme Court came closest to reversing *Plessy v. Ferguson* expressly is *Gayle v. Browder*, a piece of litigation sparked by the year-long boycott of public busses in Montgomery, Alabama in 1955–56 that was led by Martin Luther King, Jr.[17]

Browder warrants attention here for three reasons. First, that a constitutional challenge to *de jure* segregation on busses in Alabama required resolution by the Supreme Court in the aftermath of *Brown* is a clear indication of that landmark's ambiguity. Second, the sacrifice entailed in bringing such a suit is a vivid illustration of the costs generated when, as in *Brown*, the Supreme Court sends a confusing message to the citizenry. Third, the Court's resolution of *Browder* is even more unsatisfying rhetorically than *Brown*. In a one-sentence per curiam opinion it made clear that, finally, *de jure* segregation in intra-state transportation was no longer permissible under federal constitutional law. That opinion, however, offers no teaching about the social cruelty that Jim Crow seating represented. In this sense it was representative of virtually all of the Court's immediate post-*Brown* desegregation holdings. As Professor Michael W. McConnell observes, "Never did the Court get around to informing the nation of the legal basis for desegregating the South, outside the context of education."[18]

As a teacher of constitutional mores during the Second Reconstruction, the Court did, on occasion, offer useful instruction above and beyond the bottom line of its holdings. For one thing, it some-

[17] See Randall Kennedy, "Martin Luther King's Constitution: A Legal History of the Montgomery Bus Boycott," *Yale Law Journal* 98 (1989): 999–1067.

[18] Michael W. McConnell, "Originalism and the Desegregation Decisions," *Virginia Law Review* 81 (1995): 947.

times clarified the moral standing of the contending forces in the drama, distinguishing the good guys from the bad guys. Hence, in *Edwards v. South Carolina*,[19] Justice Potter Stewart, writing for the Court, spends four pages describing in detail the disciplined, heroic actions of civil rights demonstrators who were challenging their convictions for breach of the peace on First Amendment grounds. After having noted the songs they sang ("patriotic and religious songs") and the placards they carried ("I am proud to be a Negro" and "Down with segregation"), Justice Stewart does not simply state that their arrests were invalid because they were engaged in activity protected by the First Amendment. He also aptly and movingly observes that the activists were engaged in an exercise of "basic constitutional rights in their most pristine and classic form."[20]

In some cases, moreover, the Justices clearly put considerable effort into a strategy of stigmatizing the segregationists. One of the most potent tactics of this strategy involved simply quoting segregationists and thereby allowing them to discredit themselves with their own language. In *Peterson v. Greenville*,[21] a case in which the Court invalidated the convictions for trespass of civil rights demonstrators, the Court did not simply mention that the city had a segregation ordinance pertinent to the controversy. The Court took care to quote the ordinance liberally in order to reveal its malevolence. Chief Justice Warren, for example, put into the text and not simply the footnotes of his *Peterson* opinion the following excerpt from a municipal ordinance:

> It shall be unlawful for any person owning . . . any . . . hotel, restaurant, cafe, eating house, boarding-house or similar establishment to furnish meals to white persons and colored persons in the same room . . . ; provided, however, that meals may be served to white persons and colored persons in the same room where separate facilities are furnished. Separate facilities shall be interpreted to mean:
>
> (a) Separate eating utensils and separate dishes for the serving of food, all of which shall be distinctly marked by some appropriate color scheme or otherwise;
>
> (b) Separate tables, counters, or booths;
>
> (c) A distance of at least thirty-five feet shall be maintained between the area where white and colored persons are served. . . .[22]

[19] 372 U.S. 229 (1963).
[20] Id. at 235.
[21] 373 U.S. 244 (1963).
[22] Id. at 246.

In *South Carolina v. Katzenbach*, a case in which the Court upheld challenged sections of the Voting Rights Act of 1965, the Court does not simply declare that Congress acted within its authority. The Court also provides a history of efforts to nullify the Fifteenth Amendment. Seeking to bring home vividly the need for the legislation, the Court notes, for instance, that while voting registrars in the Deep South regularly barred educated blacks from the ballot on the grounds that they were supposedly "unqualified," functionally illiterate whites were typically registered with no difficulty, including the one who satisfied a registrar of his ability to interpret the state constitution by writing "FRDUM FOOF SPETGH."[23]

Similarly, in the exquisitely named case of *Loving v. Virginia* in which the Court finally invalidated laws prohibiting inter-racial marriage, the Justices' attack on segregation is decidedly more forthright than what appears in *Brown*. The Court links the prohibition against miscegenation with the history of slavery, calls it an "endorsement of the doctrine of White Supremacy," and embarrasses the proponents of the prohibition by quoting the trial judge in the case. After suspending the prison sentence of the convicted couple on the condition that the black wife and her white husband leave Virginia and not return for 25 years, the judge explained:

> Almighty God created the races white, black, yellow, malay and red, and he placed them on separate continents. And but for the interference with his arrangement there would be no cause for such marriages. That fact that he separated the races shows that he did not intend for the races to mix.[24]

At the same time that the Court increased the acerbity of its criticisms of segregation, it also pursued another strategy worth noting. It misleadingly revised the history of its own institutional stance towards racial oppression. Consider the brief history of disfranchisement that the Court sets forth in *Katzenbach*. Not once does the Court make reference to its own role in facilitating open and widespread violation of the Fifteenth Amendment. The Court never mentions, for instance, *Williams v. Mississippi*,[25] a decision favorable to racial disfranchisement that was, in Benno Schmidt's words, "as fundamental a support for legalized white supremacy as *Plessy v. Ferguson*."[26] Nor

[23] *Katzenbach*, 383 U.S. at 312.
[24] 388 U.S. at 3.
[25] 170 U.S. 213 (1898).
[26] See Alexander Bickel & Benno C. Schmidt, Jr., *History of the Supreme Court of the United States: The Judiciary and Responsible Government, 1910–21* (New York: Macmillan Publishing Co., 1984), 923.

does the Court mention *Giles v. Harris*, an extraordinary but ne-
glected case in which the Court assumed as fact that the state of Ala-
bama, in seeking to disenfranchise on racial grounds its black
population, was perpetrating "a fraud upon the Constitution of the
United States."[27] Even if that was so, the Court concluded per Justice
Oliver Wendell Holmes, there was no appropriate remedy that the
Court could offer. In light of *Giles* it is no wonder that the *Harvard
Law Review* published in 1910 an article entitled "Is the Fifteenth
Amendment Void?"[28] Yet, the only Supreme Court cases the *Katzen-
bach* Court mentions are ones in which the Justices are on the side of
the angels.[29]

Perhaps these omissions in *Katzenbach* can be explained on the
grounds that the Court's "bad" voting rights cases had been sup-
planted by decisions that consistently supported petitioners challenging invidious racial exclusions from the ballot box. That explanation
is unavailable, however, when one faces the Court's institutional historical revisionism in *Loving*. There one encounters the following
statement: "Over the years, this Court has consistently repudiated
'distinctions between citizens solely because of their ancestry as being
odious to a free people whose institutions are founded on the doctrine of equality.' *Hirabayashi v. United States*, 320 U.S. 81, 100
(1943)." That assertion is laughable. In the first place, over the years
the Supreme Court of the United States has clearly *not* consistently
repudiated invidious ancestral distinctions. Until the 1950s, the
Court had upheld *de jure* segregation—a fact certainly well known to
Chief Justice Warren, the author of *Loving* who was also the author of
Brown. Second, the reason that the Supreme Court was faced with
the task of deciding *Loving* was because it had previously upheld the
authority of states to regulate on racial grounds the sexual conduct
of adults.[30] Third, the decision cited by Chief Justice Warren—
Hirabayashi v. United States—itself flew in the face of his proposition
insofar as that decision wrongly legitimated the imposition of a ra-
cially selective curfew on all persons of Japanese ancestry during
World War II, a decision that has subsequently been repudiated by
the United States government.

[27] 189 U.S. at 486.
[28] See Arthur W. Machen, Jr., "Is the Fifteenth Amendment Void?" *Harvard Law
Review* 23 (1910): 169–93.
[29] In *Katzenbach* there is also no mention of *Grovey v. Townsend*, 295 U.S. 45
(1935), which threatened for a while to permit political parties to exclude black
participation so long as sufficient steps were taken to keep the party "private."
Grovey lasted less than a decade. It was overruled by *Smith v. Allwright*, 321 U.S.
649 (1944).
[30] See *Pace*, 106 U.S. 583 (1883).

There are reasons behind the decisions that the Court made in addressing segregation in the manner it did, although the Justices may have been more self-conscious with respect to certain rhetorical tactics than others. In *Brown*, Chief Justice Warren was quite self-conscious in crafting a narrow opinion that would give as little offense as possible. The rhetorical blandness of *Brown* was, to some extent, a calculated effort to obtain unanimous support for the decision among the Justices and to dampen opposition to it from the segregationist public. With those goals in mind, Chief Justice Warren informed his colleagues that he intended to write an opinion that would be "short, readable by the lay public, non-rhetorical, unemotional and, above all, non-accusatory."[31] The summary disposition of *Gayle* seems to have been another facet of the same strategy. The Justices apparently sought to enlarge the ambit of *Brown* in as low-key a manner as possible.

The likely strategy behind those aspects of *Katzenbach* and *Loving* that I have highlighted has two dimensions. First, the rhetorical aggressiveness I noted above seems to have been part of an effort to stigmatize segregation more directly than had been done earlier. *Brown* and *Browder* predate *Katzenbach* and *Loving* by an eventful decade. By the mid-sixties, the Justices appeared to feel confident in saying what prudence (buttressed perhaps by timidity and ignorance?) might have dissuaded them from saying previously. Second, the revisionism I noted above may have been based on a belief that it was important to imagine a tradition of judicial rectitude in order to better create such a tradition. By asserting that the Supreme Court has consistently repudiated invidious distinctions based on ancestry, the Court may have been trading on respect for precedent in order to make palatable what was in actuality a rejection of precedent, albeit a justified rejection.

What should we make of the Supreme Court's strategies? First and foremost we should embrace the main tendency of the Court's work during the Second Reconstruction which was to stigmatize segregation and its attendant sentiments and practices. The Court advanced that mission impressively when it documented in detail the horrifying facts of segregation and the attractive characteristics of the civil rights activists who battled the Jim Crow regime. The Court retarded that mission when it resorted to certain other tactics. It is unfortunate, for instance, that in *Brown* and *Browder* the Court declined

[31] Quoted In Dennis J. Hutchinson, "Unanimity and Desegregation: Decision-making in the Supreme Court, 1948–1958," *Georgetown Law Journal* 68 (1979): 42.

to educate the public more directly about the evils of segregation. Doing so might have enlightened even knowledgeable people who found themselves somewhat mystified by *Brown*'s murky pronouncement. Doing so might also have helped to enlighten the Justices themselves. It is true that Chief Justice Warren might not have been able to deliver a single-voiced, unanimous decision in *Brown* had he condemned segregation in the way that atrocious system warranted. But my impression is that the price for unanimity was greater than the cost. There are, after all, many important Supreme Court decisions that are accompanied by concurrences or dissents that have done little to undercut the influence of the majority opinion.[32] Indeed, a strong dissent or concurrence may well have strengthened *Brown* and its progeny by forcing the Court to sharpen its analysis and message, a clarifying development that may in turn have obviated various costly struggles both inside and outside of courtrooms.

Many who defend the Court against my critique will suggest that, like any teacher, the Court was limited by the expectations and capacities of its audience. In the case of the Court, the audience was the politically influential sector of the American polity. Those who defend the Court's strategy might well maintain that, unfortunately, the expectations and capacities of this audience had been shaped by segregation and all that made segregation possible, and that therefore prudence dictated evasiveness and obfuscation in the Court's movement towards desegregation. It was foreseeable, however, that almost regardless of how they were packaged, Supreme Court rulings invalidating *de jure* segregation were going to provoke strong negative reactions from segregationists. That being so, the Court should have worried less about angering those who were going to be enraged anyway and worried more about those who were undecided but persuadable. Furthermore, if it is true that teachers are to some extent the captives of their audiences, it is also true that teachers often underestimate their audiences. That may well have happened in *Brown*.

The same can be said about the Court's handling of *Browder*. Though it has been defended as a pragmatic, defensive maneuver in a hostile political environment, *Browder* may not, in fact, have been as wise a move politically as its defenders believe. By resorting to an inarticulate, summary disposition of the case, the Justices, as two keen court-watchers observe, "withdrew from the arena in which lies the Court's real strength, the arena of reason and documentation," and

---

[32] See, e.g, *The Slaughter-House Cases*, 83 U.S. 36 (1873); *Strauder v. West Virginia*, 100 U.S. 303 (1879); *The Civil Rights Cases*, 109 U.S. 3 (1883).

instead gave battle "with the weapon that [was] its opponents' choice—the bare assertion."[33]

I doubt that the revisionism that may have been exhibited in *Katzenbach* and that was certainly exhibited in *Loving* was as self-consciously designed as the planned rhetorical blandness of *Brown*. But regardless of the degree of self-consciousness, it was flawed as a strategy. Revising the Court's history was unlikely to sway anyone who would not have been persuaded anyway by the other considerations noted in the opinion. Moreover, the claim the Court makes on behalf of itself is absurd and discrediting. Anyone who knows anything about the development of American constitutional law knows that it is simply untrue that "[o]ver the years, [the Supreme Court] has consistently repudiated 'distinctions between citizens solely because of their ancestry.' " The Justices probably believed that asserting this claim about an imagined tradition would facilitate the emergence of such a tradition. But the best way of pursuing that task is not by creating illusions but rather by facing the truth and taking the steps, albeit difficult, to reach our envisioned destination. One of those steps should entail recognizing and acknowledging that the Supreme Court of the United States has been no less complicit in the moral crimes of racial injustice than other branches of government. This is a haunting lesson about which the citizenry should be informed. No people are better situated to bring this lesson home than the Justices themselves.

[33]Alexander Bickel & Harry Wellington, "Legislative Purpose and the Judicial Process: The Lincoln Mills Case," *Harvard Law Review* 71 (1957): 4.

On the Grounds of Rights and Republican Government: What the Judges May Still Teach

Hadley Arkes

THAT REDOUBTABLE CASE of *Chisholm v. Georgia*[1] stands out to us now as the first major case under the Constitution, because it was the first case in which the judges seemed to see themselves as teaching the first lessons of the American law. James Wilson of Philadelphia had taken a leading role in the framing of the Constitution, and in the debates in Pennsylvania over ratification. Now, as a member of the first Court, he evidently understood that the moment warranted a certain effort to set first principles into place. Before Wilson would speak about the text of the Constitution, he would speak about "the principles of general jurisprudence." But even before that, something else had to be set in order: Before Wilson and his colleagues would begin expounding the principles of legal judgment, he found it necessary to acknowledge something of the laws of reason and "the philosophy of mind."[2]

Wilson would begin by rejecting "scepticism"—by which he meant the doctrine that proclaimed our skepticism, or doubt, about the prospect of knowing, reliably, anything about the world, including the material objects around us. And swept into that doctrine of skepticism was of course the doubt that we could know anything of "moral truths." Wilson recognized this "scepticism" as the fount of all forms of "relativism" in morality and law, and in his understanding, the American law had to begin with the rejection of that moral relativism. In that vein, he took the occasion to point out that the law

[1] 2 Dallas 419 (1793).
[2] Id. at 453–54.

27

in America would be planted on an entirely different ground from that of the law in England. That law in England, made familiar by William Blackstone, began with the notion of a sovereign issuing commands. But the law in America, wrote Wilson, would begin "with another principle, very different in its nature and operations":

> [L]aws derived from the pure source of equality and justice must be founded on the consent of those, whose obedience they require. The sovereign, when traced to his source, must be found in the *man*.[3]

Against the legal "positivism" of Blackstone, Wilson would assert the foundation of the American law in natural right. As Locke had pointed out in the *Second Treatise*, "the constitution of the legislative being the original and supreme act of the society," it had to be "antecedent to all positive laws." The legislature might be the source of "positive" law—the law that is "law" only because it is "posited," set down, enacted by an officer, or an official body, with the authority to issue commands. But the legislature, as an artifact of the Constitution, could not itself spring from positive law. It had to find its origins, as Locke said, in that understanding "antecedent to all positive laws," and that authority was "depending wholly on the people," on their natural right to be governed with their own consent.[4]

In the same vein, George Mason would later point out, at the Constitutional Convention, that the legislatures in the states could claim no power to ratify a new Constitution. For "they are the mere creatures of the State Constitutions, and cannot be greater than their creators."[5] Madison added that it would be a "novel & dangerous doctrine that a Legislature could change the constitution under which it held its existence."[6] The appeal would have to be made, beyond the legislatures, to the authority of the people themselves. And from that power of the people, said Wilson, "there is no appeal; of their error there is no superior principle of correction."[7]

---

[3] Id. at 458.

[4] See Locke, *An Essay Concerning the True Original, Extent, and End of Civil Government*, sec. 157.

[5] Max Farrand, ed., *Records of the Federal Convention of 1787* (New Haven: Yale University Press, 1911; 1966 edition), 2:88 (Madison's notes).

[6] Ibid., 92–93.

[7] Wilson, remarks in the ratifying convention in Pennsylvania, in Jonathan Elliott, *Debates in the State Conventions on the Adoption of the Federal Constitution* (Philadelphia: J. B. Lippincott, 1888), 2:432. Wilson went on:
There can be no disorder in the community but may here receive a radical cure. If the error be in the legislature, it may be corrected by the constitu-

In the case of Wilson, there was an explicit merger of judging and teaching. When he was a member of the first Supreme Court, Wilson was appointed to a chair in law at the University of Pennsylvania, and he left us, as one of the legacies of his teaching, his engaging lectures on jurisprudence, delivered in 1790–91. In his inaugural lecture, Wilson took the occasion to mark off once again the critical differences that separated the law in America from the teachings of Blackstone and the premises of the English law. In the case of Blackstone, Wilson could open up a landscape of philosophic differences simply by beginning with Blackstone's remark that it was a "chimera" to refer to an unjust law. For Blackstone, it was a matter of incoherence to argue, in a court provided by the King, that the King's law was unjust at the root and therefore not truly lawful in the deepest sense. It was the sovereignty of the King that provided, in the first place, the authority that attached to the courts of law, and to the remedies that would be handed down by judges. And so Blackstone could regard it as a solecism on the part of Mr. Locke to contend that "there remains still inherent in the people, a supreme power to alter the legislative, when they find the legislative act contrary to the trust reposed in them; for when such trust is abused, it is thereby forfeited."[8] To Blackstone, this was a careless mode of writing that incorporated, in the standing law, the principle of revolution. And any meretricious mingling of that kind would work, inescapably, to the dissolution of the law.

Wilson recalled this argument of Blackstone's in the course of his inaugural address, in the presence of President Washington and Vice President Adams, because he meant to reject this teaching at the root, as part of his first lesson in jurisprudence. What Blackstone regarded as a "chimera," Wilson was willing to take now as part of the foundation of the American law. "A revolution principle," he said, "certainly is, and certainly should be taught as a principle for the constitution of the United States, and of every State in the Union."[9]

tion; if in the constitution, it may be corrected by the people. . . . [But from the power of the people] . . . there is no appeal; of their error there is no superior principle of correction.
Ibid., 433.

[8] Quoted by Blackstone in *Commentaries on the Laws of England* (Oxford: Clarendon Press, 1765), 1:157. I am using here the edition published by the University of Chicago Press in 1979, with a copy of the original plates and preserving the same pagination.

[9] Wilson, First Lecture on the Law, in *The Works of James Wilson*, ed. Robert Green McCloskey (Cambridge: Harvard University Press, 1967; originally published in 1804), 1:79.

The American law would begin then with the notion that the positive law, a "law" established in a thoroughly legal manner, may nevertheless be wanting in the substance of justice. For that reason, a statute might not be "lawful" in the strictest sense even if it were passed with a thorough respect for the forms of law. To put the matter another way, the American law would begin by taking as profoundly serious the existence of the natural law, as the measure of the positive law, and the ultimate guarantor of a right to revolution.

These passages in the lectures of Wilson make clear again that the task of explaining and justifying this new constitution could not be detached from the task of teaching. And the lessons taught by the Founders, of course, were the first principles of lawful government. As the Founders understood that problem, the deepest lesson they had to impart was the understanding of the difference between the positive law and those principles of lawfulness, or natural law, that lay behind the positive law. As it was said in the Bible, they would teach this lesson coming in and going out; they would teach it at almost every occasion where there were lessons to be taught.

They taught it even in the throes of political controversy, in their journalistic sallies in the Federalist papers. In *Federalist* 81 Hamilton sought to counter the alarms, cast up by Anti-federalist writers, over courts that would be armed now with powers of judicial review. The charge had been made that the new government would surrender the supremacy of the legislature and concede a sovereignty, in certain matters, to the unelected judges. In the face of these arguments, Hamilton observed that neither Britain nor the American states could furnish an example of parliamentary supremacy over the courts. For under none of these constitutions was it understood that the legislature was at liberty to revise the verdict or judgment of a court. As Hamilton put it more precisely, "A legislature, without exceeding its province, cannot reverse a determination once made in a particular case; though it may prescribe a new rule for future case."[10] That is to say, the legislature would not seek to interfere with the disposition of a case; it would act *prospectively* by legislating a new rule for all similar cases that are yet to arise. That arrangement seems quite consistent with the moral discipline of a constitutional government, and yet, as Hamilton noted, it was set down nowhere in the Constitution. If the question were posed then as to why the legislature may not overturn the judgment of a court in a particular case, Hamilton explained that "the impropriety of the thing, on the general principles of law and reason, is the sole obstacle."[11]

[10] *The Federalist* (New York: Random House, n.d.), 526.
[11] Ibid.

Just a bit earlier, in *Federalist* 78, Hamilton remarked on the rule of construction in applying statutes. "The rule which has obtained in the courts," he said, "for determining their relative validity is, that the last in order of time should be preferred to the first." The common sense of the matter was that a later statute superseded an earlier one. That was not, of course, the rule of construction that came into play in measuring statutes against the Constitution. In that event, the basic law would always claim a logical preeminence, even against a statute that came much later. These understandings were bound up with the authority that attached to the laws, but once again they were nowhere to be found in the body of the Constitution. On what ground then did they form our understanding of "the laws"? Once again, Hamilton explained, the answer was not "derived from any positive law, but from the nature and reason of the thing."[12] It was part, that is, of those first principles of our understanding, which were bound up with the first principles of the law.

By any reckoning, John Marshall had to stand as a chief among the republican schoolmasters, for it was evident, in certain landmark cases, that Marshall had to understand himself as working, quite consciously, as a teacher. Few of his opinions seem more self-consciously didactic than the opinion in *McCulloch v. Maryland*,[13] on the constitutionality of the national bank. Of course, Marshall was teaching quite as surely in cases like *Ogden v. Saunders*[14] or *Cohens v. Virginia*,[15] but *McCulloch* probably sounded more like a lecture offered by a grammarian or by a philosopher of ordinary language as Marshall interpreted the "necessary and proper" clause and moved, precisely, through the tiers of meaning that may affect the notion of "necessary." Of Marshall, it is hardly possible to say enough—and indeed, much has already been amply said. He has left us, in his writings, a curriculum on the first principles of republican government, and in the course of that achievement, he may also be credited with one of the most elegant turns of reasoning in the judicial records of this country. I pick it out here, as the pivot of this essay, because the elegance was drawn in large part from the surpassing importance of the point he was conveying. But beyond that, it stands out as a distinct act of teaching because it was entirely gratuitous: He did not need to flex himself in this show of artistry for the sake of deciding the case. The only reason for the effort had to be found in the purpose of teaching itself.

[12] Ibid., no. 78, 507.
[13] 17 U.S. (4 Wheaton) 316 (1819).
[14] 25 U.S. (12 Wheaton) 213 (1827).
[15] 19 U.S. 264 (1821).

The case in question was *Fletcher v. Peck*, in 1810.[16] And in that celebrated case, the legislature of Georgia had acted, through a statute, to rescind a grant of lands made by an earlier legislature. The law was a response to the famous "Yazoo scandals," in which legislators had been bribed by speculators as an inducement to make a grant of public lands. But the problem had become complicated by the fact that the land had since been sold, in many parcels, to third parties, who were innocent of the original wrongdoing. *Fletcher v. Peck* would become notable as an early test of the provision in Article I, Section 10 of the Constitution, which barred the states from passing any law "impairing the Obligations of Contracts."

To compress a story that is familiar in its main lines, Marshall argued that the rescinding of the grant, the annulling of the conveyance of property, was equivalent to an act "discharging the vendors of property from the obligation of executing their contracts by conveyances." It was the equivalent then of a law impairing the obligation of contracts. In that event, Marshall would have said enough to bring the law in Georgia under the proscription of the Contract Clause of the Constitution. And yet, Marshall did not choose to settle the case in that way. Instead, he went on to show that the wrong engaged in this case could be *deduced* from the principle on "ex post facto" laws.

From Marshall's day to our own there has been a certain confusion over the question of whether a retrospective law counts as an ex post facto law if it is not attached to a criminal penalty. Marshall fell into that group among the Founders that regarded the distinction as a difference without substance. As Marshall put it, a legislature would be "prohibited from passing a law by which a man's estate, or any part of it, shall be seized for a crime which was not declared, by some previous law, to render him liable to that punishment." But Marshall then asked, What would be the distinction between that arrangement and one in which the legislature claims the power of "seizing, for public use, the estate of any individual in the form of a law annulling the title by which he holds that estate?" He saw in fact no distinction:

> This rescinding act [in Georgia] would have the effect of an *ex post facto* law. It forfeits the estate of [the buyer] for a crime not committed by himself, but by those from whom he purchased. This cannot be effected in the form of an *ex post facto* law, or bill of attainder; why, then, is it allowable in the form of a law annulling the original grant?[17]

[16] 6 Cranch 87.
[17] Id. at 138–39, emphasis original.

When Marshall appealed to the principle of ex post facto laws, he understood that he was invoking a principle that was regarded among the Founders as one of those first principles bound up with the notion of lawfulness itself. In fact, it was so widely understood as a principle of law, before the framing of the Constitution, that a serious question arose as to whether there was any need to mention it within the body of the document. When the question had arisen, during the debates at the Constitutional Convention, James Wilson and Oliver Ellsworth expressed deep reservations over this exercise of naming one or two principles of law in the text of the Constitution. They found something artless, even embarrassing, in the prospect of mentioning ex post facto laws, along with one or two other principles, and omitting, by implication, any reference to other principles. Ellsworth thought that the point on ex post facto laws was too obvious, that "there was no lawyer, no civilian who would not say that ex post facto laws were void in themselves." And indeed, that sense of the matter was expressed quite emphatically by Marshall's colleague, Justice Johnson, in his concurring opinion in *Fletcher v. Peck.* "I do not hesitate to declare," he wrote, "that a state does not possess the power of revoking its own grants. But I do it on a general principle, on the reason and nature of things: a principle which will impose laws even on the Deity." Johnson wished to have it understood, in that vein, "that my opinion on this point is *not founded on the provision in the constitution* . . . relative to laws impairing the obligations of contracts." Marshall drew out the import of this point with a further, and novel, recognition. He remarked that Georgia was "part of a large empire; she is a member of the American union," and the union had a Constitution that was supreme over its separate parts. But as a result of the argument that Marshall and Johnson had made here, Marshall could point out that the rescinding act passed by the legislature of Georgia "might well be doubted, were Georgia a single sovereign power."[18] That is, even if Georgia had not come under the Constitution and the restrictions of the Contract Clause, the action of the legislature would still have been wrong. For the legislature had violated a principle that did not depend, for its validity, on the explicit provisions of the Constitution, or on the membership of Georgia in the American Union.

To restate the problem, then, Marshall could have settled the case neatly by bringing it under the Contract Clause, Article I, Section 10, of the Constitution. But instead, he sought to show that the Contract Clause could be drawn *deductively* from a deeper principle of law

[18] Id. at 136.

that did not depend for its validity on its mention in the Constitution. Marshall understood that, when he drew a conclusion deductively, he drew it with all of the force of necessity that attached to conclusions drawn through a syllogism. And as he completed the scheme in this way, he left us with this construction: The law in Georgia was not wrong because it ran counter to some local rules adopted in this tribe of Americans. But rather, the Constitution itself, in this respect, represented something more than the local rules of a club, or of positive law. It stood on a higher epistemic plane than an expression of "how we do things here." What Marshall managed to show was that the Constitution had the deeper claim of being the fundamental law because it was founded on principles that did not finally depend for their truth, or authority, on the fact that they had been set down in the text of the Constitution.

With judges like Marshall and Wilson, it is apparent that the furnishings of mind among the jurists bore a favorable comparison to the most accomplished philosophers of their age.[19] We would not expect, from our current college of jurists, minds of the same reach, though it is clear that we can find, among them, an abundance of estimable and lively characters. I would pick out here a few instances in which a judge came closer to the example of Marshall in this respect: that he was not writing for the sake of settling the case, or sounding lofty themes for the anthologies; that the writing could have been animated solely by the purpose of teaching.

I would draw my examples here from our former colleague in the professoriate, Justice Antonin Scalia. He has been, we know, a lively presence in oral arguments, and a scrappy participant in the ongoing argument of the Court. But Scalia's main genius has been shown at those times when he has leaned in to offer some guidance to the readers who are trying to follow the cross-cutting lines of argument in the Court. At those moments, he has offered a line of counsel, or the kind of example, that serves to illuminate the landscape in a flash of recognition.

In my own reckoning, none of them had quite the same dramatic force as the aside he offered in the course of his concurring opinion in the *Cruzan* case in 1990.[20] The problem in that case, of course, was the so-called "right to die." The Court backed away from articulating

[19] Another striking example on this head—if any further examples were needed—may be found in Wilson's essay, "Of the Nature and Philosophy of Evidence, " in *The Works of James Wilson*, ed. James DeWitt Andrews (Chicago: Callaghan and Co., 1896), 1:477–522.

[20] *Cruzan v. Director, Missouri Health Department*, 111 L.Ed.2d 224.

any such curious construction of a right. But the Chief Justice managed to create a bit of haze about this question as he merely sought to confirm the understanding, long settled, that patients had the right to consent, or withdraw their consent, on the matter of their own treatment. Under that principle there seemed to fall a certain right to back away from unwanted medical treatment. Of course, that understanding had been planted for many years without commentators drawing the extravagant conclusion that it implied anything that could be described as a "right to die." And yet, in March of 1996, Judge Stephen Reinhardt, in the federal court of appeals for the Ninth Circuit, sought to extract just that kind of significance from the *Cruzan* case.[21]

There is then, today, a certain ambiguity about the *Cruzan* case, because there was a certain ambiguity about it at the time. And sensing the problem, Scalia offered certain words of counsel or guidance to people who needed to draw some practical instruction from the ruling of the Court. They might be the people who drive ambulances and participate in "emergency" medical units; they were people who made a vocation of flying to the rescue to save lives. Scalia directed to them these telling words:

> The state-run hospital, I am certain, is not liable under 42 USC Sec. 1983 . . . for violation of constitutional rights, nor the private hospital liable under general tort law, if, in a State where suicide is unlawful, it pumps out the stomach of a person who has intentionally taken an overdose of barbiturates, despite that person's wishes to the contrary.[22]

The people who rush to the rescue, who resuscitate a victim, or preserve a life, should not expect then that the victim, when he revives, will sue them under the Civil Rights Acts for depriving him of a constitutional right: namely, his "right to die."

With that commentary, as I say, Scalia illuminated the landscape. There are so many soaring words about constitutional "rights" that the notion may often float off, untethered in the world of abstraction. But I would leave aside for a moment the host of serious problems that arise when the logic of rights is attached to the taking of one's own life. Scalia's observation puts things instantly back in their proper scale, anchored in the natural goods of this world. In the world of the federal courts, people have managed these days to get past the threshold of litigation with claims of the following kind:

---

[21] See *Compassion in Dying v. State of Washington*, 79 F. 3d 790 (9th Cir., 1996).
[22] *Cruzan*, 111 L.Ed. 2d at 254–55.

- A student on a college football team misses a punt. He is benched, he is eventually dropped from the team; and as a consequence he loses his football scholarship and drops out of school. He then launches a lawsuit against the coach who benched him. Since this is a state university, the coach is described as an official in an instrument of the state, acting "under the color of law." On that event, he becomes vulnerable then to a suit launched by the student, claiming that he had suffered, at the hands of the coach, a violation of his civil rights.[23]
- The warden of a prison in Pennsylvania is sued by one of the inmates because the library of the prison receives 123 magazines, but only two of those journals are directed to the interests of blacks.[24]

These two cases did not advance very far within the federal courts. Still, what is interesting is that they did manage to get past the threshold and get a hearing. Scalia's commentary on the right to die gains its fuller force when set against that background. For what Scalia is saying is that the so-called "right to die" does not state a claim even as faintly colorable as these cases that made it, at least, to the threshold of the courts. In the scale of things, the so-called "right to die" was not even near the alleged right not to be benched for missing a punt.

That sober ordering of these claims—that placing of things in their proper scale—may quickly lead the curious mind to work back to the explanation. And what is likely to be discovered, at the bottom of it all, is that ancient recognition that death simply cannot stand on the same plane, as a rival to the good of life. If death were a "good," on the same level as the good of life, then we should expect the babysitter, just as plausibly, to leave her charges inside the burning house, rather than remove them. For if death is a good, quite as good as life, why should she not choose it for the children as readily as she would choose life? Or, why would it not be plausible for her to impute to the children an "interest" in death at least as weighty as their interest in preserving their lives? For those with a touch of imagination, Scalia's gentle intervention not only gave us a more realistic reading of the legal landscape. It directed us to an understanding of those basic goods—we might even say, those *natural* goods—that form the most coherent ground of the law. They would also mark the intelligible ends that animate and direct our own acts.

[23] *Rutledge v. Arizona Board of Regents*, 660 F. 2d 1345 (1981).
[24] *Owens v. Brierly*, 52 F. 2d 640 (1971).

I would attach to this account one other case, in which Scalia once again used the occasion to expose some current cliches, offering themselves as principles of the law. And in the course of administering these lessons, he managed to reveal contradictions running back to the root in some of the recent and novel claims to "rights": What Scalia managed to expose, in a series of cases, was the logic that attached to new claims of rights—rights so sublime and so insistent that they virtually obliterated themselves.

Such was the nature of the right that Scalia's colleagues brought forth, in June 1992, in the case of *Lee v. Weisman*.[25] The case involved a commencement at a public high school in Providence, Rhode Island. Principals in the public school were permitted to invite clergy to offer invocations and benedictions as part of the ceremony. But in this instance, a young woman and her father objected to the presence even of the thinnest version of a prayer at this public ceremony, encompassing students of many faiths and—even more to the point—families professing to bear an objection in principle to religiosity. In this case, the invocation and benediction were framed by a rabbi, who carefully avoided any sectarian shading to these prayers. The prayers were cast, sparely, as an expression of gratitude to the God shared by Christians and Jews. In fact the references to God were no more extended or elaborated than anything found in the Pledge of Allegiance, or in the fleeting reference to God that is made in closing sessions of the Supreme Court. And so, as one commentator observed, if Ms. Deborah Weisman suffered a violation of her constitutional rights because she had been compelled to sit in silent respect during an invocation, she would have been compelled to suffer precisely the same wrong if she had decided to attend the session of the Supreme Court in which her cause was being argued.

For the peculiar, novel claim here was that Ms. Weisman had been subjected to a kind of "psychological coercion" in being asked to sit in silence during the recitation of a prayer. Her silence, it was argued, could be construed as a tacit endorsement of prayer and of the God who was the object of the prayers. I say it was a peculiar and novel claim because there has been no particular reason to attach this kind of significance to the act of sitting silently. Some of us, who do not say grace before meals, find ourselves often in the company of friends, or families, who do. It would be graceless in turn if we made a show of absenting ourselves from the table, or taking our presence as a ground for insisting that the grace be suspended on this occasion. Our inclination is to sit in silent respect. And for guests

[25] 120 L.Ed.2d 467 (1992).

who share no religious commitments, no one ever seems to draw the inference that the guests, with their respectful silence, have signalled their endorsement.

The question naturally arises then of why a nation that cultivates religious tolerance cannot take these public ceremonies as an occasion for showing that fellowship through the modest touch of simply sitting in quiet respect. But Justice Kennedy and a majority of the Court thought that this gesture of respect or tolerance could not possibly form an *obligation* for Deborah Weisman under the Constitution. In their judgment, the Constitution was the source of an even deeper claim not to suffer the expressions of religiosity in a civic occasion, sponsored by the government. That Deborah Weisman had not been strictly compelled to attend the ceremony, or that she had not been required herself to speak any words or make any sign, was regarded by the Court now as essentially beside the point.

But to people of ordinary wit, untutored in the law, there is the most obvious and telling difference between sitting in silent respect and being coerced to speak things one finds repugnant. And for judges tutored in these cases on religion, that distinction should have set off bells and sirens because it marked the difference between *Lee v. Weisman* and that classic case on the Jehovah's Witness and the "flag salute," *West Virginia Board of Education v. Barnette*.[26] For judges, who work through making comparisons among cases, the comparison with *Barnette* should have tripped off the warnings. In *Barnette*, the students were indeed forced to speak the pledge of allegiance and render the salute to the flag—words and gestures that signified, to them, a form of idolatry. If the Court was now taking a critical step beyond the *Barnette* case, it seemed to neglect the fact that it was bearing, along the way, the entire freight of *Barnette*. When *Barnette* was added to the *Weisman* case, the mixture produced a result that evidently ran beyond the wit of the Court. The Jehovah's Witnesses might have borne a religious objection to the requirement of saluting the flag, but the Court, in sustaining the Witnesses, did not create a special exemption for the religious, or find, in the policy, an establishment of religion. Justice Jackson cast the opinion of the Court along different lines, and years later Walter Berns would point up the significance of Jackson's move. Instead of articulating a claim of religious freedom, Jackson framed a broader argument, under the First Amendment, to protect people from the imposition of political orthodoxies:

[26] 319 U.S. 624 (1943).

The flag salute requirement was held to be unconstitutional, a violation not, however, of the free exercise of religion clause of the First Amendment but of the free speech provision. Stated otherwise, the Court held that *no one*, pious sectarian or militant atheist, could be required to salute the flag.[27]

Scalia was apparently attentive to this refined point in a way that his colleagues were not. He reminded them that, under the ruling in *Barnette*, "the government can . . . no more coerce political orthodoxy than religious orthodoxy."[28] He also recalled that, since the *Barnette* case in 1943, the words "under God" had been added to the pledge of allegiance. If there was a constitutional violation now when people were asked to sit silently, then Deborah Weisman could object, quite as tenably, to a requirement that she sit silently through the pledge of allegiance. The implication was that Deborah Weisman could command the deletion of the pledge of allegiance, as she could command now the deletion of prayers.

But that was not all, especially when the holding in *Weisman* was joined with the holding in *Barnette*. For Deborah Weisman could hold now a trumping power, a power to override and silence that was not confined any longer to references to God or expressions of religiosity. The holding in *Barnette* referred, as Scalia said, to the imposition of political orthodoxies as well as religious doctrines. People who have made their lives in the academy have long settled in with those conventions of courtesy that oblige them to sit in silent respect and acquiescence during the commencements of our colleges and universities, even as these rituals have acquired the most emphatic political cast. That cast has become even clearer over the past thirty years, and its character is readily disclosed in the parade of people and causes who are held up on these occasions as figures to be honored and celebrated: leaders of such estimable groups as the American Civil Liberties Union, Common Cause, and the Sierra Club; figures who have led the fight against apartheid in South Africa, or the attack on corporations in America; leaders and writers in the cause of "feminism." And the figures have become familiar, especially as they are recycled through the circuit of schools and commencements: the Ellen Goodmans, the Jesse Jacksons, the Ralph Naders. Even people who are rather dim in these matters will have no trouble in decoding the message or noticing the political cast: As it happens, that cast is pronounced and unmistakable on the side of liberalism; the com-

[27]Walter Berns, "The Importance of Being Amish," *Harper's* (March 1973): 39–40.

[28] *Weisman*, 120 L.Ed.2d at 514.

mencements have become rituals of celebration for the culture of
liberalism. At certain moments in these ceremonies, with high-mind-
edness rising in its pitch, the audience is often expected to rise in
a standing ovation. Those professors who do not share the political
passions of the event may decline at times to rise. Yet, they too may
rise, simply in courtesy, rather than making a show of their reservations; and in any event, their inclination has been to bite their lips
and hold their peace.

But with the innovation in *Lee v. Weisman,* these members of the
audience might have a new lever at hand if they happened to be in
public universities. For it should be evident now that they could not
bear an *obligation* to sit in respectful silence, because that silence
could be taken as an endorsement. And the state has no authority to
compel, in this way, their endorsement of sectarian political doctrines
that they may find deeply repugnant. After all, if these professors follow the line of the Court, they would not have the claim merely to
absent themselves. They would have the right to insist that they not
be affronted by the presence of the Harry Blackmuns and the Kate
Michelmans. They would have the right, in effect, to purge them
from the program, as much as Deborah Weisman had the right to
purge from the program the prayers that other students and their
families wished to have.

Or this would be the result, at any rate, if the Court recognized
the logic of its own work. The justices may choose, for obvious reasons, to feign ignorance or obtuseness, but this charade may be rendered all the more implausible for them after Justice Scalia has gone
to the trouble of setting before them the implications that spring
from their own work: What Scalia's colleagues have created, in the
Weisman case, is the novelty of a right that extinguishes itself—and
more besides.

As for the litigants, they seem rather heedless here, as in other
cases, of the principles they are willing to foist on the courts as the
means of attaining their ends. And in that event, it is not only fair,
but especially apt, that someone in a position of judicial authority
finally administer a lesson in sobriety. Who would be better placed in
fact than the judges to instruct citizens, in this setting, about the
grounds of principle that a decent people should never wish to put
in place, even in advancing their own interests? As Harry Jaffa once
put it, in summing up Lincoln's teaching on this point, a free people
must learn to respect, in the first instance, the premises on which its
own freedom rests.[29]

---

[29] Harry V. Jaffa, *Crisis of the House Divided: An Interpretation of the Issues in the
Lincoln-Douglas Debates* (Chicago: University of Chicago Press, 1982; originally
published 1959), 305–07.

With that concern, at the root, for the premises or the "first principles" of the law, I return where I began, to James Wilson and his colleagues in *Chisholm v. Georgia*, the first major case to elicit a set of opinions from the Supreme Court in 1793. Among those opinions was a trenchant analysis offered by the Chief Justice, John Jay, along with a statement by Wilson so elegant, and so drawn to first principles, that it deserves to stand among the first of our "State papers" as a virtual primer on the American law. Wilson and Jay offered, on that day, nothing less than syllogisms, arresting and compelling: arresting in the style of their construction, and utterly compelling in producing conclusions that have the force of logical necessity. And yet, it would put the matter mildly to say that they were met with a show of incomprehension on the part of the politicians and the voting public. The political class surveyed this elegant first opinion, and then responded by enacting the Eleventh Amendment for the purpose, in effect, of overriding the decision reached by the Court. But if we look at the matter again—and look as though we were looking for the first time, reading with a due respect what Jay and Wilson were putting before us as a syllogism—I think we would have to render a verdict rather different from the verdict dished up at that moment by the politics of this new nation.

The question before the Court was whether a state could be sued against its wishes, in a federal court, by an individual, a single person, litigating a personal interest. The concern of the political class was with loyalists, displaced from their property during the war, and making use now of the federal courts to extract compensation. Hamilton had remarked in passing, in *The Federalist Papers*, that "it was inherent in the nature of sovereignty not to be amenable to the suit of an individual without its consent."[30] But this might have been one of those rare instances in which Hamilton assimilated too readily the conventions long settled around him. In any event, he was not as sensitive as his fellow nationalists, Wilson and Jay, to the implications that sprung from the logic of this new national government.

I would not try to reconstruct here all of the intricate arguments fashioned by Wilson and Jay as they sought to demonstrate the structure of logic that made it indeed possible for a state to be brought to the bar in the federal courts by an individual person. I would pick out only a couple of fragments that convey adequately, for our purposes here, the sense of their argument. Wilson offered a chain of reasoning rather similar to one offered by Hamilton in *Federalist* 33: The authority to legislate for the nation meant the authority to make rules that were binding on all of the lesser units or associations, which

[30] See Hamilton in *The Federalist* no. 81, 529.

included then the states. Citing from Bracton, he pointed out that
the authority to legislate had to entail the authority to enforce or
to administer, in particular cases, the acts that were legislated. The
operations of a court offered merely another instance in the administration of the laws. If laws could be passed then, binding on the states,
they could be enforced by the executive against the resistance of the
states. And if the same laws, administered by the executive, came
under challenge, that challenge could be addressed, and the laws
administered, in the courts.[31]

Wilson pointed out that, under the Constitution, the judicial
power extended to "controversies between two States." But then, Wilson asked, how could a controversy of this kind be brought before
the federal courts "and yet neither of these States be a Defendant?"[32]
And if a state could be a defendant in a federal court, could it be a
matter of significance then as to whether the plaintiff was a state or a
person? Evidently, many jurists at the time thought there was a certain point of complication: On the surface, there seemed to be a notable difference between being sued by another state or by individuals
unencumbered by the restraints of official responsibility. Yet, Wilson
raised the question of how free men, or states, may bind themselves
to the law, and come under the authority of the courts:

> The only reason, I believe, why a free man is bound by human laws,
> is, *that he binds himself.* Upon the same principles, upon which he
> becomes bound *by the laws,* he becomes amenable to the *Courts of
> Justice,* which are formed and authorized by those laws. If one free
> man, an original sovereign, may do all this; why may not an aggre-

---

[31] See *Chisholm*, 2 Dallas at 464–65:
In order, ultimately, to discover, [wrote Wilson] whether the people of the
United States intended to bind those States by the Judicial power vested by
the national Constitution, a previous enquiry will naturally be: Did those
people intend to bind those States by the *Legislative* power vested by that
Constitution? . . . [I]t cannot, surely, be contended that the Legislative
power of the national Government was meant to have no operation on the
several States. The fact, uncontrovertibly established in one instance,
proves the principle in all other instances. . . . We may then infer, that the
people of the United States intended to bind the several States, by the
Legislative power of the national Government. [And since the judicial authority is merely another instance in the enforcement of the laws, it fol-
lows] from the second to the third and last step of our deduction. Fair and
conclusive deduction, then, evinces that the people of the United States
did vest this Court with jurisdiction over the State of Georgia. [Emphasis
in original.]
[32] Id. at 466.

gate of free men, a collection of original sovereigns, do this like-wise?[33]

Chief Justice Jay picked up that same thread, in his own opinion: It was axiomatic that one free citizen may sue another, and therefore, he could sue as many citizens as were the objects, fairly, of his complaint. In certain cases, said Jay, he may sue forty thousand, as he might if he lodged a suit against the forty thousand individuals who constituted, at that time, the city of Philadelphia. "For where a corporation is sued," wrote Jay, "all the members of it are *actually* sued, though not *personally*, sued."[34] There were, at the time, but fifty thousand people in the whole state of Delaware. Was it to be assumed then, asked Jay, that a free person had a right to sue the forty thousand individuals who made up Philadelphia, but not the fifty thousand people who made up Delaware? "Can the difference between forty odd thousand, and fifty odd thousand make any distinction as to right?"[35]

To put it another way, it was plain, in the text of the Constitution, that "any one State in the Union may sue another State, in this Court." But what does that mean except that "all the people of one State may sue all of the people of another"? And if *all* the people of Pennsylvania, say, could sue *all* the people of Delaware, then it would seem to follow that the "all" *must encompass the individuals who compose it*: If *all* the citizens of Pennsylvania may sue *all* the citizens of Delaware, then one of those citizens of Pennsylvania must be able to sue all the citizens of Delaware. As Jay remarked, "it is plain that no degradation to a State is thought to accompany her appearance in this Court."[36] And if a state is not degraded when it is sued by another state, how could it be degraded when it is sued by one of the free citizens who make up that other state? Of course, there was the sovereignty that attached to the community itself, constituted as a body politic. But as Wilson had observed at the beginning, "the sovereign, when traced to his source, must be found in the *man*."[37]

These opinions by Wilson and Jay were not offered as exercises in abstraction. They were attended with historical citations, with all of the earmarks of scholarship, and they were offered by one member of the Constitutional Convention and one contributor to *The Federalist Papers*. These judges were, in other words, men of deep experience

[33] Id. at 456, emphasis original.
[34] Id. at 472, emphasis original.
[35] Ibid.
[36] Id. at 473.
[37] Id. at 438.

in politics, and their writing was informed by a direct engagement with the framing of the Constitution. But when they composed their arguments, they also annexed to their experience the force of syllogisms. Yet, the political class viewed their handiwork, pronounced it wrong, and passed the Eleventh Amendment. Over the next several generations, however, judges would be forced to tie themselves in knots as they tried to construe the Eleventh Amendment and explain how a Constitution containing the Eleventh Amendment must nevertheless make it possible, on occasion, for the officers of states to be sued. The problem would be abated in large part with the advent of the Fourteenth Amendment, and yet, at one telling moment, in a case in 1890, the first Justice Harlan appended a note to a concurring opinion and admitted what deserved to be said: that all of the judicial acrobatics were unavailing and rather silly, because the first Court, in *Chisholm v. Georgia* got it right.[38] We might add: irresistibly, and finally, right.

Much has been made over the years of that line of Justice Holmes in the *Eisner* case, that "a page of history is worth a volume of logic."[39] I would suggest that, if we read in the classic cases, we would find there a quality of teaching that rather belies Holmes's glib dictum. If we opened ourselves anew to the lessons taught by our best jural minds, we would discover that an ounce of logic is worth several generations of misspent history.

I have come back full circle now to the *Chisholm* case and that first generation of judges as teachers, but the problem of the judge as republican schoolmaster had its more engaging expression, of course, by Alexis de Tocqueville, in his account of the jury as a political institution. Tocqueville's account of the jury paralleled his account of political life itself "as a gratuitous public school." And what was learned in this school were the principles of justice. People were compelled to argue about the things that were right and wrong, and about the principles that underlay their judgments. In the case of the jury, Tocqueville observed that

> every juror learns his rights, enters into daily communication with the most learned and enlightened members of the upper classes, and becomes practically acquainted with the laws, which are brought within the reach of his capacity by the efforts of the bar, the advice of the judge, and even the passions of the parties.

As for the judge, the jurors "look up to him with confidence"; they will need his guidance in sifting the evidence, and sorting out

---

[38] See *Hans v. Louisiana*, 134 U.S 1, 21.
[39] *New York Trust Co. v. Eisner*, 256 U.S. 345, 349 (1921).

the points of judgment. And he will need to tell them "how to answer the question of law." In this way, as Tocqueville said—not again, spinning out fables, but reporting soberly on what he saw—"the American magistrates imbue even the lower classes of society with the spirit of their profession." The difference between Tocqueville's day and ours is that we have suffered a kind of reversal: The law seems ever more disconnected from natural justice, and from the language in which people of ordinary wit understand matters of right and wrong. The exclusionary rule, affirmative action, claims of "autonomy," and the fables that support these slogans, require the kinds of arguments that can be contrived only in the pages of the law journals. They have meaning only there, or in the offices of the clerks newly sprung from the law reviews. But those arguments rarely make contact with the world inhabited by the rest of us, and they almost never make sense to people who have not had their ears tuned to the language, and state of mind, of the law reviews. It is not the people, these days, who need to be instructed in the premises of constitutional government in order to be rendered into citizens fit for a republic. Curiously, it is their "betters" who seem in most urgent need of this instruction.

To the extent that I can summon, to this point, the aid of personal experience, I have the melancholy duty of reporting that my principal evidence would have been drawn from the state of Ohio. I was engaged, in 1994, as a consultant in the litigation over gay rights and the amendment to the charter of Cincinnati. Even now, it seems rather bizarre that this litigation, in Cincinnati and the state of Colorado, should bring forth academic "witnesses" such as Harvey Mansfield, Robert George, and me. Or it seems bizarre until we encounter the things that federal judges profess these days not to know. The policies at issue in Colorado and Cincinnati were cut from the same cloth: In both instances there was a movement, through a popular referendum, to amend the constitution of the state or the city. The amendments in either case were substantially the same: They would foreclose legislatures from treating gays and lesbians as a protected minority, on the same plane as the groups that suffer discrimination based on race, religion, or gender. The purpose of the legislation was not to license a regimen of prosecutions against gays and lesbians. The aim, rather, was to hold back the club of the law, and confirm to people, in their private settings, the freedom to honor their own moral or religious judgments on the matter of homosexuality.

In Cincinnati, the amendment to the city charter would have had the effect of superseding the Human Rights Ordinance of 1992, which barred virtually all species of discrimination, including the discriminations based on "sexual orientation." But for Judge Arthur

Spiegel, in the federal court in Cincinnati, this precise effect of the amendment marked one of its fatal defects: The amendment would remove gays and lesbians from the sweeping protections that were cast over so many other groups. It seemed to escape the recognition of Judge Spiegel that the constitutional amendment in Cincinnati had superseded the ordinance. Quite the reverse: Spiegel seemed to treat it as a telling flaw in the amendment that it ran counter to the ordinance.[40] At this moment, it fell to the attorneys and professors to remind the judge of the lessons taught by Chief Justice Marshall in *Marbury v. Madison*: Behind the ordinary laws were the "basic laws," the laws that told us, in effect, just what constitutes a "law." The fundamental law of a constitution bears then a *logical precedence* over the statute or the ordinary law. Spiegel complained that the amendment to the constitution removed from the legislature the power to pass the laws sought by gays and lesbians. But he had to be reminded that this was precisely the function that constitutions were meant to have in relation to legislatures—that they may limit the power of legislatures, in part by limiting the ends that the legislatures may reach. For Spiegel, there seemed to be something faintly disreputable in appealing to the voters at large when the local legislature showed in its work a large, liberal sympathy. What seemed to have vanished, however, from the judge was that understanding, expressed by Madison, Mason, and Wilson, that legislatures could not be the sources of the constitution; that there had to be an appeal beyond the legislature to the people themselves as the source of authority; and that, as James Wilson had said, "from [the power of the people] there is no appeal; of their error there is no superior principle of correction."[41]

I restate my point bluntly: This late in the seasons of our experience, federal judges should not be in need of this kind of instruction, on the rudiments of constitutional government. That a tuition in these matters would have to be administered to the judges could not have been what the Founders expected when they anticipated that the judges, and especially the judges of the Supreme Court, would have to engage in some public teaching. They did not suspect that the main instruction would have to be offered to the lawyers and judges themselves, and to the resident wits in the schools of law. That is not where the Founders thought that our most inventive judges would have to be directing their own genius, or their own arts as teachers. But that project has become, in our own day, steady work.

[40] See *Equality Foundation of Greater Cincinnati v. City of Cincinnati*, 838 F. Supp. 1235, 1238 (S.D. Ohio 1993).
[41] Elliot's *Debates*, 2:433.

THE IDIOM OF COMMON LAW IN THE FORMATION OF JUDICIAL POWER

James R. Stoner, Jr. *

> Laws based on unwritten customs are more authoritative, and deal with more authoritative matters, than those based on written rules; so if it is safer for a human being to rule than laws based on written rules, this is not the case for rules based on custom.
>
> —ARISTOTLE, *Politics* III (1287b1)

IN THE PITCHED battles of the "culture wars," whatever the field of our engagement, we soldiers of fortune quickly forget our victories and defeats, and sometimes even mistake the one for the other. Something like this must explain the disappearance in the past decade or so of the question whether we Americans have, in some respects, an unwritten constitution. While scholars then divided between "interpretivists" and "non-interpretivists," the partisans of the written and the unwritten, today the conservative insistence on the priority of the written text and the authority of the original understanding of that text by those who wrote and ratified it frames the terms of debate.[1] Perhaps it is only a matter of language; advocates

*The author wishes to express his gratitude to the National Endowment for the Humanities, for a fellowship that provided the time to prepare this essay.

[1] Thomas C. Grey, "Do We have an Unwritten Constitution?" *Stanford Law Review* 27 (1975): 703–18; "Origins of the Unwritten Constitution: Fundamental Law in American Revolutionary Thought," *Stanford Law Review* 30 (1978): 843–93; John Hart Ely, *Democracy and Distrust* (Cambridge, Mass.: Harvard University Press, 1980). The exception to the rule about disappearance of interest in the unwritten constitution is a fine article by Suzanna Sherry, "The Founders' Unwritten Constitution," *University of Chicago Law Review* 54 (1987): 1127–77. The "Jurisprudence of Original Intention" was thrust into public debate by a much-publicized speech to the American Bar Association by then-Attorney Gen-

of an evolving or "living" Constitution have developed theories of interpretation sophisticated enough to permit them to reach the same results based on the text as they had sought in unwritten principle.[2] Still, the Supreme Court today seems more scrupulous in attaching even its innovations to the written word. In the watershed issue of whether the Constitution licenses an abortion right, the justices have replaced their reference in *Roe v. Wade*[3] to a "right of privacy," supposedly found in the shadows of the text, with reference to the protection of "liberty" in the Due Process Clauses of the Fifth and Fourteenth Amendments, all the while reaffirming that an abortion right is present. That the definition they give of "liberty" in the Constitution's text—"the right to define one's own concept of existence, of meaning, of the universe, and of the mystery of human life"—is obviously expansive enough to enact the whole agenda of sexual liberation and much more by judicial decree might counsel caution of those who think the bare text enough to confine those who would use judicial power as an instrument of what they favor as reform.[4]

In this context, I propose reopening the question of the unwritten constitution, or rather, the question of the implications for the written Constitution we have of the tradition of unwritten law in the midst of which that Constitution was written. While others have for similar reasons turned their attention to natural law or natural rights,[5] I recommend, not instead but in tandem, attention to the common law. Theories of natural law or natural rights are perhaps more satisfying to the mind, but they are for the same reason more contentious in the polity; let it be enough for now to point to the radically different conceptions of law and political life in classical natural law on the one hand and modern natural rights on the other.[6]

eral Edwin Meese, III, published as "The Supreme Court of the United States: Bulwark of a Limited Constitution," *South Texas Law Review* 27 (1986): 455–66. For a more developed account, see Robert Bork, *The Tempting of America: The Political Seduction of the Law* (New York: Free Press, 1990), and the essay in this volume by Robert P. George and Gerard V. Bradley.

[2] See, e.g., Ronald Dworkin, *A Matter of Principle* (Cambridge, Mass.: Harvard University Press, 1985), ch. 6.

[3] 410 U.S. 113 (1973). The "shadows" are the "penumbras" announced in the basic "right of privacy" case, *Griswold v. Connecticut*, 381 U.S. 479, 484 (1965).

[4] *Planned Parenthood v. Casey*, 112 S.Ct. 2791, 2807 (1992).

[5] See especially the important work of Hadley Arkes, *Beyond the Constitution* (Princeton, N.J.: Princeton University Press, 1990), and *The Return of George Sutherland: Restoring a Jurisprudence of Natural Rights* (Princeton, N.J.: Princeton University Press, 1994).

[6] See Leo Strauss, "Natural Law," in *International Encyclopedia of the Social Sciences*, ed. David L. Sills (New York: Macmillan, 1968).

Grounded in custom, and so in consensus, common law gained in practical authority what it yielded in intellectual simplicity. Moreover, at the time of the Founding, natural law and common law were seen as complementary, and more than one effort was made to assimilate the one to the other. My argument for the importance of common law is partly historical: Not only the original intention of the Constitution but the value of recourse to original intention is oblique if common law is overlooked, for the great document and the Bill of Rights that soon joined it were written in the idiom of common law, and the authority of legislative intent was among the common law's many maxims. Besides, for a century or more, American constitutional development took place in a legal context that took its bearings from common law, and even today our law is replete with precepts and institutions of common law descent.

I also think that renewed appreciation of common law, not so much in its modern as in its classic meaning, offers for our consideration, if not a promise of truce in the "culture wars," at least a way toward restoring what Robert Nagel has called our "constitutional culture,"[7] now divided into warring camps. I will not present common law constitutionalism as an alternative constitutional *theory*, for it is part of the genius of common law to be skeptical of comprehensive theory in the law, thinking it certain to simplify and thus oppress some realm of human experience. Nor do I mean to revive lapsed ethnic privilege: Although I suppose the eclipse of common law in recent years owes something to the rise of a multi-ethnic America and thus to the decline of Anglo predominance in the culture, common law here was always distinct from its English parent and was a powerful means of assimilating the foreign-born into a shared world. Quite simply, the common law has had, along with natural law, liberalism, capitalism, Christianity, and much else, a formative influence on the American character, and a recognition of what it is and has become is an essential part of understanding our constitutionalism, our possibilities, and ourselves. Let me try, in what follows, to sketch what that understanding might entail.

THE ORIGINAL UNDERSTANDING OF COMMON LAW

Like a well-fit ring or watch, ever on the hand but never in mind, the common law is rarely noticed by most scholars of the law, and especially of the Constitution. More importantly, if attended to at all,

---

[7] See Robert Nagel, *Constitutional Cultures: The Mentality and Consequences of Judicial Review* (Berkeley and Los Angeles: University of California Press, 1989).

it is understood in a way that is at odds with its original understanding, that is, with the way it was seen by the Framers of the Constitution and by the English authors whom they read. Ask any lawyer or professor today to define "common law" and he will answer that it is "judge-made law," devised in cases, extended by precedent, and limited only by the consensus of the bench and bar or by legislative intervention. This opinion was not entirely unknown to the Founders, but it was the cynic's perspective, to which no self-respecting lawyer or judge, much less republican citizen, could admit. The transformation in the meaning of common law was the work of Oliver Wendell Holmes, Jr., in his lectures called *The Common Law* and in his influence from the bench, first of the Supreme Judicial Court of Massachusetts and then for almost thirty years of the Supreme Court of the United States. I will have more to say about Holmes later, but it is essential at the outset to suspend allegiance to Holmes's definition if the original understanding of common law is to be grasped.

Common law was, in the first place, the immemorial customary law of England, enforced in the Court of Common Pleas and the King's Bench, and throughout the realm in the assizes. These were not the only courts in England nor was common law the only law of the realm; ecclesiastical law and admiralty were separate jurisdictions, both operating on civil law principles, and equity was administered by the court of Chancery in cases where strict law was thought not to satisfy the demands of conscience. Common law governed matters of estate and also crime and punishment (the chief business, respectively, of its two principal courts), and by the seventeenth century, its classic era, its principles gave form to English law as a whole. Lacking a written code, the written evidence of common law was to be found in the records of cases previously decided. To learn the law meant to learn these precedents and the rules of law they established, but also to understand the reasons behind them, for it was a maxim at common law that a precedent that ran against reason was no law; to decide a case at common law required a determination of what precedents were appropriate to the case at hand. It was settled in the rhetoric of common law, and held to be fixed in the character of a common law judge, that in deciding cases it was the judge's duty to discover, not invent, what law governed the case at hand, and if the case seemed genuinely novel, the judge was to proceed by analogy to the appropriate precedent. As statutes were made they were assimilated to common law, for the common law had rules by which statutes were to be interpreted. While it was among the maxims of common law that a rule of statute law supersedes a contrary, unwritten common law rule, it had first to be determined whether the statute in question modified the common law or simply declared it in writing. To the most characteristic and perhaps the greatest of the English common law judges, Sir Edward Coke, the whole array of customs, maxims, precedents, and statutes appeared as an "artificial perfection of reason," and he meant by that phrase to refer, not to an edifice of science established in a treatise, but to the learning and the judgment—that is, the art—that took form in the mind of a well-read and experienced judge.[8]

The law of what came to be called the English constitution was not strictly speaking common law, since Parliament had its own law and custom and the king his own prerogatives, but the constitution of the courts was a part of common law and the larger principles of the English constitution clearly bore the stamp of common law thinking. That the English constitution is unwritten astonishes us today, but it was reasonable and indeed expected in a common law setting. As statutes were held to declare the law as well as make it, the unwritten character of the constitution was not inconsistent with a tradition of great constitutional documents, from Magna Carta (1215) to the Petition of Right (1628) to the Bill of Rights (1689), that declared the privileges and immunities of subjects of the realm. Besides, as precedents had the force of law, so what Albert Venn Dicey was in the nineteenth century to call the conventions of the constitution could by analogy be considered authoritative, even if their violation would find no remedy in court.[9] That judges were appointed from the bar was among these conventions; lawyers were already considered officers of the court, after all, and so their elevation to the bench had something of the character of a promotion, not a change of profession. That judges declared the law in cases before them, with the facts determined by a jury of "twelve good men and true," was well-established by the seventeenth century as a matter of common right.[10] Indeed, trial by jury was as much as its unwrittenness the distinctive mark of common law, and not by accident, for both customary law and jury verdict might be said to register the understanding of justice in the common mind.

To Coke and his fellows, the common law was the guarantor of English liberties; its Great Charter was called a charter of liberties, he

[8] I discuss these matters at greater length in *Common Law and Liberal Theory: Coke, Hobbes, and the Origins of American Constitutionalism* (Lawrence: University Press of Kansas, 1992), esp. ch. 1.

[9] A. V. Dicey, *Introduction to the Study of the Law of the Constitution* (reprint, Indianapolis: Liberty Press, 1982).

[10] See, for example, Thomas Andrew Green, *Verdict According to Conscience* (Chicago: University of Chicago Press, 1985).

explained, because the effect of its many privileges was to make men free, especially by its assurance in its twenty-ninth chapter of what by Coke's time was already called "due process of law."[11] The liberty protected by common law was achieved through the law, not outside it; it was characteristic of common law to protect men's estates or their right to earn a living, and thus no accident that Parliament anchored its authority then not in a general assertion of sovereignty but in its power over taxation. A liberty that considered due process its expression and "no taxation without representation" its guarantor was not defined as personal autonomy; it was taken for granted that crimes were moral wrongs, not just behavior deemed undesirable by the social power or minimal restrictions on the license of each in the name of the others. Due process, and the jury trial at its heart, was a promise that legal proceedings would uncover the truth and that conviction would follow proof of guilt. That it afforded special protection for the accused, forbidding torture and thus involuntary self-incrimination, revealed something of the genius that ran throughout the common law, tender towards the innocent and respectful of free will.

When liberal political theory first arrived in the work of Thomas Hobbes, it was as opponent of the common law, not as its champion, even though on some matters, such as self-incrimination, the traditions converged. By the eighteenth century, however, several great attempts at synthesis were attempted, first by John Locke, who aimed to reconcile liberal philosophy and the English constitution, then by William Blackstone, whose *Commentaries on the Laws of England*, appearing in the 1760s, reworked the common law from a liberal perspective and presented its chief rules and maxims in accessible, literary form.[12] Blackstone's contemporary, William Murray (Lord Mansfield), meanwhile, had undertaken from the King's Bench to reform common law, most successfully in incorporating into what had been predominantly a law of landed estate the principles of the law merchant and thus developing the common law of contract. Reforming common law from within, Mansfield and Blackstone also taught the sovereignty of Parliament, thus preparing the eclipse of common law even as they infused it with modern ideas.

To assume that the Americans of the Revolutionary Era simply

---

[11] *The Reports of Sir Edward Coke*, ed. George Wilson (Dublin: J. Moore, 1793), vol. 8, preface; Sir Edward Coke, *Institutes of the Laws of England*, part II (London, 1642; reprint, New York: Garland Publishing, 1979), 47. See also Stoner, *Common Law and Liberal Theory*, 21.

[12] See Stoner, *Common Law and Liberal Theory*, chaps. 8, 10.

accepted the dominant understanding of common law in contemporary Britain would be a serious error. Although Blackstone was within a generation to replace Coke as the favorite authority on common law among Americans, it was understood that his account of parliamentary sovereignty was inapplicable here—the Revolution might even be said to have been fought against the assertion of that principle in the colonies—and Mansfield had been an outspoken foe in the struggles leading up to independence. Still, in the course of their struggles, and even on the brink of separation, Americans claimed the common law as their inheritance, most dramatically in the "Declaration and Resolves" of the First Continental Congress, who resolved "That the respective colonies are entitled to the common law of England, and more especially to the great and inestimable privilege of being tried by their peers of the vicinage, according to the course of that law."[13] In the more famous Declaration of Independence not two years later, the choice of independence—or its defense to the world—mandated that appeal be made to the law of nature rather than the law of England, but when abstract terms like "absolute Despotism" were given concrete meaning, it was by reference, in the largely unread catalogue of grievances, to numerous rights and privileges at common law, against which the king and his Parliament now were found to have transgressed.

Meanwhile, as the colonies reformed themselves into states, they all adopted, often by statute or constitutional provision, the common law as the basis of their jurisprudence—not the common law of England in its entirety, to be sure, but, as Joseph Story was to write in 1837 for a commission on codification in reference to his native Massachusetts,

> that portion of the common law of England, (as modified and ameliorated by English statutes,) which was in force at the time of the emigration of our ancestors, and was applicable to the situation of the colony, and has since been recognized and acted upon, during the successive progresses of our Colonial, Provincial, and State Governments, with this additional qualification, that it has not been altered, repealed, or modified by any of our subsequent legislation now in force.[14]

[13] Reprinted in *Colonies to Nation, 1763–1789: A Documentary History of the American Revolution,* ed. Jack P. Greene (New York: W.W. Norton & Co., 1975), 245.

[14] "Codification of the Common Law," in *The Miscellaneous Writings of Joseph Story,* ed. William W. Story (Boston: Little, Brown, 1852), 701. On the more general question of the reception of common law in America, see Kermit Hall, *The Magic Mirror: Law in American History* (New York: Oxford University Press, 1989), 12 ff.; and William E. Nelson, *Americanization of the Common Law: The Impact of*

To the modern reader this sounds so qualified as to sever all relation, but Story is merely writing with his customary precision; although such important parts of the common law as many of the feudal tenures and all that related to "the ecclesiastical establishment" had never been known in Massachusetts, it is clear he thinks the essence of the common law was successfully transplanted and grew strong and free in its new soil. In Virginia, where the established church and many feudal tenures had indeed come across, the project of adjusting the common law upon independence was more urgent, hence the appointment of a Committee of Revisors in 1776, with Thomas Jefferson, Edmund Pendleton, and George Wythe among its members. But even here, the decision was simply to draft model statutes for reform, not to try by code to introduce a wholly new order. As Jefferson was to write of the Revisors' deliberations, looking back in 1821,

> to abrogate our whole system would be a bold measure, and probably far beyond the views of the legislature; . . . to compose a new Institute . . . would be an arduous undertaking, of vast research, of great consideration & judgment; and when reduced to a text, every word of that text, from the imperfection of human language, and it's [*sic*] incompetence to express distinctly every shade of idea, would become a subject of question & chicanery until settled by repeated adjudications; . . . this would involve us for ages in litigation, and render property uncertain until, like the statutes of old, every word had been tried, and settled by numerous decisions, and by new volumes of reports & commentaries.[15]

The decision of the colonies becoming states to adhere by and large to their common law tradition, indeed to make their case for independence by appeal to ancient rights they had by common law, makes plain enough that, even as they introduced to the world the written constitution, they had no intention of replacing the unwritten law on which their properties were founded and by which their moral and social lives were ordered. This helps explain an overlooked peculiarity in the Declaration of Independence itself, namely its reference, when condemning acts of parliamentary oppression, to "our constitution," eleven years before the Philadelphia Convention and before the committee to draft written Articles of Confederation were even appointed, much less successful in their work.[16] Jefferson's draft had

Legal Change on Massachusetts Society, 1760–1830 (Cambridge, Mass: Harvard University Press, 1975).

[15] Thomas Jefferson, *Writings* (New York: The Library of America, 1984), 38.

[16] I discuss this matter at greater length in *Common Law and Liberal Theory*, 188–89.

the word in the plural (indeed reprints of the Declaration can be found today with this error), and while the referent then would have been the constitutions of the colonies or states, these too were still for the most part unwritten, Congress just having issued on May 10, 1776, a call to the colonies to suppress crown authority and adopt their own forms of government. But Jefferson's "constitutions" was changed to the singular in committee, leaving no alternative but to suppose an unwritten constitution of British North America, defined in the Declaration itself by the violations alleged to have been made upon it by the British Parliament and king. One might say that the constitution there mentioned was dissolved by the very document that names it, but it is not obvious that to "dissolve the Political Bands" between two peoples was the same thing as undoing a constitution, even or especially an unwritten one. Besides, it might be recalled that the Second Continental Congress operated without a written constitution for the course of the fighting, the Articles lying unratified for four years because of disputes among the states over the future of the western lands.

Here, then, is a sketch of the understanding of common law on the eve of the Philadelphia convention. It was proudly claimed by Americans as their inheritance, modified to fit the more democratic circumstances of the New World. It was known to have its roots in England, but it was thought to have survived transplanting and to be on the verge of becoming its own tradition. It was, like the legislative power, still principally at home in the colonies-become-states, but such federal action as had begun was not thought formed on hostile principles, and indeed relied at least in part on principles familiar from common law. It formed the law administered in courts, again more democratically than in the mother country, since juries played a greater role and since judges, appointed in colonial times by the crown, were viewed with some suspicion.[17] And it also gave form to the politics of the Revolution itself, which framed the dispute with England in legal terms and so saw the war that followed from it as a sort of trial by battle. My argument is not to deny that, when the break came, it was defended in the natural rights language of Lockean liberalism or of a radical Whiggism that was influenced by this. It is rather to say that liberalism served to provide, not a theory for the ordering of the whole society, but a program to explain the unusual or extreme case in which the colonists found themselves as the British govern-

[17] Nelson, *Americanization of the Common Law*; see also Shannon Stimson, *The American Revolution in the Law: Anglo-American Jurisprudence Before John Marshall* (Princeton, N.J.: Princeton University Press, 1990).

ment moved to crush the assertion of what they saw as their constitutional rights. Liberalism grows in influence as the United States develops, not least as the federal government expands, and liberalism eventually grows away from its natural rights foundation, but its role at the outset was to sever "political bands" that had grown destructive and to suggest reforms in the common law order, something that that order had always allowed. That the change of regime from monarchy to republic occurred with such restraint in America is testimony, in part, to the continuous power of a common law that focused its attention, not on the question of regime, but on the rights of individuals in particular cases and thus on the whole array of institutions in civil society in the midst of which the people went about their lives. That we today find our lives so thoroughly politicized, and thus our politics so bitter, might be testimony to the consequences of dismantling the buffer of common law that stood between the individual and the legislative will.

COMMON LAW IN THE CONSTITUTION

The original understanding of common law, which I have laid out at such length because it has been largely forgotten, colors every aspect of the Constitution and thus is essential to a complete account of the original understanding of the Constitution itself. Let me try to put the matter more precisely. That the Constitution concentrates on establishing the structure of the federal government; that it organizes its institutions according to the principles of the separation of powers and federalism, and that it understands the latter especially on a novel scheme; that it insists on a form of government that is at once strictly republican, in the sense of drawing all its power directly or indirectly from the people, and entirely representative, in removing the people from the administration of the government; that it puts this all in a positive, written document to be ratified by extraordinary conventions in the states—all of this owes little or nothing to common law and much to the "great improvements" in "the science of politics" praised by Alexander Hamilton in *The Federalist Papers*, as well as to the "manly spirit" of the Founding generation, who had not, in his co-author James Madison's words, "suffered a blind veneration for antiquity, for custom, or for names, to overrule the suggestions of their own good sense, the knowledge of their own situation, and the lessons of their own experience."[18] But if the Constitution

[18] *The Federalist*, ed. Jacob E. Cooke (Middletown, Conn.: Wesleyan University Press, 1961), no. 9, 51, and no. 14, 88.

made an "experiment of an extended republic," its genius was to build with materials at hand, to temper its innovations with the familiar, to establish a government that was limited not only in its power over individuals but in its sovereignty over what they accounted law. The Constitution was, to be sure, meant to be a written instrument of government, and its engineers were trained in a liberal school, but that does not establish that it undertook to remake man on liberal principles or to narrow all authority to what the new federal government was enabled to achieve.

To fully establish the argument I have just sketched would require an investigation—beyond the bounds of the current essay—into law and politics in the states in 1787, which the Constitution was meant, of course, to constrain but not to replace. What is worth examining here is the presence of common law in the Constitution itself. This appears in the first place, as mentioned before and as universally acknowledged, in the language in which the document is written. Whether at issue is "the Privilege of the Writ of Habeas Corpus" or "ex post facto Law," or "natural born," or "good behavior," recourse must be had to common law for definition. Moreover, in contrast to the Virginia Plan at the Convention, which spoke of the National Legislature and the National Executive, the Constitution proceeds, common law-like, even when fashioning new institutions, to give them established names, most obviously in the case of Congress, but even in the use of "President" for the chief executive. The influence of common law appears not only in the words but also in the style of the document, most especially in the way the Constitution articulates rather by enumeration than by definition, most famously in the list of the powers of Congress in Article I, section 8. Here again the contrast to the Virginia Plan is instructive. It would have defined rather than enumerated the power of the National Legislature: "to legislate in all cases to which the separate States are incompetent, or in which the harmony of the United States may be interrupted by the exercise of individual Legislation."[19] Although the Convention at first approved such an approach, the Committee of Detail returned to an enumeration of powers, as in the Articles of Confederation, and the delegates readily acquiesced.

My point in drawing attention to the common law language in the Constitution is not to deny that old words can assume new meanings, but rather to suggest that the presumption was meant to run the other way, to presume stability in language and continuity in law, ex-

---

[19] In Max Farrand, *The Framing of the Constitution of the United States* (New Haven: Yale University Press, 1913), Appendix II, 226.

cept where there was explicit, written text to the contrary or a clear, logical implication derived from the text. That at least was the practice in interpreting statutes at common law, and there is no reason to suppose that the Framers meant for their Constitution to be read any differently, at least in court. The Constitution was a new kind of statute, of course, a fundamental law stamped with popular approval. How that Constitution was to be read, whether strictly, as were penal statutes, or liberally, as were statutes against frauds[20]—or whether powers were to be read one way and rights another—thus needed fresh determination, and so it was no accident that constitutional law in its early years was concerned with precisely this. But to allow for a liberal interpretation of congressional powers need not deny stability in meaning, and may even be thought to demand it, for the Framers' having anticipated the need for flexibility in government to meet changing exigencies is an argument against their having left their words infinitely supple. As for the persistence of enumerating powers and rights rather than defining them abstractly, it betrays a common law willingness to respect the multiplicity of human concerns, rather than to insist on theoretical perfection.

In the second place, common law appears in the Constitution specifically in Article III, where the judicial power is established, and again it appears not in terms but as presupposition. Ironically, this is clearest in the text at the very moment the Framers depart from common law practice by assigning "all Cases, in Law and Equity," to a single set of courts, for the understanding of "law and equity" here is quite obviously specific to the English tradition, where a settled practice of equity adjudication developed alongside the common law courts. Likewise, trial by jury, the trademark of common law, is guaranteed, although again a few modifications of common law practice are indicated—the subject of much dispute in ratification debates, by the way. That the judicial power was understood in common law manner is nowhere more evident than in *The Federalist Papers*, where Hamilton, in No. 78, takes it for granted that judges will be "bound down by strict rules and precedents"; that they must devote themselves to "long and laborious study" of "the records of precedents[, which] must unavoidably swell to a very considerable bulk"; and that they will have to "quit[] a lucrative line of practice to accept a seat on the bench"—that is, he takes for granted that they will, in common law fashion, be appointed from the bar, and that they will study and judge

[20] See the rules for interpretation of statutes in William Blackstone, *Commentaries on the Laws of England* (reprint of 1765 original, Chicago: University of Chicago Press, 1979), 1:87–91.

in the common law mode. Nor in this light is it accidental that their power to set aside unconstitutional statutes remains unwritten, to be deduced on analogy to the rule for interpreting conflicting statutes, a "mere rule of construction, not derived from any positive law, but from the nature and reason of the thing," in Hamilton's words again in No. 78. That he expects federal judges to protect individual rights even when no written constitutional command is crossed, by "mitigating the severity, and confining the operation of such laws" as are "unjust and partial" further suggests that he expects them to possess, by virtue of the judicial power itself, the common law judge's tools of art.[21]

A third place where the common law way of thinking appears in the Constitution is in the Supremacy Clause of Article VI: "This Constitution, and the Laws of the United States which shall be made in Pursuance thereof; and all Treaties made, or which shall be made, under the Authority of the United States, shall be the supreme Law of the Land; and the Judges in every State shall be bound thereby, any Thing in the Constitution or Laws of any State to the Contrary notwithstanding." What is remarkable here is not the fact of federal supremacy but the manner in which it was to be secured, namely, through the courts of law. Once again the Virginia Plan had some thing very different in mind, a power in the National Legislature "to negative all laws passed by the several States, contravening in the opinion of the National Legislature the articles of Union." The Supremacy Clause, instead, comes from the alternative New Jersey Plan, where it appeared in a version very similar to its final form. (Interestingly, this plan refers several times, in a different context, to the "Common law Judiciary" in the several states.)[22] What made possible the unique arrangement of American federalism, at least in the early years of the republic, was its mediation by a judiciary trained to focus not on abstract questions of sovereignty but on questions of right and power as they arise in a particular case. This allowed for the logic of the novel system to be worked out over time, as issues develop, rather than forcing a settlement before the advantages and disadvantages of any scheme had become clear. It allowed the judiciaries of each part of the system to reach unobtrusively into the other as needed to settle the case at hand: the state courts enforcing claims under federal law when these arose in cases within their jurisdiction, the federal courts deferring to the law of the states in settling diversity suits and even,

[21] *The Federalist*, 529, 526, 528.
[22] Farrand, *The Framing of the Constitution*, Appendix II, 226; Appendix III, 232, 229.

under the original Judiciary Act, in ordering their own legal process. Moreover, it allowed state law to develop in parallel fashion in the several states, as common law precedents came to be cited across state boundaries and as legal treatises of national scope, for instance those of Supreme Court Justice Joseph Story or the *Commentaries on American Law* of New York Chancellor James Kent, made American common law readily available to lawyers and judges in a land growing and changing at a rapid pace. How much of this can be attributed to the intention of the Framers is uncertain, but it is clear, at least from Hamilton's papers in *The Federalist*, that they understood that no written constitution by itself will anticipate every difficulty:

> The erection of a new government, whatever care or wisdom may distinguish the work, cannot fail to originate questions of intricacy and nicety; and these may in a particular manner be expected to flow from the establishment of a constitution founded upon the total or partial incorporation of a number of distinct sovereignties. 'Tis time only that can mature and perfect so compound a system, can liquidate the meaning of all the parts, and can adjust them to each other in a harmonious and consistent WHOLE.[23]

Although the passage occurs in the context of a discussion of the relation of state and federal courts, Hamilton does not suggest that only the judiciary is involved in the work of maturity and adjustment. Indeed, no one should expect such a suggestion from a mind trained, like Hamilton's, in the common law, where courts settle novel issues when they arise in the context of a legal dispute, but legislatures can alter, not past verdicts, but the future course of the law.

To these three aspects of common law in the Constitution was added a fourth, the Bill of Rights. Enumerated in traditional fashion, drawn from the English experience, many (especially in Amendments IV through VIII) concerned specifically with legal process, the rights here protected against federal infringement make explicit the common law demeanor of the new federal government, reinforced by the story of their enactment. Over the protests of leading Federalists, who thought such a catalogue of rights unnecessary or positively dangerous, many of the state ratifying conventions insisted on a promise of amendments to insure traditional rights thought insecure, if not positively threatened, by the new federal regime. The case of trial by jury, that emblem of common law, is most indicative. Though established in general terms for criminal trials in Article III of the original document, it was not above criticism in *The Federalist*, where

[23] *Federalist* no. 82, 553.

its virtue in civil cases is somewhat impeached and the difference between Federalists and Anti-Federalists on trial by jury is aptly captured: "the former regard it as a valuable safeguard to liberty, the latter represent it as the very palladium of free government."[24] The Bill of Rights edges the government toward the palladian view, specifying in some detail the rights of the criminal jury trial and adding, in the Seventh Amendment, protection for juries in "Suits at common law." That James Madison and other Federalists in Congress were readily able to introduce a series of amendments that would meet the promise of the ratification compromise without undermining the original document suggests that enough of them saw the amendments as merely declaring unwritten law—if at the price of reducing Congress' future room for maneuver—rather than as retrenchment on the Constitution's own reforms.[25] Moreover, the Ninth Amendment, a written tribute to unwritten rights, loses much of its uncertainty if understood from the common law perspective, for it then appears not as a license for inventive judges but as testimony to the unwritten store of rights discovered in common law privileges and immunities, perhaps the very sort of thing Hamilton had in mind when he attributed to judges a duty to mitigate and confine the statute law.

COMMON LAW IN CONSTITUTIONAL LAW: PAST AND PROSPECTS

Until well into the twentieth century, common law not only helped shape American law and legal culture generally and American constitutional law in particular, but had a specific role in federal law in its own right. As announced by Justice Story in the 1842 case, *Swift v. Tyson*,[26] the federal courts thought themselves bound, when deciding common law matters under their diversity jurisdiction (that is, in cases between citizens of different states), to rest their decisions on "the general principles and doctrines of commercial jurisprudence." At issue in the case was the interpretation of section 34 of the Judiciary Act of 1789, "that the laws of the several States . . . shall be regarded as rules of decision in trials at common law in the courts of the United States, in cases where they apply," and in particular whether the "laws of the several States" includes precedents of their courts, even when these run against general legal practice, as did

[24] Ibid., no. 83, 562.
[25] See Herbert J. Storing, "The Constitution and the Bill of Rights," in *Essays on the Constitution of the United States*, ed. M. Judd Harmon (Port Washington, N.Y.: Kennikat Press, 1978).
[26] 16 Peters 1.

some of the New York precedents arguably applicable here. Determining that "the decisions of courts . . . are, at most, only evidence of what the laws are, and are not of themselveś laws," since such decisions "are often re-examined, reversed, and qualified by the courts themselves, whenever they are found to be either defective or ill-founded, or otherwise incorrect," Story concluded that "The laws of a State are more usually understood to mean the rules and enactments promulgated by the legislative authority thereof, or long established local customs having the force of laws."[27] Thus, while common law could acquire a local character concerning local matters, such as real estate, the federal courts would settle common law cases that came within their jurisdiction by what would come to be known as federal common law.[28]

The demise of *Swift v. Tyson* came in 1938 in an opinion by Justice Louis Brandeis in the case of *Erie R. Co. v. Tompkins*,[29] and it was part and parcel of the "Constitution Revolution" that precipitated the year before. Like *Swift*, *Erie* turned on interpretation of section 34 of the Judiciary Act of 1789; but Brandeis chose not to reverse the long-standing statutory reading solely on the basis of better information about its framers' original intent—perhaps because it is generally held that precedent ought to be especially strong in the interpretation of statutes, since legislative acquiescence even in a historical error is presumed to indicate current legislative will.[30] Although the bulk of Brandeis's discussion was to illustrate what he held to be "the mischievous results" of the *Swift* doctrine, he relied on what he called "the unconstitutionality of the course" of decisions under *Swift*, which had the effect of discriminating in favor of non-citizens over citizens of a state, the former of whom could choose the forum of the federal courts when these decided cases under a more favorable rule than was available in the courts of the state where the complaint arose, and which thus "rendered impossible equal protection of the law." Instead, Brandeis would read the Judiciary Act's command to include among the "laws of the several States" not only their statutes

[27] Id. at 18–19.
[28] For a fine discussion of *Swift v. Tyson* and of its constitutional implications, see William T. Braithwaite, "The Common Law and Judicial Power: An Introduction to Swift-Erie and the Problem of Transcendental versus Positive Law," in *Law and Philosophy: The Practice of Theory, Essays in Honor of George Anastaplo*, ed. John A. Murley, Robert L. Stone, and William T. Braithwaite (Athens, Ohio: Ohio University Press, 1992), 2:774–818.
[29] 304 U.S. 64 (1938).
[30] See Edward H. Levi, *An Introduction to Legal Reasoning* (Chicago: University of Chicago Press, 1949), esp. 27 ff.

but the entire common law of the state as it now stood established by precedent in the state whose laws would apply. The federal judiciary would subsequently have no recourse of its own to common law, but must defer to whatever was announced as common law by state judges.

Erie has been thought responsible for the death of federal common law, in its technical sense, but in fact it was only its death knell, for underlying the opinion was the radical reorientation in the meaning of common law that had been introduced in the generation leading up to *Erie* by Justice Holmes: If judges are law-makers, then it is surely perverse to exclude their decisions from the law of the states to which the federal courts must defer. Holmes's project, introduced as early as his 1881 lectures, was first of all "to insist on a more conscious recognition of the legislative function of courts."[31] If this statement contains the germ of a critique of the Constitution, structured as the latter is on the notion of separate and analytically distinct powers of government, Holmes's strategy is not to assault the Constitution or, for that matter, American constitutional law head-on, but rather to act by indirection, as it were through the underbelly of that constitutionalism in common law. In a speech on John Marshall delivered from the Massachusetts bench, he confessed:

> My keenest interest is excited, not by what are called great questions and great cases, but by little decisions which the common run of selectors would pass by because they did not deal with the Constitution or a telephone company, yet which have in them the germ of some wider theory, and therefore of some profound interstitial change in the very tissue of the law.[32]

His book, *The Common Law*, is a study of just such change, usually unintentional, initiated by judges whose views of policy inevitably colored their decisions at law. The book is historical, but as he explains in his celebrated essay, "The Path of the Law," he is interested in history because "it is the first step toward an enlightened skepticism, that is, toward a deliberate reconsideration of the worth of those rules" that govern common law adjudication, now on self-conscious policy grounds. "For the rational study of the law, the black-letter man may be the man of the present, but the man of the future is the man of statistics and the master of economics. It is revolting to have

[31] *The Common Law*, ed. Mark DeWolfe Howe (Cambridge: Harvard University Press, 1963), 32.
[32] Holmes, *Collected Legal Papers* (New York: Harcourt, Brace and Howe, 1920), 269.

no better reason for a rule of law than that so it was laid down in the time of Henry IV."[33] Still, Holmes's economist does not work as a classical legislator; he is no architect of comprehensive political and social change. Rather, as a judge, he legislates little by little, adjusting the rules of decision case by case on the basis of a larger theory. He is a craftsman of judicious or surreptitious change, and thus he shies away from constitutional law, with its bright spotlight in the midst of party politics, or rather, he makes his contribution to constitutional law as he would to common law, quietly adjusting doctrine in the direction, but not the name, of new principles—as, it might be noted, Holmes succeeded in doing with the constitutional law of free speech. He is rather guided towards than confined by "interstices," for like the modern atom discovered by his contemporaries, Holmes's law is wide open between charged particles, though its surfaces seem solid to superficial minds.

The school of legal analysis Holmes fostered has come to be called legal realism, and Holmes's claim was first of all to describe what judges actually do, and only then to teach them better ways to do it. As I noted before, his basic account of common law as a process of judicially managed legal change is now orthodox in the legal academy, even if only occasionally employing economists as its priests.[34] Was it a fair description of the American common law judge in Holmes's time? Perhaps, but Holmes did not do justice to the serious reflection on the relation between permanence and change in the great publicists of common law in the early republic. As we saw above, already by the time of the Revolution the notion was alive, through the practice of Lord Mansfield and the writings of Blackstone, that the common law carried within it a reforming principle, at least in commercial matters, where the current practice of merchants was held to be entitled to respect in the courts. Moreover, in the early years of the American republic, the maxim that nothing against reason could be lawful itself became an engine of common law reform, in two related, but distinguishable ways. In the first place, the power of the common law judge to confine a precedent and even control a statute that went against reason seems to have referred most especially to his duty to keep the law consistent with itself.[35] The demand here was not that he deduce a fully articulated theory or model of

---

[33] Ibid., 186–87.

[34] See, e.g., Melvin Aron Eisenberg, *The Nature of the Common Law* (Cambridge: Harvard University Press, 1988); for the dean of the school of law and economics, a self-conscious Holmesian and now an influential federal judge, see Richard A. Posner, *Economic Analysis of Law*, 4th ed. (Boston: Little, Brown, 1992).

[35] See Stoner, *Common Law and Liberal Theory*, 53 ff.

the law from a few axioms; again, the common law welcomed a multiplicity of rules, even of kinds and sources of law, that any rigorous demand for consistency would have squelched. At the same time, contrary rules brought to bear on the same case could not be tolerated, and one must be obliged to yield. In the early years after the Founding, with the change of regime from monarchy to republic and with a vast expansion in the sources of law—the addition of a federal government with its own Constitution, legislature, and judiciary; the political independence and growing economic interdependence of the states, not to mention the steady growth in their numbers—numerous questions of law for which there were no adequate precedents were only to be expected, and the courts at every level had to reason their way through the new order of things. In the second place, however, under the influence of the same Enlightenment that helped set in motion these changes, the meaning of reason in the public sphere began to alter, so that courts might be called to consider not so much the consistency of law within its own immemorial order as its compatibility with the discoveries of modern social science, and especially the new science of political economy. Here the common law became an important part of the story of the economic development of the continent, the old genius of individual initiative embedded in the common law now allying with modern reforms in certain rules concerning the rights of property to give the edge to commercial improvement and acquisition over landed and inherited wealth.[36]

Let me illustrate these trends with two abbreviated examples. First, the controversy over the Alien and Sedition Acts from 1798 to 1800 is an important chapter in the history of common law in relation to the Constitution, not least because the ruling Federalists had begun common law prosecutions for seditious libel even before the Sedition Act was passed and because they argued that the Act itself was an improvement over the common law of libel in that it allowed for a jury determination of malicious intent and admitted proof of the truth of an assertion as a defense.[37] The newly formed Republicans countered that the federal government had no constitutional authority to prosecute crimes in the absence of a statute, but rather that libel, whether criminal or civil, was a matter for the common law courts in the states. Besides, they argued, the common law of sedi-

---

[36] See Morton J. Horwitz, *The Transformation of American Law, 1780–1860* (Cambridge, Mass.: Harvard University Press, 1977).

[37] See James Morton Smith, *Freedom's Fetters: The Alien and Sedition Laws and American Civil Liberties* (Ithaca, N.Y.: Cornell University Press, 1956).

tious libel was necessarily modified by the fact of republican government: "No previous restraint" might be an adequate definition of freedom of speech in a monarchy, where the parties to be feared were executive censors, but wider protection was imperative in a republic, where by statutes punishing defamation of government officials, a legislative majority might seek to entrench itself in power and stifle the public debate on which free elections depend.[38] The Republicans, of course, won the immediate battle, taking the presidential and congressional election of 1800, allowing the noxious act to expire, pardoning those still undergoing punishment because of it, and insuring an end to the doctrine of federal common law crimes. Still, with libel returned to the states, the Federalists too won a victory. Thanks to an argument by Hamilton in the name of common law (which he defined as "Natural law and natural reason applied to the purposes of Society") that lost in state court but won in the hearts and minds of the state legislators who came to hear him speak, they established in the law of New York that truth should be admitted as evidence in a libel case and the jury should be allowed to consider the intent of the publisher in determining its verdict—and from New York the rule went out into America through the *Commentaries* of Hamilton's friend and admirer, James Kent.[39]

The second illustration, even more foreshortened, concerns the course of economic liberty in American law. Drawing on the old common law contempt for monopolies, finding expression in the presidency of Andrew Jackson and his promise of "equal protection" against economic privilege, the movement for entrepreneurial liberty found expression in the antebellum years in such policies as the establishment of general incorporation statutes in the states and the decision not to renew the charter of the Second Bank of the United States.[40] After the Civil War this movement turned with eventual success to the federal judiciary, who found by interpretation a liberty of contract in the Due Process Clauses of the Fifth and Fourteenth Amendments that scuttled economic and social regulations which, in the judgment of the Court, impaired the individual's liberty to manage his own affairs free of such legislative interference as proceeded,

[38] See Madison's 1800 "Report on the Resolutions," in *The Writings of James Madison*, ed. Gaillard Hunt (New York: G.P. Putnam's Sons, 1906), 6:341–406.

[39] Julius Goebel, Jr., ed., *The Law Practice of Alexander Hamilton* (New York: Columbia University Press, 1964), 1:775 ff.; the quotation is from 830.

[40] See generally James W. Ely, Jr., *The Guardian of Every Other Right: A Constitutional History of Property Rights* (New York: Oxford University Press, 1992). The quotation is from Jackson's "Bank Veto, July 10, 1832," in *Messages of Gen. Andrew Jackson* (Concord, N.H.: John F. Brown and William White, 1837), 167.

not from a genuine concern for the public welfare, but from the attempt to privilege a particular economic class. Although recent scholarship has stressed the moral basis of laissez-faire constitutionalism in the right of the individual to equal standing before the law in his efforts to determine his own affairs,[41] the argument in court drew not only on the modern moral theory of natural rights but also on the assurance of the coincidence of private liberty and common wealth supplied by the modern economic theory of the invisible hand. Developed in the name of reasonableness, it pushed to the background common law doctrines such as nuisance that restricted noxious or uncustomary use of property, even as it promoted the individual initiative which balanced these at common law.

The malleability of common law supposed by Holmes thus had some precedent in American common law, partly in the adjustment of English practices to fit the circumstances of the American federal republic, partly in a more open-ended engagement with the developments in science and economy characteristic of the modern world. Nor was change in common law innocent of hope of moral improvement; while common law in England was more or less independent of ecclesiastical law, it still accommodated an established church, which American law was soon enough to do without. Still, for all his Unitarian optimism, Joseph Story could proclaim, "One of the beautiful boasts of our municipal jurisprudence is, that Christianity is a part of the common law, from which it seeks the sanction of its rights, and by which it endeavors to regulate its doctrines. . . . There never has been a period, in which the common law did not recognize Christianity as lying at its foundations."[42] With Holmes, that period arrives, for he reserves his religious awe for the dispensations of unfathomable fate, even as he reserves for himself the role of oracle. The detachment of common law from its ancient ground, whether in natural law or in Christian faith, makes inevitable its becoming an empty form of flux and so prepares the course by which, in a constitutional jurisprudence that unfolds like Holmes's common law, the right to procreate and educate one's children becomes the right to abort.[43] Immemorial

[41] Michael Les Benedict, "Laissez-Faire and Liberty: A Re-evaluation of the Meaning and Origins of Laissez-Faire Constitutionalism," *Law and History Review* 3 (1985): 293–331; Arkes, *The Return of George Sutherland*, 20 ff.

[42] Joseph Story, *A Discourse Pronounced Upon the Inauguration of the Author as Dane Professor of Law in Harvard University* (Boston: Hilliard, Gray, Little, and Wilkins, 1829), 20–21. As a young man, Thomas Jefferson wrote an essay in which he attempted to expose this proposition as a seventeenth century error or fraud, and in his later years he digs it out again and stands by his youthful opinion. See Jefferson, *Writings*, 1321–29, 1494–95.

[43] Compare *Roe v. Wade* with *Skinner v. Oklahoma*, 316 U.S. 535 (1942), *Meyer v. Nebraska*, 262 U.S. 390 (1923), and *Pierce v. Society of Sisters*, 268 U.S. 510 (1925).

customary law, now revolted by its own antiquity, rushes headlong into the brave new world.

Is common law, then, dead to us today, at least in any sense that adheres to its original understanding? I think not, for several reasons. First, if the bark of precedential development has lost its anchor, still many of the forms of common law retain their vitality. It suffices here to mention the jury, which, in America at least, though the source of much controversy of late, seems to be rediscovering its authority, even or especially as long excluded populations enter the box. Second, the interest in original intention, which has an intelligent, if minority foothold even on the Supreme Court, and which is echoed in a re-awakening interest in the Founders throughout our society, seems to point in its favor, at least to the extent it is recognized that that intent incorporated rather than discarded the understanding of common law in whose midst the Constitution was formed. Third, the growing sense of a crisis in moral authority today seems to beg for a revival of unwritten law, still arguably in force if not on notice. As for the adage, just quoted, that "Christianity is a part of the common law," it seems poised, for the first time in a generation or two, to attract more than it would repel, at least outside the academy—and, I should add, seems poised to instruct, for the adage meant, as when the same was said of natural law, only that there was nothing in common law that was contrary to Christianity (or natural law), the business of the common law, even in the enforcement of morals, being rather to form sturdy, free wills and to protect the possibility of innocence, than to gather souls into the Church. Indeed, the common law, offering a middle way between the theocratic and the secular state, for that reason alone merits our attention. Finally, it should be said that the present eclipse of common law is no argument against its possible revival, for in the seventeenth century common law, so to speak, came out of the shadows of Tudor despotism to lead, in the name of its ancient and then almost-forgotten basic charter, a revival of constitutionalism the effects of which linger even in our day. Naturally enough a revitalized common law would look different now than before its slumber. The unwritten needs articulation in our cacophonous age, and an appeal to political theory by the normally and rightly theory-shy cannot be eschewed. I do not think, if a restoration of common law is in the offing, that it will be brokered by the Supreme Court, at least with its current majority. But neither should that Court have an incentive, or at least an honorable incentive, to stand in the way.

The Court as Astigmatic Schoolmarm: A Case for the Clear-Sighted Citizen

Stanley C. Brubaker

IF THE CONSTITUTION is the supreme law of the land—as it claims to be in Article VI—how should we look at it? Where should we stand, in a sense, to gain the best view of its full and true character? The question may seem precious, since the answer appears obvious: it is the judicial perspective. So widely is this perspective presumed to be both authoritative and exclusive that a recent survey to test civic competence (conducted by the *Washington Post*, the Kaiser Family Foundation, and Harvard University) posed this question—"Who has the final responsibility to decide if a law is constitutional or not?"—and counted any answer other than "the Supreme Court" as wrong.[1] For the moment, let me set aside the fact that by this measure Jefferson, Jackson, Lincoln, Franklin Roosevelt, and many more would rank as civic incompetents and acknowledge that the inquiry appears precious. What difference can it make from what perspective we see the Constitution, for is not the law the law however we look at it? Even when the aforementioned presidents challenged the Court's claim to finality, they did not argue that the law looked different from the perspective of the presidency, but that the Court was mistaken in its interpretation and they were not bound by that interpretation.

Yet perspective does make an enormous difference. Consider for instance what happens to the character of the Constitution as law if we adopt the perspective urged by Oliver Wendell Holmes. "If you want to know the law and nothing else," he wrote, "you must see it

[1] Richard Morin, "Who's in Control? Many Don't Know or Care," *Washington Post*, January 29, 1996.

69

as a bad man, who cares only for the material consequences such knowledge enables him to predict, not as a good one, who finds his reasons for conduct . . . in the vaguer sanctions of conscience." For the bad man, the law is "nothing more pretentious" than "prophecies of what the courts will do in fact."[2] By adopting the perspective of the bad man, we do clear from our vision obligations that are moral rather than legal in character as well as moral connotations that are misleading.[3] And that was the primary intent of Holmes's essay. But the bad man perspective also clears from our view the claim of obligation that is essential to the concept of law itself.

We can see this point more clearly by drawing on a distinction observed by H. L. A. Hart between "being obliged" and "having an obligation." One "is obliged," say, to hand over a sum of cash, when confronted by a weighty threat. Such would equally be the case whether the threat comes from a robber's gun or a court's injunction. By contrast, one may "have an obligation" to hand over the cash only in the latter case. In asking us to think of law as a "prediction," Holmes allows us only to see rules in terms of "being obliged," that is, "how far [bad men] run the risk of coming against what is so much stronger than themselves." But he blinds us to rules in terms of "having an obligation." Or phrased another way, Holmes gives us a clear view of the rules from an "external" perspective, that is, the perspective of one who stands apart from the authority of the law. But he blinds us to that dimension of authority, which can only be seen from the "internal" perspective, that is, from the standpoint of one who accepts the authority of the law. His "bad man" perspective allows us to see rules, in the empirical sense of predicted regularities, but it does not allow us to see authoritative rules, that is, law.[4]

[2] Oliver Wendell Holmes, "The Path of the Law," *Harvard Law Review* 10 (1897): 459, 461.
[3] Tortious "wrongs," Holmes accurately observed, are often best seen as merely the price of a course of action.
[4] In his otherwise insightful analysis of Holmes's perspective on the law, Thomas Grey obscures this point by arguing that Holmes meant this perspective to illuminate private law rather than criminal law. "Holmes and Legal Pragmatism," *Stanford Law Review* 41 (1989): 834. The difficulty with this interpretation is that Holmes makes no such distinction in the text. Certainly there is none implied in Holmes forthright invitation to consider the law from the perspective of the bad man "who cares only for the material consequences which such knowledge enables him to predict." Also, whether law is civil or criminal, it terminates in language of duty and rights, not options. The millowner might have the option of building a dam or not, but he has no option to comply or not with the judgment of the court—or at least there is no question of his having an obligation to comply.

To an extent Holmes masks this deficiency by making his "bad man" parasitic on the perspective of another who does see the law from the internal perspective, that is, the judge. But the judge himself cannot look at the law in the same way as does the bad man; he cannot, that is, determine the law by making prophecies about how he will decide the case. The judge's internal perspective must include the sense of obligation that the bad man lacks. The judge cannot look at law simply as a *prediction* of whether his court will apply force; he must also see law as a *reason* for the imposition of force.

A related and similarly obscuring perspective comes from political scientists of the behavioral persuasion, who, in order to extend the mantle of modern "science" to their profession, seek models and variables that will enable them to explain an event. By "explain," they mean to find the efficient cause. So how can the Constitution be looked at scientifically? How can it be an event to explain? Prior to gaining his seat on the Supreme Court, Charles Evans Hughes, stated, "We are under the Constitution, but the Constitution is what the judges say it is."[5] If this is true, the Constitution becomes an event, or a series of events, which the political scientist can seek to explain: it is the decisions of the justices.

The justices themselves, of course, very kindly supply explanations for their decisions, that is, their opinions. One might think that the political scientist could study these, inquire into their worth and consistency, and thereby develop a "science of the law." But the scientist of the behavioral persuasion seeks a knowledge that is more certain than the opinions of the justices and therefore, in his mind, superior to it. A "science of the law" in the above sense would place the knowledge of the political scientist on the same level as that of the justice; his would be just one more opinion about what the Constitution means. In fact, for the behavioralist, the opinions of the justices fall so far short of what can be called knowledge that they become matters of taste or attitude, not reason.

In this perspective one can say knowledgeably, that is, with certainty, that the justices have these opinions, but one cannot say anything about the reasonableness of these opinions. So instead of the reasoning of the justices, the behavioralist looks at the reasons for those reasons. That is, he looks for something knowable, but itself sub-rational, to explain the reasons. He looks, therefore, to the inarticulate and even unconscious "attitudes" of the justices.

---

[5] Hughes later claimed he did not wish the comment to convey cynicism. *The Autobiographical Notes of Charles Evans Hughes*, ed. David J. Danelski and Joseph S. Tulchin (Cambridge: Harvard University Press, 1973), 143.

Now here is a cause that the behavioralist perspective can behold and measure. He looks directly at votes, not the reasons given for these, as evidence of attitudes, then scales these attitudes along some continuum, for example, the propensity to decide for the defendant rather than the government in search and seizure cases. Consistency of decisions according to this propensity thus counts as evidence that the justice is really deciding according to an attitude, a more scientific explanation than found in opinions and their references to legal texts or other authoritative sources. Such a "psychometric" model, one pioneering enthusiast explained in the leading journal of the profession, "proceeds on the premise that a justice reacts in his voting behavior to the stimuli presented by cases before the Court in accordance with his attitudes toward the issue raised for decision." It provides a "better and more reliable" approach than studying the "values articulated in the opinions of the justices."[6] Thus the Constitution is what the judges say it is, and what they say it is derives not so much from their "judgment," but their attitudinal "reaction to stimuli" presented by cases.

Despite the accuracy with which these political scientists have been able to predict Court decisions,[7] we have good reason to question the fit between their perspective and the Constitution. To begin, the fact that their predictions are often accurate explains less than the behavioralist would wish, for these are only comparable to what a student of judicial opinions would also predict. And the reason for this is rather obvious. A Justice brings to the job, or develops while on it, a philosophy of the Constitution and the judicial role. This philosophy results in a coherent pattern of voting. By studying this voting pattern, the scientist will be able to predict how the Justice will decide similar cases in the future. The "attitudinal hypothesis"—i.e., that Justices decide according to their attitudes—would fail only if Justices functioned with no philosophy of the law, making wildly idiosyncratic decisions.

Moreover, the perspective of the scientist on the law, like that of the bad man, is derivative. The scientist does not look at the law itself, but at the judge who is looking at the law—rather like the truffle hunter who relies on a pig to sense what he cannot. The scientist himself cannot comprehend the law as such because he cannot com-

---

[6] Glendon Schubert, "The 1960 Term of the Supreme Court: A Psychological Analysis," *American Political Science Review* 56 (1962): 107.

[7] Jeffrey A. Segal and Harold J. Spaeth, *The Supreme Court and the Attitudinal Model* (Cambridge: Cambridge University Presss, 1993) presents the most self-congratulatory account of this perspective and its ability to predict.

prehend the claims of authority and duty that all law must make and that the judge must take seriously if he is to perform his job and justify, through opinions, the decisions he makes. If the judge could no longer see the law from his "internal perspective" and instead had to rely on the eyes of the scientist, he could not possibly do his job, for his most basic material, claims of authority and duty, would have vanished. If all of us would view the Constitution scientifically, it would disappear entirely.

But if these examples show that the question of perspective is not entirely inconsequential, is not the answer still obvious, i.e., the judicial perspective? Certainly there is much to recommend this perspective. Situated internal to the law and specially trained in it, capable of seeing the Constitution as supreme law and law as an authoritative rule, conducting his affairs with gravity and solemnity, through procedures designed to minimize the distractions and distortions of partisan consideration, the judge—and thus ultimately the Supreme Court—seems to enjoy a privileged perspective. Indeed, both Holmes's bad man and the political "scientist" could see the law at all only by linking their lenses to those of the judge.

Yet we should attend with care to what recommends the judge's perspective first and foremost—that he sees law from the internal perspective. For this same authority that defines the internal perspective may additionally restrict the manner in which, and the extent to which, the judge may see the Constitution.

The Constitution may authorize judges to interpret only portions of itself or to interpret itself in a particular way. Under the British constitution, for instance, courts only consider whether an act brought before them has indeed been enacted according to constitutional procedures, i.e., by Parliament, rather than, say, a rabble assembly at Hyde Park. Under the French constitution, despite the fact that it is written, ordinary courts may see no further into the constitutionality of laws than may the British. Constitutional questions are reserved for a *Counseil Constitutionnel*, which can be called a "court" only in a loose sense of the word, and which may consider the constitutionality of a law only when it has been referred to them by the president, premier, leaders of the two houses of Parliament, or by a group of sixty deputies or senators—and assuredly not in ordinary litigation.[8]

[8] Henry J. Abraham, *The Judicial Process*, 6th ed. (New York: Oxford University Press, 1993), 289–93. See also Alec Stone, *The Birth of Judicial Politics in France: The Constitutional Council in Comparative Perspective* (New York: Oxford University Press, 1992).

So although we occasionally hear claims to the contrary, it does not follow from the fact that we have a constitution, even a written constitution, that the best perspective for viewing it will be that of the Court. The breadth and clarity of the judicial perspective can be assessed only after we ascertain the authority granted courts by the Constitution. That is, we must consider the authority and scope of judicial review.

The locus classicus for judicial review of federal legislation is of course *Marbury v. Madison*.[9] In that case Chief Justice Marshall employs two distinct modes of interpretation, textual exegesis and inference from structural principles of the regime. The textual argument is notoriously weak. Marshall points to three passages: the oath of office, the supremacy clause, and article III's statement of jurisdiction. The oath of office is taken by all persons holding authority under the Constitution of the United States, whether federal or state—legislators, executive officials, municipal councils, police officers, jurors. If the oath of office obliges one never to give effect to a law one thinks unconstitutional—the claim that Marshall was making—it would grant the power to void laws to any executive official. The prison warden who thought his inmates confined contrary to his understanding of due process would be obliged to set them free. The supremacy clause answers what is not in question—whether the Constitution is the supreme law of the land—and is silent on what is in question—whether federal courts have authority to determine the constitutionality of federal laws. And while article III's statement of jurisdiction does extend the "judicial Power of the United States" to all cases "arising under this Constitution," it too sheds no light on the question of what this judicial power consists, only the cases to which it extends.[10]

Marshall's more substantive argument is the structural one, and it runs essentially as follows: 1) "It is emphatically the province and duty of the judicial department to say what the law is." 2) "If two laws conflict with each other, the courts must decide on the operation of each." 3) "If, then, the courts are to regard the constitution, and the constitution is superior to any ordinary act of the legislature, the constitution, and not such ordinary act, must govern the case to which they both apply."[11]

---

[9] 5 US 137 (1803). My analysis of the legitimacy of judicial review concentrates on the review of federal rather than state law.

[10] Alexander Bickel, *The Least Dangerous Branch* (Indianapolis: Bobbs-Merrill Company, 1962), 4–7; William Van Alstyne, "A Critical Guide to *Marbury v. Madison*," *Duke Law Journal* (1969): 26–29.

[11] *Marbury v. Madison*, 5 U.S. 137, 177–78 (1803).

In this argument, Marshall assimilates the extraordinary power of judicial review to the ordinary judicial function of resolving conflicts of law in favor of that which has greater authority. In a conflict between a statute and a common law precedent, courts would govern the case according to the statute; in a conflict between an old statute and a new one, courts would govern the case according to the new. Yet the authority to declare a law unconstitutional, especially federal law, does not follow so smoothly from these analogies, for there are strikingly disanalogous features as well. While the Constitution is law, it is also a quite distinct sort of law; thus, courts in many countries have accepted Marshall's premises—that courts say what the law is and that a constitution is supreme law—but do not accept his conclusion of judicial review. Ordinary law flows *from* the regime and is directed to the governed. As fundamental law, on the other hand, the Constitution *defines* the regime and is directed to the government. With ordinary law, courts adjudicate as an integral part of the regime, functionally aligned with the executive, both broadly engaged in the application of this law to the governed. Violations of ordinary laws are common, but the will of the regime to act upon the Court's interpretation is rarely in doubt. If the regime doubts the fidelity of the Court's interpretation, it has a convenient remedy: enact a law clarifying the point in dispute. By contrast, with fundamental law, as the rules *of* the regime, courts would apply rules to the government itself. Violations are less common, but the will to act upon the Court's interpretation may be less than wholehearted. There is less need for a definitive interpretation and greater difficulty of enforcement.[12] Constitutional amendments to "correct" mistaken Court interpretations are possible, but difficult.

Problems of this sort, following Alexander Bickel's description, are often addressed as the "countermajoritarian difficulty."[13] But the point should be made in a broader context and seen as a "counter-regime difficulty." When a court rejects the lawmakers' interpretation of their constitution, whether that constitution is democratic, aristocratic, or monarchic, the court is asserting its authority contrary to the defining principle or principles of the regime, though ironically, it does so in the name of the regime. Were a court to void a law enacted by an aristocratic assembly in the name of the aristocratic

[12] See, e.g., Sylvia Snowiss, *Judicial Review and the Law of the Constitution* (New Haven: Yale University Press, 1990), esp. 197–201; Gerald Rosenberg, *The Hollow Hope: Can Courts Bring About Social Change?* (Chicago: University of Chicago, 1991); Louis Fisher, *Constitutional Conflicts between Congress and the President* (Lawrence, Kansas: University Press of Kansas, 1991).

[13] *Least Dangerous Branch*, 16–23.

constitution, its action would be in tension with the defining principle of the regime. Similarly, were a court to void the pronouncement of a monarch in the name of the monarchic constitution, its action would be in tension with the defining principle of the regime.

In each case, of course, the court would have an obvious response to the complaint of the lawmakers. Yes, we void your democratically (or aristocratically or monarchically) enacted law, but we do so in the name of democracy (or aristocracy or monarchy). Yours may be the more recent expression of the regime, but ours is the deeper one. And that is essentially the response of Marshall. The Constitution, he writes, derives its authority from the "original right" of the people in their supreme authority to establish such principles of government as "shall most conduce to their own happiness." When the Court voids a law contrary to this fundamental law, it is not acting against the will of the people, but in the name of the people. The Court is the ally of the people, in the exercise of their "original and supreme will," resisting the encroachments of the legislature or the temporary delusions of the people themselves. Marshall implies that the choice is stark. Either courts enforce these limits or our Constitution is essentially without limits.

Yet surely the dilemma is a false one. Other nations have written constitutions of limited powers, do not rely on the courts for their enforcement, and have not found their foundations entirely subverted. Further, it is far from clear that a court is a better equipped institution to give more authentic expression to the underlying character of the regime. In an aristocratic constitution, why should the courts give deeper or more authentic expression than the aristocratic lawmakers to the character of their previous aristocratic commitments? In a republic, why should courts give deeper or more authentic expression than the people's representatives to the character of their previous republican commitments?

At the outset of his argument for judicial review, Marshall had asked "whether an act, repugnant to the constitution, can become the law of the land." But as Bickel has pointed out, that's the wrong question. The real question is not "whether?" but "who?" Who is to say that a law violates the Constitution? Marshall made a case for the courts, but as we have seen, the logic is not entirely unassailable. Thus, the case for the courts can be assessed only by looking at other possibilities, two of which are prominent contenders, each backed by regime principles and by distinguished proponents.

One is legislative supremacy. This leaves the final say as to what the Constitution means in the hands of Congress and the president in his lawmaking capacity. Courts would exercise only "procedural" judicial review, recognizing as law only what has been enacted according to constitutional procedures, that is, bicameral support and presentation to the president. Beyond such minimal assurance of appropriate procedures, substantive interpretation would be in the hands of the lawmakers. Much is to be said in favor of legislative supremacy.[14] Its authority derives from the democratic republican character of the Constitution and the capacity of the legislature to give expression to that authority. A well-structured assembly, it might be argued, is more likely to express the "cool and deliberate sense of the community" than is a nonrepresentative court, a single executive, a massive assembly of the people themselves, or a popular referendum. If well structured, the assembly is likely to yield an expression "more consonant to the public good than if pronounced by the people themselves, convened for the purpose."[15] That the legislature is well structured of course is the proposition defended by Madison in *Federalist* 10. With an extended commercial republic forming a social basis for moderate, coalitional majorities, it becomes possible to structure political institutions that attract representatives "whose wisdom may best discern the true interest of their country and whose patriotism and love of justice will be least likely to sacrifice it to temporary and partial considerations."[16] In fact, though he was not entirely consistent on the subject, legislative review seems to have been the mechanism of constitutional enforcement favored by James Madison, the acknowledged father of the Constitution.[17]

Another possibility is coordinate review. According to this doctrine, it is the responsibility of each branch of government, within its own sphere of activities, to interpret authoritatively the Constitution. This doctrine is grounded in the fundamental regime principle of the separation of powers, which in turn is integrally tied to the regime

[14] See the opinion of Pennsylvania's Judge John Gibson in *Eakin v. Raub*, 12 Sergeant & Rawls (PA) 330 (1825).

[15] *Federalist* no. 10.

[16] Ibid.

[17] See, e.g., his speech on the power of the president to remove officers whom he has appointed by and with the consent of the Senate, and more to the point, the authority of deciding this question through the legislative process. *Annals of Congress* (June 17, 1789), 1:519–21. See also, his letter to John Brown, commenting that to allow final determinations of constitutionality to rest in the hands of the judiciary "was never intended and can never be proper." *The Writings of James Madison*, ed. Gaillard Hunt (New York: Putnam's Sons, 1900–1910), 5:294. Madison also expressed support for coordinate review. See note 18 below as well as the several statements collected in Walter F. Murphy, James E. Fleming, and Sotirios Barber, *American Constitutional Interpretation*, 2nd ed. (Westbury, New York: Foundation Press, 1995), 277–81.

character of democratic republicanism and its principle of liberty. Like legislative supremacy, coordinate review has its distinguished proponents. Madison, for instance, occasionally migrated the short distance to this position from that of legislative supremacy.[18] And Jefferson in a letter to Abigail Adams, concerning the enforcement of the Alien and Sedition Laws, advocated it forcefully:

> You seem to think it devolved on the judges to decide the validity of the sedition law. But nothing in the Constitution has given them a right to decide for the Executive, any more than to the Executive to decide for them. The judges, believing the law constitutional, had a right to pass a sentence of fine and imprisonment, because that power was placed in their hands by the Constitution. But the Executive, believing the law to be unconstitutional, was bound to remit the execution of it; because that power has been confided to him by the Constitution. That instrument meant that its coordinate branches should be checks on each other. But the opinion which gives to the judges the right to decide what laws are constitutional, and what not, not only for themselves in their sphere of action, but for the Legislature and Executive also, would make the judiciary a despotic branch.[19]

Neither of these alternatives to judicial review is unassailable. Against legislative supremacy, it might be said that it leaves lawmakers as judges in their own case, where their interests are likely to skew their interpretation. When their constituents wish it, their reelection is enhanced by it, and their career on the Hill is rewarded by it, legislators are likely to follow convenience over accuracy in constitutional interpretation. And against coordinate review, it might be said to allow for too much conflict and uncertainty on constitutional meaning, with too much power flowing into the hands of the executive as the final enforcer of the law.

There are replies to these points. Judges too have interests that may skew their judgments. On such decisions as jurisdiction and justi-

---

[18] See his statement given under the pseudonym, Helvidius: "It may happen . . . that different departments . . . may, in the exercise of their functions, interpret the constitution differently, and thence lay claim to the same power. This difference of opinion is an inconvenience not entirely to be avoided. It results from what may be called . . . a *concurrent* right to expound the constitution." *Writings of James Madison*, 6:155, emphasis original.

[19] Jefferson to Abigail Adams, September 11, 1804. *The Writings of Thomas Jefferson*, ed. Paul Leicester Ford, 12 vols. (New York: G. P. Putnam's Sons, 1904–5), 8:310. For a more recent as well as more moderate statement in favor of a coordinate review, see Walter F. Murphy, "Who Shall Interpret the Constitution?" *Review of Politics* 48 (1986): 401–23.

ciability, salary increases, decorum to be observed in and around the courtroom,[20] liability for judicial decisions, or even vindication of their own idea of right, the self-interest of judges may be engaged and they may become judges in their own cases. *Marbury* itself involves a remarkable instance of self-interested interpretation.[21] And, concerning coordinate review, while it may be disturbing to have constitutional interpretation never at rest, always subject to challenge, there is one thing worse: to have constitutional interpretation resting always and forever with the judiciary. As Lincoln stated in his first inaugural, concerning the *Dred Scott* decision and whether the political branches should accept it as the final word on constitutional meaning, "[I]f the policy of the government, upon vital questions affecting the whole people, is to be irrevocably fixed by decisions of the Supreme Court, the instant they are made, in ordinary litigation between parties in personal actions, the people will have ceased to be their own rulers, having to that extent practically resigned the government into the hands of that eminent tribunal."[22]

Even if we do not grant legislative supremacy and co-ordinate review the full force claimed for them by Madison, Jefferson, and Lincoln, we must acknowledge that they grow out of fundamental principles of the regime and that in the name of those principles they confront judicial review with hard questions. From legislative supremacy: When the legislature enacts a law according to an interpretation of the Constitution that a judge has to admit is plausible, and possibly correct, by what right does he void the law in the name of an interpretation of the Constitution he prefers? From co-ordinate review: By what right can the Court extend its interpretation into the "sphere of action" of the other branches of government? Neither legislative

---

[20] This is an especially revealing area where the decorum the Court claims for its proceedings diverges dramatically from the decorum it allows other institutions to claim for themselves. See Jules Gerard, "May Society Preserve a Modicum of Decorum in Public Discourse?" in *The Bill of Rights: Original Meaning and Current Understanding*, ed. Eugene W. Hickok, Jr. (Charlottesville: University Press of Virginia, 1991), 94–113.

[21] Van Alstyne, "A Critical Guide to *Marbury v. Madison*"; Robert G. McCloskey, *The American Supreme Court* (Chicago: University of Chicago, 1960), 40–44. It is hard to explain Marshall's strained reading of section 13 of the Judiciary Act of 1789 except as a way of rendering that provision contrary to the Constitution, thus giving the Court the opportunity to claim for itself the authority of judicial review and at the same time to avoid a political confrontation with the Jefferson administration that it was bound to lose.

[22] For a fuller statement of Lincoln's position, see his response to Stephen Douglas, Springfield, July 17, 1858. *The Collected Works of Abraham Lincoln*, ed. Roy Basler (New Brunswick: Rutgers University Press, 1953), 2:516.

supremacy, co-ordinate review, nor judicial review seems capable of mustering a knockdown argument in its behalf and flooring the opposing two. Although judicial review seems to have won in practice, it has done so, at least in its classical defense, only by recognizing the credibility of the other two possibilities, and with the traditional doctrines confining its exercise, answering the hard questions posed by them.

Legislative supremacy and its grounding in democratic republican authority are recognized in the doctrine of "deference." On most questions likely to come before the Court, the Constitution provides no singular, crisply defined answer, plain for all to see, but rather a range of interpretations among which "reasonable persons may differ." The doctrine of deference holds that a court should declare a law unconstitutional, not when it thinks that the law in question runs afoul of its own reasonable interpretation of the Constitution, but only when the law falls outside the range where reasonable people may differ.[23] This doctrine thus asks the Court to bow to democratic authority, without, as the pure doctrine of legislative supremacy would ask of it, falling on its face.[24]

Co-ordinate review and its grounding in separation of power are recognized by several doctrines designed to ensure that judicial review is indeed "judicial" rather than legislative or executive. These doctrines ensure, in other words, that the exercise of judicial review will be confined to the resolution of concrete cases and controversies, according to discernible standards, recognized as law.[25] Such are the function of the "who, what, when" doctrines. "Who" may bring a case before the courts is confined to those with proper "standing," that is, suffering a "concrete injury in fact" likely to be relieved if they are successful in their suit. As Justice Frankfurter once wrote,

---

[23] The classical statement is found in James Bradley Thayer's 1893 essay, "The Origin and Scope of the American Doctrine of Constitutional Law," *Harvard Law Review* 7 (1893): 129–56. See also, Stanley C. Brubaker "Reconsidering Dworkin's Case for Judicial Activism," *Journal of Politics* 46 (1984): 503–519.

[24] In his classic defense of judicial review in *Federalist* No. 78, Alexander Hamilton seems to acknowledge the doctrine of deference. He writes of the judicial duty to declare "all acts contrary to the *manifest* tenor of the Constitution void" (emphasis added), not just a "*plausible* interpretation" of the Constitution or even the judge's "best judgment" of the Constitution's meaning. Further, he writes that a court should declare a statute void only if there is an "irreconcilable variance" between it and the Constitution, implying that the court should first try to find an interpretation of both statute and constitution that would preserve the statute.

[25] I say "recognized" rather than "enacted" to characterize the judicial function in order to include judicial resolution of cases according to common law.

"The Court is not the forum for a chivalrous or disinterested defense of the Constitution. Its business is with self-regarding, immediate, secular claims."[26]

"What" may be brought before the courts is limited to questions that are legal in character; it is not extended to questions that are merely "advisory" or "political" in character. The doctrine of "political questions" is complex, but two strands are prominent and reasonably clear. One is that a case should not be brought before the courts if its final resolution is entrusted by the Constitution to another branch of government. The prime example is impeachment, committed by article I, sections two and three, to the House and the Senate.[27] The other strand is that a case should not be brought before the courts if its resolution lacks "judicially discoverable and manageable standards." "Discoverable" means that the Constitution, with its text or history or other sources of interpretation, provides sufficient guidance so that the court is not "creating" the law by which it decides the case, so that it is not, in other words, exercising a legislative function. A common illustration of the lack of discoverable standards is the Ninth Amendment, which reads, "The enumeration in the Constitution of certain rights shall not be construed to deny or disparage others retained by the people." Other aspects of the text, the structure of the Constitution, and the intent of its framers and ratifiers, may shed light on the meaning of this sentence, but not enough, most agree, to spare the Court from the charge of legislating, were it to base a decision on this amendment. And, even through the heyday of noninterpretive review, the Court never has.[28] "Manageable" means that even if the central legal question could be answered by the courts, problems of implementation require tools essentially executive and legislative in character.[29]

"When" doctrines restrict the courts to instances that are nei-

[26] Felix Frankfurter and Adrian S. Fisher, "The Business of the Supreme Court at the October Terms, 1935 and 1936," *Harvard Law Review* 51 (1938): 623.

[27] See, e.g., *Nixon v. United States*, 506 U.S. 224 (1993). Chief Justice Rehnquist emphatically affirms that this is a question for the Senate to decide.

[28] Further, in only two instances have any Justices relied on it in the more limited sense of an aid to interpretation: Justice Goldberg in *Griswold v. Connecticut*, 381 U.S. 479, 486–93 (1965) and Justice Burger (joined by Justice White and Justice Stevens) in *Richmond Newspapers, Inc. v. Virginia*, 448 U.S. 555, 579–80 (1980).

[29] Robert Nagel, "Separation of Powers and the Scope of Federal Equitable Remedies," *Stanford Law Review* 30 (1978): 661–724. Admittedly the doctrine has thinned remarkably. See, e.g., *Missouri v. Jenkins*, 495 U.S. 33 (1990) where the Court upheld the authority of a lower court to order the raising of revenue to fund a desegregation order.

ther "too soon," the parties having not yet been brought into real legal conflict (the matter is not yet "ripe") nor "too late," a judicial decision making no material difference for the plaintiff (the matter is "moot").

So, as we have seen, to the hard questions posed by legislative supremacy and coordinate review, democratic authority and separation of powers, classical judicial review has a response. By what right does the Court void a law that can reasonably be said not to violate the Constitution? In the classical defense of judicial review, the Court does not claim such a right, but declares a law void only when it falls outside the boundaries of reasonable interpretation. By what right can the Court extend its interpretation into the sphere of action of the other branches? In the classical defense, it does not do this, but confines itself to actions that are judicial in character.[30]

Although controversy surrounds the doctrine of deference as well as those doctrines concerning who, what, and when, virtually all of that controversy concerns the *scope* of these doctrines, not their existence. And as long as these doctrines are accepted as legitimate, as constitutionally required, they mean that a good court will provide an imperfect perspective on the Constitution. This imperfection is comparatively mild. Unlike the French or British constitution, the Constitution of the United States does not render its ordinary judges blind to its substance. But it does in effect fit its courts with a peculiar set of lenses overlying those that define the internal perspective.

The result is a sort of astigmatism. In optometry, this condition is defined as the distortion of vision caused by asymmetrical curvature of the cornea so that its refractive power varies in different axes. As a result, some lines—e.g., vertical or horizontal—will be in focus, but not others; the lines that are out of focus will appear as fuzzy stretches along their axes. With severe asymmetry in portions of the cornea, the individual has virtual blind spots. Deference means that on those portions of the Constitution where the doctrine is appropriate, the Court will see a fuzzy range of meaning rather than bright lines. Who,

---

[30] Though today *Marbury v. Madison* is usually read to have grander ambitions, the opinion seems to acknowledge coordinate review and strives to find the proper place for the courts within that doctrine. Note, for instance, that after listing clauses especially addressed to the courts, Marshall writes, "it is apparent that the framers of the constitution contemplated that instrument, as a rule for the government of *courts*, as well as of the legislature" (original emphasis). *Marbury*, 5 U.S. at 179–80. For simplicity, I will not consider here the closely related question of the finality of the judicial decisions, except to note that the doctrine of coordinate review implies that the other branches need not, at least not always, regard decisions of the Supreme Court as binding them in their sphere of action.

what, when doctrines mean that where cases do not meet these requirements, the Court will have blind spots. Let me develop some of these imperfections.

According to the doctrine of deference, the proper question in judicial review is not what does the Constitution mean, but, as James Bradley Thayer argued, what range of judgment on meaning is "permissible" to the political branches of government.[31] Accordingly, courts are to define not the precise and true meaning of the Constitution, but to defer to the reasonable and sustainable judgments of that meaning by the political branches. They are to declare an enacted law invalid only when it falls outside the scope of reasonable judgment. In effect, the Court does not look at the Constitution directly, but through the lens of a reasonable person, or rather, the lenses of reasonable people, since reasonable people may differ.

In using the metaphor of astigmatism to describe the import of deference, I imply that on some matters the Court does see clearly, just as the astigmatic individual will see the lines on some axes clearly. For Thayer, what could be seen clearly were the democratic republican character of the Constitution and the judicial character of the Court; from these two clear features, he inferred that the rest had to be seen as open to a range of meaning, or out of focus. For Justice Stone as well, the democratic republican character of the Constitution was clear, but he drew a couple of inferences from this that Thayer had not: that deference should be abandoned on questions of political process (upon which the operation of a democratic republic depends) and on questions concerning discrete and insular minorities (prejudice against whom may prevent their effective participation in democratic politics).[32] On questions of federal and state authority, Stone agreed with Thayer, the Court was to defer. There are other possibilities,[33] but outside of the lines the Court sees clearly, wherever it exercises deference, what it announces as "constitutional law" will not be its opinion of what the Constitution really means, but the outer boundary of what meanings it thinks are reasonable.

The who, what, when doctrines imply more severe perceptual

---

[31] "Origin and Scope," 144.

[32] *U.S. v. Carolene Products*, 304 U.S. 144 (1938), note 4. Justice Stone also thought he could see "specific prohibitions" clearly, but only if they were not economic in character.

[33] One of the more extreme is offered by Jesse Choper, who argues, in effect, that the Court must render itself blind to all questions of federalism and separation of powers in order to see and act clearly on questions of individual rights. *Judicial Review and the National Political Process* (Chicago: University of Chicago Press, 1980).

impairments, suggesting that for certain provisions of the Constitution the Court will not be able to see them at all. On some doctrines, to be sure, the limitation is merely procedural and thus temporary. If, for instance, lack of standing inhibits the Court from hearing, or seeing, the question presented by a particular case, it may be able to address it in a later case. Yet later may be much, much later, as in the case of the legislative veto. This odd procedure for making and "braking" law had been around since 1932, but it was only a half century later that an individual was able to satisfy the Court that he had suffered the concrete personal injury as a result of the veto necessary to challenge to it.[34] And on some questions—such as aid to a religious institution, expenditure of funds beyond the authorizations of article I, section 8, or the limits of the Tenth Amendment, or the failure to publish a regular "Statement of Account of the Receipts and Expenditures of all public Money"—it may be difficult for an individual ever to show concrete, personal injury, at least under traditional doctrines of standing.[35]

The blind spots posed by the doctrine of political questions are even more severe and unyielding. As mentioned above, by the "commitment to another branch of government" strand of the doctrine, courts should not consider, thus cannot see, the scope of impeachable offenses, the standard of proof, the adequacy of the evidence in a specific instance of impeachment, and so forth.[36] Similarly, it is up to the political branches of government to judge whether a state has a "Republican Form of Government" as required by article IV, section 4,"[37] how the Militia are to be organized, armed, and disciplined under art. 1, sec. 8,[38] what constitutes reasonable time for ratification

[34] *INS v. Chadha*, 462 U.S. 919 (1983). Chadha was an unusual case in that the legislative veto in question reversed an exception to a deportation order, meaning that because of the legislative veto, Chadha was about to be deported. More typically, legislative vetoes block the implementation of the law; standing then is difficult to gain in that one has to show legal injury by virtue of a law's not taking effect. In "Slouching Toward Constitutional Duty," *Constitutional Commentary* 1 (1984): 81, I argue that the real constitutional defect lies not in the legislative veto itself but in the law authorizing the legislative veto procedure since such law contains a reservation of the legislative will. In that sense the law fails to meet the bicameral enactment requirements of Art. 1, Sec. 7. If that is the constitutional defect of the laws containing a legislative veto, standing would go to anyone injured by the law, not the legislative veto of it.
[35] *Valley Forge College v. Americans United*, 454 U.S. 464 (1982); *Frothingham v. Mellon*, 262 U.S. 447 (1923); and *United States v. Richardson*, 418 U.S. 166 (1974).
[36] On this, Raoul Berger stands as an exception, *Impeachment: The Constitutional Problems* (Cambridge: Harvard University Press, 1973), 103–21.
[37] *Luther v. Borden*, 7 How. 1 (1849).
[38] *Gilligan v. Morgan*, 413 U.S. 1 (1973).

of a constitutional amendment under art. 5,[39] and the "Elections, Returns, and Qualifications of [the] Members" of each chamber of Congress.[40] By the "lack of discoverable standards" strand of the doctrine, the Ninth Amendment and the vast realm of the unwritten Constitution should be virtually out of sight. The "lack of manageable standards" strand of the doctrine—i.e., unmanageable by the tools that distinguish the judicial from the legislative or executive functions[41]—sets, or at least should set, a range of remedial questions beyond the purview of the Court.

Paradoxically, when the answer to a constitutional question is in a sense too easily discoverable, or too obvious, the question also never finds its way into the Court's range of vision. No one has brought to the Court the contentions of a thirty-three year old wannabe president; no court has had to rescind congressionally granted titles of nobility. A typical text today in "constitutional law," that is, a study of major decisions of the Court, will devote one third of its pages to equal protection and due process, another third to First Amendment freedoms of speech and religion, and another third to everything else. Constitutional law thus exaggerates the importance of some provisions of the Constitution and minimizes the importance of others that rarely if ever find their way into court. Robert Nagel refers to these provisions as the "uninterpreted Constitution" and their importance cannot be gainsaid.

> Congress "assembles" every year as the Constitution requires. Despite the temptation of power, presidents routinely relinquish office when their constitutional terms expire. The provisions for replacement of a president after death or during periods of incapacity have never been abused. The rules controlling impeachment and removal of civil offices have rarely been used and have never led to removal for purely partisan reasons. Procedures for amending the Constitution have been followed some twenty-six times without judicial intervention.
>
> . . . With the remotely possible exception of West Virginia, territorial integrity of the states has been respected, as article IV, section 3 requires. Soldiers have not been quartered in homes. A census has been conducted every ten years, as required by article I, section 1, without the aid of the Supreme Court. All the presidents have been older than thirty-five. Although the difference between a "treaty," which requires ratification by the Senate, and an executive agreement, which does not, has never been formalized

[39] *Coleman v. Miller,* 307 U.S. 433 (1939).
[40] *Roudebush v. Hartke,* 405 U.S. 15 (1972).
[41] Cf. *Missouri v. Jenkins,* 495 U.S. 33 (1990); Nagel, "Separation of Powers."

by the Court, the ratification provisions of article II, section 1 have
never fallen into disuse. The import of "advice and consent" was
determined by the behavior of George Washington and the subsequent presidents who have followed his example.[42]

Nagel's list goes on, but the point should be clear. Viewing the Constitution through the perspective of the Court is rather akin to viewing
the United States through the perspective of the New Yorker carica-
tured in Saul Steinberg's famous cartoon,[43] with Madison Avenue
looming far larger than the entire midwest and Los Angeles, somewhere "over there." Though Nagel's uninterpreted Constitution
would barely find a place on a map charted through the perspective
of the Court, it is almost certainly the larger and more important part
of the continent.

If we accept the premise of judicial exclusivity, these doctrines
place the Court on the horns of a dilemma. It can forget the limits in
order to see, and enforce, the entire Constitution. Or it can remember the limits, but forget and encourage the rest of us to forget about
those large portions of the Constitution falling outside of its clear
limits. Each alternative has its advocates. The Warren Court moved
towards an ardent embrace of the first alternative. Justice Brennan
led the way on the question of standing by famously asserting that its
function was to ensure that the litigant has "such a personal stake in
the outcome of the controversy as to assure that concrete adverseness
which sharpens the presentation of issues upon which the Court so
largely depends for illumination of difficult constitutional questions."[44]
    This restatement turns the traditional function of standing on
its head. Instead of functioning to keep the Court a court, resolving
concrete disputes, Brennan has it helping the Court give the right
answers to constitutional questions. With this statement as its guide,
it is no wonder that the Warren Court found it so easy to forget the
traditional limits of standing in order to reach important constitutional questions. Thus, the Warren Court set aside the traditional doctrines concerning a taxpayer's standing to sue, embracing in their

[42] Robert Nagel, *Constitutional Cultures: The Mentality and Consequences of Judicial Review* (Berkeley: University of California Press, 1989), 13, footnotes omitted. See also Frederick Schauer, "Easy Cases," *Southern California Law Review* 58 (1985): 399–440.

[43] I am indebted to Sanford Levinson for the analogy, which he puts to distinct use in "The Embarrassing Second Amendment," *Yale Law Journal* 99 (1989): 637–59.

[44] *Baker v. Carr*, 369 U.S. 186 (1962).

stead the "nexus" theory.[45] Without much exaggeration, this doctrine may be restated as the proposition that when there is a connection between the plaintiff's status as a taxpayer and a question that the Court thinks too important to leave to the political branches of government, the Court will grant standing. As Warren Court holdovers, Brennan, Douglas, and Marshall would have taken the logical further step of forgetting the fiction of "taxpayer" standing and substituting that of "citizens standing," i.e., it is sufficient injury for an individual to believe that his country operates according to laws that contravene the Constitution, which means for all practical purposes that one has eliminated the doctrine of standing all together.[46]

So also the Warren Court would not let the absence of discoverable and manageable standards stop it from addressing a significant constitutional question. Thus in *Baker v. Carr*[47] the Court abandoned the long held view[48] that reapportionment presents a political question concerning Article IV's guaranty of a republican form of government, and without indicating just what standards the lower courts should rely upon, declared the matter justiciable under the equal protection clause. The Court quickly followed that *ipse dixit* with the even bolder, though unstated, conclusion in *Reynolds v. Sims*[49] that the absence of an equal protection standard that was discoverable could be remedied by creating one that was at least manageable—"one man, one vote." Not surprisingly, Earl Warren concluded his tenure as Chief Justice with a bold claim that ignores all the aforesaid limitations designed to keep the Court as a court and to respect the authority of the political branches of government: "it is the responsibility of this Court to act as the ultimate interpreter of the Constitution."[50]

The second alternative—to remember the limits, but forget the Constitution—also seems to have its advocates. Robert Bork, for instance, would have us simply forget those portions of the Constitution that lack judicially discoverable standards, such as the Ninth Amendment or the Privileges and Immunities Clause. When a case raises questions concerning such provisions, a judge "is in exactly the same circumstance as a judge who has no Constitution to work with," he writes. "There being nothing to work with, the judge should refrain

[45] *Flast v. Cohen*, 393 U.S. 83 (1968).
[46] *Schlesinger v. Reservists to Stop the War*, 418 U.S. 208 (1974).
[47] 369 U.S. 186 (1962).
[48] See, e.g., *Luther v. Borden* 48 U.S. 1 (1849) and *Colegrove v. Green*, 328 U.S. 549 (1946).
[49] *Reynolds v. Sims*, 377 U.S. 533 (1964).
[50] *Powell v. McCormack*, 395 U.S. 486, 549 (1969). See Terrence Sandalow, "Comments on Powell v. McCormack, *U.C.L.A. Law Review* 17 (1969): 164–74.

from working. A provision whose meaning cannot be ascertained is precisely like a provision that is written in Sanskrit or is obliterated past deciphering by an ink blot."[51] This is a fair enough statement as far as the Court's responsibilities go, but for Bork, such provisions appear to remain Sanskrit or ink blots for the rest of the polity as well and serve as no impediment to the majoritarian will.[52]

Justice Black presented an interesting variation on this alternative. He insisted adamantly that the function of the Court was to discover legal meaning, not to create it. And he insisted further that the only meaning to be discovered was the one placed there by the framers. But what to do where the framer's intent was unclear, such as the meaning of Due Process or Privileges and Immunities in the Fourteenth Amendment? Black's solution was to *create* a clear history, which would then provide the clear meanings he could purport to discover. Thus, he claimed it was the intention of the framers of the Fourteenth Amendment to incorporate the first eight amendments of the Bill of Rights—but only these eight amendments. Nothing more or less. Although the intention of the framers and ratifiers of the Fourteenth Amendment is the subject of intense debate,[53] the one thing that can be said with confidence is that there is no evidence that anyone favored Black's meaning. Black's strongest evidence comes from the speeches of Jacob Howard, who did indeed argue for the incorporation of the first eight amendments, but who also urged that the Fourteenth Amendment should encompass other fundamental privileges and immunities "whatever they may be—for they are not and cannot be fully defined in their entire extent and precise nature."[54] But the indefiniteness of that addition was exactly the sort of thing that Black would prefer to forget. So he did.

These alternatives present a dilemma. If we accept the premise of judicial exclusivity, is it better to scrap the limitations rendering judicial review compatible with the regime in order to see the Constitution whole, or to scrap portions of the Constitution in order to adhere to the limits that render judicial review compatible with the regime? When impaled on the horns of a dilemma, it is perhaps prudent to consider the premise that placed one there: "*If* we accept the premise of judicial exclusivity." But of course we need not accept that premise. And neither should the Court.

---

[51] Robert Bork, *The Tempting of America* (New York: The Free Press, 1990), 166.

[52] Ibid., 167. For further statements by Judge Bork identifying the Constitution with what can be enforced through judicial review, see ibid., 78, 139, and 147.

[53] For the most significant of the recent historical analyses, see Akhil Reed Amar, "The Bill of Rights and the Fourteenth Amendment," *Yale Law Journal* 101 (1992): 1193–1284.

[54] *Congressional Globe*, 39th Congress, 1st Session (1866), 2765–66.

In searching for the best perspective we could examine others whose authority is defined by the Constitution, most notably the legislative and executive perspectives. But the analysis of the judicial perspective should teach us an inherent problem in specialized perspectives: they are partial, they see only a part of the Constitution. A more fruitful approach is to seek a more comprehensive view by finding what is common among the internal perspectives. Article VI gives us an important hint. It reads: "The Senators and Representatives before mentioned, and the Members of the several State Legislatures, and all executive and judicial Officers, both of the United States and of the several States, shall be bound by Oath or Affirmation, to support this Constitution."

Taking this oath is common to all internal perspectives. It is likely to be one of the more solemn moments in the life of a public official, and it certainly is a transformative one. Without the oath to support "this Constitution," no one, though duly elected or nominated, can become a public official. With it, the individual is authorized to speak in the name of the state. With it, powers are vested that otherwise exercised would be theft, robbery, assault, or murder; and similarly, limits are imposed that could not restrict one in a private capacity. Taking this oath, as is customarily done, from a previous oath taker, links the public official in chains of obligation reaching back to that first generation which we call our founding fathers. More broadly, we can speak of this perspective as encompassing those willing and qualified to take the oath and thus to act in the name of the state. So extended, we can identify this as the perspective of the citizen and an ideal form of this perspective as that of the "good" or "serious" citizen.[55]

The good citizen accepts and fosters the ends of his constitution. His constitution is distinct from his country and thus the good citizen is distinguished from the patriot. The patriot loves his country above all else, and thus he says, "my country, right or wrong." The country's constitution may change radically, but the loyalty of the patriot remains. The good citizen's loyalty by contrast is to the regime, the constitution. He says, "my constitution, because it is right." If his constitution changes in character, he will reassess his loyalty. From a broader perspective, we might say of the loyalty of the citizen, "his country, because he *believes* it is right," for his goodness *is relative* to his constitution. A citizen good for a regime dedicated to communism will not be good for a regime dedicated to the rights of private property; a citizen good for a constitution founded on Islamic funda-

---

[55] Aristotle, *Politics*, Bk. 3, 1276b16–1277b33.

mentalism will not be good for one dedicated to the separation of state and religion. A good citizen is thus not good in an absolute sense, or at least not necessarily, for his constitution may not serve good ends. Further, politics itself may not provide an arena fit for the full expression of human excellence. Perhaps in the end we will need to seek a perspective that encompasses and surpasses that of the citizen.[56] Our immediate concern, however, is not how good is the citizen as measured by some sort of absolute standard, but how well he can see the Constitution—if it is what it claims to be, i.e., the supreme law of the land.

We can assess the perspective of the citizen by comparing it with other perspectives we have considered. Where the political "scientist" or the bad man sees the Constitution through the eyes of a judge, the citizen sees it with his own eyes. Where the scientist is blind to authority, the citizen comprehends it. Where the bad man undermines the Constitution, the citizen supports it. Comprehending authority and taking the Constitution as his standard of judgment, the citizen is similar to the judge, but he suffers none of the latter's disabilities. Where the judge can see only what is fit for adjudication, the citizen sees the whole Constitution. Where the lens of the judge is adjusted to accommodate the "countermajoritarian" or "counterregime" difficulty, the lens of the citizen is direct and unfiltered.

The latter point is worth expanding. There may be some tension between one's authority as a good judge to pronounce what the Constitution permits and one's capacity as a good citizen to decide what the Constitution really means. Thus, one may have an obligation as a good judge to pronounce: "This court cannot dispute the conclusion of Congress that the petitioner's conduct constitutes an impeachable offense. That is a political question." But in his identity as a good citizen, this same person may decide that the conduct is *not* an impeachable offense. Or, one may have an obligation as a good judge to pronounce: "Because it lies within the realm of reason to say that the activity in question concerns commerce among the states, this court must uphold the federal law." But in his identity as a citizen, this same person may decide the activity is *not* really commercial in

[56] Ibid. Cf. Leo Strauss, *What is Political Philosophy?* (Glencoe, Ill.: Free Press, 1959; Chicago: University of Chicago Press, 1988), 26–27: "[The classical philosophers] look at political things in the perspective of the enlightened citizen or statesmen. They see things clearly which the enlightened citizens or statesmen do not see clearly, or do not see at all. But this has no other reason but the fact that they look further afield in the same direction as the enlightened citizens or statesmen. They do not look at political things from the outside, as spectators of political life."

character and thus lies beyond federal authority.[57] A large part of what is often called "constitutional theory" is actually about such tensions which inhere in the practice of judicial review. Such tensions arise because judicial review looks at the Constitution through the perspective of a specialized role, a part that must accommodate itself to other parts and principles of the regime and whose goodness therefore must always be partial, incomplete. But with the citizen as citizen, there is no tension, for the goodness of the citizen is coterminous with that of the regime. There can be no tension between his goodness and the principles of the regime, for he is the embodiment of the regime.

If then the Constitution is supreme law, the case seems strong that we can see it best through the eyes of the good citizen, not the astigmatic lens of the Court.

[57] Similarly, one might have to say as a good president: "I cannot enforce this law that the Supreme Court has declared unconstitutional," though as a good citizen, this same person may think the law valid. Or one might have to say as a good prison warden: "I cannot set this prisoner free," though as a good citizen, this same person may think the confinement unconstitutional.

DON QUIXOTE AND THE CONSTITUTION

George Anastaplo

The spell of the steel itself draws men on to fight.

—Odysseus[1]

I.

I have been invited to provide for this volume the reflections of "an elder statesman." I cannot help but recall that Harry Truman considered *statesman* a fancy term for a *dead politician*. Since I am still alive the "statesman" title for me may simply be a generous courtesy. Even so, I take it that I am being asked to draw in this essay upon my public career which has run between the ages of seventeen and seventy.[2]

---

[1] Homer, *Odyssey*, XIX, 13 (incorporated in a lulling speech that Odysseus prepared for his son to use). I am glad to accept the invitation to expand the modest notes originally prepared for this occasion, if only to suggest those materials of mine from which I have distilled many of the observations in this essay. I devote too much care to the things I prepare for publication to allow them, without an effort on my part, to be lost from view thereafter either because of my obscurity or because of the quite limited circulation of the journals in which I happen to be published. My model in self-advertisement is Don Quixote, who seems to have reckoned that if he (as an artist of knight-errantry) went to the trouble of doing useful things, others should benefit from learning about them.

[2] See, on that career, Anastaplo, *The American Moralist: On Law, Ethics, and Government* (Athens: Ohio University Press, 1992), 582–91; Anastaplo, "Lessons for the Student of Law: The Oklahoma Lectures," *Oklahoma City University Law Review* 20 (1995): 153–79. See also interviews by Studs Terkel, in John A. Murley, Robert L. Stone, and William T. Braithwaite, eds., *Law and Philosophy: The Practice of Theory* (Athens: Ohio University Press, 1992), 1:504–38. See as well the collection of essays, "The Scholarship of George Anastaplo," *Political Science Reviewer* 26 (1997): 1–247. That symposium was anticipated by a panel discussion sponsored by the Claremont Institute at the 1995 Annual Convention of the American Political Science Association in Chicago. See note 3 below.

There is all too much about that career which can remind one of the follies of Don Quixote. The obsessiveness of Don Quixote is tempered somewhat by his faithful companion, Sancho Panza. Such a companion, whether the Lone Ranger's Tonto or a contemporary dissident's long-suffering spouse, can provide a steadying influence.[3]

Three of my own follies, or "projects," over the years, point to problems that we are all familiar with, whatever we may now believe about our right and ability as a community to do much if anything about them. The bearing of the judiciary upon these matters will be noticed with a view to the theme of this book, *The Supreme Court and American Constitutionalism.*

II.

Each of my projects has constitutional implications. This is not the same as saying that the Supreme Court can, or should try to,

---

[3] See, for how a long-suffering spouse can find relief in poetry, Murley et al., *Law and Philosophy*, 2:1033–45. See also Anastaplo, *The Artist as Thinker: From Shakespeare to Joyce* (Athens: Ohio University Press, 1983), Dedication. A different kind of "faithful companion" has been Harry V. Jaffa from whose scholarship on Abraham Lincoln and on others I have learned much. See, on our decades-long "collaboration," Laurence Berns, "Aristotle and the Moderns on Freedom and Equality," in Kenneth L. Deutsch and Walter Soffer, eds., *The Crisis of Liberal Democracy: A Straussian Perspective* (Albany: State University of New York Press, 1987), 156–58. Professor Jaffa's generosity is evident in the instruction and reassurance he provides in a statement prepared by him for the 1995 APSA Convention (see note 2 above), "A Tribute to George Anastaplo" (dated August 25, 1995):

With the publication of his Commentary on the Amendments, Anastaplo has complemented and completed his Commentary on the Constitution of 1787. This is a major event in the history of the Constitution itself. George's commentaries, unlike any others, belong to a tradition very different from that of legal commentaries, as usually understood. They have more in common with Leo Strauss's *The Argument and the Action of Plato's Laws* than with any other contemporary work. As Strauss approached the Torah of reason with the reverence of the Torah of revelation—Anastaplo has brought a lifelong devotion to the American Constitution to his task.

Since it will be some time before I can have assimilated this magisterial work, I mention here only one of its features. The chapter on the Thirteenth Amendment is preceded by one on the Emancipation Proclamation. This is absolutely necessary, although George is perhaps the only one who would have recognized that fact. After nearly a half century of constant reading of Lincoln, and about Lincoln, I can say categorically that this chapter is the finest scholarly writing on Lincoln's words that I know. My feeling is that George must have sat at Lincoln's elbow as he composed the Proclamation of September 22, 1862, and discussed it with him, paragraph by paragraph. As a proof of the possibility that one can understand a great writer as he understood himself, it is the definitive refutation of historicism.

do much about them. Indeed, it is sometimes useful to notice the limitations of the Supreme Court in dealing with our most troublesome issues ranging from abortion to race relations. The principal official guide for us in such matters should usually be the legislature, not the judiciary.

A modern complication in dealing with our constitutional and political problems—at the highest level, the constitutional and the political may not be distinguishable (which is itself an argument against judicial review)—a modern complication is that we *are* dealing now with a country of a quarter of a billion people. It is difficult to avoid regarding so large an association as a *mass*, borrowing thereby a term from modern physics. And *masses*, we are now taught, can be adequately studied only by the use of statistics; they cannot be properly seen and understood otherwise. A sense of humanity, including a recognition of the efficacy if not also the primacy of reason, is easily sacrificed in such circumstances—especially when it is recalled that *masses* can be moved only by *forces*.

We have "advanced" here far beyond the Leviathan of the seventeenth century, which was already a repudiation of the possibility, as well as of the relevance, of the *polis* with its grounding in that meaningful political discourse which depends, in part, upon intimate and continuing personal contact. On the other hand, we contributors to this volume, and others like us elsewhere, know each other or at least *can* know each other, indirectly if not directly, reminding us thereby of what a genuine community can be like. We are, then, part of a vital *polis* within this vast American empire.

Is it quixotic for us to try to rein in and guide our country as we do, believing that we can somehow make a difference?

III.

The first of my own quixotic projects (I notice in passing that *project* itself is a modern term, going back perhaps to the eighteenth-century Enlightenment if not even to Francis Bacon and René Descartes)—the first of my projects incorporates my response to the Cold War.

My service in that war began within a decade after my service during the Second World War, which had begun for me with my volunteering at age seventeen for the Army Air Corps, where I earned

See John A. Murley, "Our Character Is Our Fate: The Constitutionalism of George Anastaplo," *Political Science Reviewer* 26 (1997): 12–13, 36f. See also notes 11 and 25 below.

my wings and commission, having had to persuade one flight surgeon
after another that I was fit to fly despite a heart murmur. Those forty
months of service in a great cause proved for me a liberating experience, the kind of experience as a patriot that has been hard for
youngsters to benefit from in the decades since. I am reminded here
of Lord Charnwood's perceptive observation in his biography of
Abraham Lincoln:[4]

> His muscular strength was great, and startling statistical tales are
> told of the weight he could lift and the force of his blow with a
> mallet or an axe. To a gentle and thoughtful boy with secret ambi-
> tion in him such strength is a great gift, and in such surroundings
> [as Lincoln grew up in] most obviously so.

One's proper service during the Cold War all too often obliged
the conscientious citizen to urge restraint upon his fellows—and to
try to do so without seeming to countenance dreadful tyrannies
around the world. The Cold War was pervasive in its manifestations
among us, leading (in the awesome name of national security) to
many distortions of our way of life. We all suffered the consequences
of executive usurpations, loyalty programs, and a waste of vast resources that should have been put to other uses both at home and
abroad, constructive uses that would probably have contributed to
genuine security.

Our misconceptions and miscalculations can be said to have culminated in the Vietnam War. Vietnam meant not only the deaths of
some fifty thousand American soldiers and of hundreds of thousands
of others. It meant also—partly because it came to be widely regarded
as perhaps in vain for us—the corruption of a generation of citizens,
contributing significantly to the distrust, especially among the young,
of our institutions. This development may have reinforced "natural"
tendencies among us to justify more and more personal privacy and
looking out primarily for oneself.[5]

Jim Wright, the former Speaker of the House of Representatives,
has reported what Lyndon Johnson said to him and others about that
war, evidently after retiring from the presidency: "The kids were
right. I blew it."[6] It is not a healthy state of affairs when "kids" come

[4] Lord Charnwood, *Abraham Lincoln* (Garden City, NY: Garden City Publishing
Co., 1917), 8.
[5] See, on the Vietnam War, Anastaplo, *The American Moralist*, 225–60. See also
Anastaplo, "On Freedom: Explorations," *Oklahoma City University Law Review* 17
(1992): 589–630; Anastaplo, "First Impressions," *Political Science Reviewer* 26
(1997): 248–57. See, as well, note 2 above, note 7 below.
[6] See Jim Wright, *Balance of Power* (Atlanta: Turner Publishing Co., 1996), 136.

to be regarded as having been right, especially when it has to be done at the expense of the stature of our leaders and hence of our political morale.[7]

One overarching question, in assessing the Cold War and our responses to it, is what we should have expected from, and how we should have dealt with, the Russian tyranny. Our point of departure should have been an early, sound estimate of the relative strengths of the United States and the Soviet Union. What I saw in Russia in the summer of 1960 confirmed what I had long believed about the primitive condition (relatively speaking) of the Russian economy and the precarious standing of Marxism there and in Eastern Europe. That visit to Russia and its obviously unreliable satellites was in the course of a six-month, seventeen-thousand-mile camping trip in a Volkswagen Microbus that our family took across Europe. Our Intelligence people should have long before seen what was obvious to us during our weeks behind the Iron Curtain about the vulnerability of the Russians, a vulnerability that the better informed among the Russian leaders were probably always aware of.[8]

The oppressiveness of the Soviet regime was obvious to any sensitive visitor, so much so that it was a great relief for us to leave Russia. One could be reminded by this kind of exposure not to want such moral as well as political and economic deterioration for one's own country. One could also recognize that we had to do the serious political thinking for the Russians as well as for ourselves that was required if worldwide devastation was to be avoided.[9]

In dealing with these matters in the 1950s and 1960s, one could reasonably come to the conclusion that the United States Supreme Court would not be of much help. In fact, it probably would have been better if the Court had simply stood aside instead of ratifying, in effect, some of the worst excesses of the Cold War in this country. Be that as it may, the decisions by the Supreme Court in the *Dennis*

[7] See, for example, Anastaplo, "In re Allan Bloom: A Respectful Dissent," in Robert L. Stone, ed., *Essays on The Closing of the American Mind* (Chicago: Chicago Review Press, 1989), 267–84. See also James C. Thomson, Jr., "A Memory of McGeorge Bundy," *New York Times*, September 22, 1996, E3.

[8] See, for example, James Burnham, "Through the Mirror," *National Review*, November 11, 1977, 1288.

[9] See Anastaplo, "Clausewitz and Intelligence: Some Preliminary Observations," *Teaching Political Science* 16 (1989): 81. See, on my expulsion from the Soviet Union (and also from the Greece of the Colonels), Anastaplo, *Human Being and Citizen: Essays on Virtue, Freedom, and the Common Good* (Chicago: Swallow Press, 1975), 5–7, 226–27; *The Artist as Thinker*, 331–33; *Law and Philosophy*, 1:539. See also Anastaplo, *The American Moralist*, 537–69; note 13 below.

case (1951) and in the *Rosenberg* case (1953) contributed to developments which culminated, as I have said, in the Vietnam War.[10]

We should be thankful, in any event, that the Supreme Court did not undertake to review the constitutionality of the Vietnam War as well, for that probably would have resulted in still another unfortunate ratification of Cold War measures. The proper forum among the branches of government for debating that and like issues is the Congress, where the Vietnam War (including how the United States was taken into it) was eventually faced up to. The way we *were* taken into that war, succumbing perhaps to "the spell of the steel itself," deprived the president of the counsel and support that proper congressional debate can provide.

Among the consequences of the Cold War in this country was what it did to that freedom of speech which we have to rely upon in governing ourselves properly. Perhaps more salutary than anything the Supreme Court did, for the cause of our constitutional liberties in the 1950s and 1960s, was what the Senate did in censuring Joseph McCarthy. (Curiously enough, on the other hand, the Cold War may have enhanced the Court's contributions to the cause of just race relations in this country. But even here, it should be noticed, the Court was in part correcting the mistakes of the late-nineteenth-century Court which had undermined the contributions which post-Civil War Congresses had tried to make on behalf of the newly-emancipated slaves.[11])

IV.

The second of my projects—or, one might say, my lost causes—is with respect to the special form of devastation that we have permitted

---

[10] See *Dennis v. United States,* 341 U.S. 494 (1951), *Rosenberg v. United States,* 346 U.S. 273, 322, 324 (1953). See also Anastaplo, *The Constitutionalist: Notes on the First Amendment* (Dallas: Southern Methodist University Press, 1971), 824, 825; Anastaplo, "On Trial: Explorations," *Loyola University of Chicago Law Journal* 22 (1991): 994–1011; Anastaplo, "The Occasions of Freedom of Speech," *Political Science Reviewer* 5 (1975): 390–97; Anastaplo, "Freedom of Speech and the First Amendment," *Texas Tech Law Review* 21 (1990): 2041–51; Anastaplo, "On Freedom," 518–40. On the other hand, summary execution would be appropriate for the likes of Aldrich Ames upon exposure.

[11] See Anastaplo, "Slavery and the Constitution: Explorations," *Texas Tech Law Review* 20 (1989): 696–766; Anastaplo, *The Amendments to the Constitution: A Commentary* (Baltimore: Johns Hopkins University Press, 1995), 168–85. See, on race relations today, Anastaplo, " 'Racism,' Political Correctness, and Constitutional Law: A Law School Case Study," *South Dakota Law Review* 42 (1997): 108–64; Anastaplo, "The O. J. Simpson Case Revisited," *Loyola University of Chicago Law Journal* 28 (1997): 489–503. See also note 3 above, note 25 below.

television to inflict upon us. I developed in 1972 the proposal that broadcast television in the United States should be abolished.[12] A quarter of a century later the damage of television has become even worse, far, far worse, than it was then. The Cold War meant that grand mistakes abroad corrupted us here in the United States. Television has meant that grand mistakes in the United States are corrupting many abroad who have become addicted to our television programs.

I recognize, of course, that the prospects of my television-abolition proposal are even slimmer than they were a quarter of a century ago—and they were virtually *nil* then. But we have celebrated the "unthinkable" in the collapse of the Soviet Union. What will it take, one might well wonder, to undermine our own tyrannical, albeit somewhat benign, television empire?[13]

I will not impose upon you my litany of the evils for which television is largely responsible. It suffices to notice how television has distorted (sometimes with the best of intentions) our entertainment, our sports, our news reports and, perhaps worst of all, our politics. Underlying these distortions is what has happened to our character and to our sense of what is needed to understand serious matters. Furthermore, we (and our language) are very much infected by the desire to sell. For example, it remains a mystery for me why people put up with the cynical (and hardly hidden) commercial butchery of the movies that are broadcast on television. Fundamental here is the damage done to American souls, a degradation that is testified to by (but is far from limited to) what is now freely talked about in public and how it is talked about. A related casualty here is practice in, and hence a general respect for, prudence.[14]

A serious effort to abolish television would face constitutional challenges to which the Supreme Court would probably be receptive. *Due process, privacy,* and other constitutional challenges would be

---

[12] See Anastaplo, *The American Moralist,* 245–74. See also the 1976 film, *Network,* for suggestions about flaws and dubious tendencies intrinsic to television. See as well Anastaplo, *The Artist as Thinker,* 322–30.

[13] See, on the vulnerability of tyrannies, Anastaplo, *The American Moralist,* 144–80. See also note 9 above.

[14] Consider, for example, how the Clarence Thomas Hearings should have been conducted: the more salacious matters, insofar as they were relevant in judging the nominee's qualifications for the Supreme Court, should have been assessed behind closed doors by Senators whom the Senate (and the country?) could trust to be sensible. But this would have required something which the Vietnam War helped subvert, a general respect for our institutions. This subversion is, unfortunately, a tendency that has been evident in the Western World even without the influence of the Vietnam War, as may be seen in how shabbily more and more English newspapers have been dealing with their somewhat reckless Royal Family.

mounted against this or any other such effort by the community to
do something useful about the character of the American people. In
addition, vigorous First Amendment complaints can be expected to
be made about any measures which presuppose that there are enduring moral standards to be drawn upon. The authority of the community is thus called into question in still another way.[15]

It is not only the abolition of television (even if done in a way
not favoring one party, political or religious, over another) that faces
constitutional challenge. Modest regulations can also run into trouble in the Supreme Court, as may be seen in how people such as Ross
Perot and Malcolm Forbes have come to be exempted on so-called
First Amendment grounds from the campaign-expenditures limitations imposed upon the rest of us.[16]

Then there are the obstacles that regulation, as well as the abolition, of television faces on related "freedom of expression"
grounds.[17] *Freedom of expression* has come to mean, in large part because of the Supreme Court, that we are entitled, if not even obliged,
to be on our own, to develop ourselves as we happen to please, etc.
Civic-mindedness and with it a reliance upon prudence suffer as a
result, with radical individualism taking over (reinforced, or given a
more and more materialist bent, by ever more intensive commercial-
ization). My television-abolition proposal, however quixotic it may
seem (with forests of television antennas taking the place of my great
Spanish predecessor's windmills) does encourage us to examine first
principles.

That proposal can include, as a useful corollary, reconsideration
of the practice of judicial review of acts of Congress. Indeed, many of
the issues considered in the instructive essays in this volume would
be far less troublesome if the Framers' original intention of a very
limited scope for judicial review had been honored by the Supreme
Court.[18]

[15] See Anastaplo, "The Public Interest in Privacy: On Becoming and Being
Human," *DePaul Law Review* 26 (1977): 767–71. See also note 26 below.

[16] See *Buckley v. Valeo,* 424 U.S. 1 (1976); Anastaplo, *The Amendments to the Constitution,* 230–31.

[17] *Freedom of expression* has usurped the proper place of *freedom of speech [and] of
the press* in our constitutional system. See, on freedom of expression, Anastaplo,
The Amendments to the Constitution, 459. See also Anastaplo, "How to Read the
Constitution of the United States," *Loyola University of Chicago Law Journal* 17
(1985): 37–49; Anastaplo, *Human Being and Citizen,* 117–38. See, on the age-old
attractions of freedom of speech, Euripides, *The Phoenician Women,* 387 sq.

[18] See, on judicial review, Anastaplo, *The Constitution of 1787: A Commentary*
(Johns Hopkins University Press, 1989), 335; Anastaplo, "Mr. Crosskey, the Amer-
ican Constitution, and the Natures of Things," *Loyola University of Chicago Law
Journal* 15 (1984): 185–88, 202–03, 208–14. See also note 21 below.

V.

The third of my projects is with respect to the education that is required today, especially for the training of lawyers and hence jurists. Consider, for example, what Edmund Wilson said in recalling "the great American jurists." They had, he said, "subtle intellect, philosophic and literary interests, a long view of human history . . . and a combination of moral anxieties with an ironic sense of humor."[19]

I have several times invoked a reliance upon *prudence*—and, for this, properly educated citizens are usually needed. It is striking, however, how shallow the intellectual foundations of students can be when they come to us in law school. It is hard to build much, or for long, on such foundations. It is remarkable what even the law students who elect to take my jurisprudence courses, who can be presumed to be more interested than most of their fellow students in philosophical matters, simply do not know about the heritage upon which our institutions depend.

This sad state of affairs prompted me to launch a few years ago my third, perhaps my most quixotic, proposal: I have suggested to my law faculty colleagues that we institute a required year-long "secular" course in the Bible and Shakespeare. Through Shakespeare, students have useful access as well to Classical thought.[20]

It should not require an argument to persuade the participants

[19] Edmund Wilson, "Conversations with Malcolm Sharp," *University of Chicago Law Review* 33 (1966): 200. See, on Malcolm P. Sharp, Anastaplo, "Lessons for the Student of Law," 133–52. See also Jonathan Sharp, "Malcolm Pitman Sharp," *American National Biography* (forthcoming).

[20] This is related to the Chaucer seminar I conducted on the Ashland University campus before the conference for which this essay was prepared started. See also Anastaplo, "Rome, Piety, and Law: Explorations," *Loyola of New Orleans Law Review* 39 (1993): 108–10; Anastaplo, *The Artist as Thinker*, 15–28. See, as well, Anastaplo, "Individualism, Professional Ethics, and the Sense of Community: From Runnymede to a London Telephone Booth," *Loyola University of Chicago Law Journal* 28 (1997): 308–16; Anastaplo, "Law & Literature and the Bible" (to be published in 1998 by the *Oklahoma City University Law Review*). I originally suggested to my law school colleagues that we add required Bible and Shakespeare courses to the first year of our law school curriculum. But it is difficult to squeeze anything new into the very crowded first-year schedule. Besides, after a year or two, law students become much more receptive to something different (which, in this case, would be something refreshingly old and even natural). I have observed a healthy response by law students to both the Bible and Shakespeare when I have used them in my upper-level jurisprudence courses. Our Spring 1997 Shakespeare course culminated in a staged reading by the class of *The Tempest*, a public reading which was well received by the student body of the law school.

in this volume that our law students would become better, not only as human beings but also as lawyers, if they knew much more than they do now about the Bible, Shakespeare, and the Classics. The prudence and enduring standards that I have been invoking are nourished by such texts. Even more critical here for men and women of the law is how they may be helped to *read* both the Constitution and the other constitutional documents (such as Magna Carta and the Declaration of Independence) that the Constitution takes for granted.

A proper reading of the Constitution would lead to a much-restricted scope for judicial review and to a much-enlarged respect for natural right and the Common Law. It should contribute thereby to a repudiation of the positivism and legal realism with which we have been saddled.

VI.

Permit me to restate briefly, and in less quixotic forms, the three proposals that I have described with respect to the Cold War, to television, and to the education of lawyers.

1) We need a reassertion of legislative supremacy, not only vis-a-vis the executive (for example, with respect to declarations of war) but also vis-a-vis the judiciary. To rely more than we now do upon legislatures means that the key issues are more likely to be considered in a political manner. If the relevant legislatures had been more deferred to, the Vietnam War would probably have had a different effect among us, just as our festering abortion controversy would have had if it had continued to be dealt with primarily in legislatures. (All this bears as well upon such prosaic but still dubious exercises in judicial legislation as the many so-called "burdens on interstate commerce" cases that the Supreme Court routinely considers.) In any event, it would contribute to a healthier constitutionalism if we should be led to a better recognition of what courts are like and should do. The Common Law aspects of judicial work could well be revived, along with a respect for natural right.[21]

---

[21] The implications here of *Erie Railroad Company v. Tompkins,* 304 U.S. 64 (1938), are not generally appreciated. See Anastaplo, "The Supreme Court Is Indeed a Court," in Robert A. Licht, ed., *Is the Supreme Court the Guardian of the Constitution?* (Washington, DC: The AEI Press, 1993), 22–33; Anastaplo, *The Constitution of 1787,* 333; Anastaplo, *The Amendments to the Constitution,* 458. See also William T. Braithwaite, "The Common Law and the Judicial Power: An Introduction to *Swift-Erie,*" in Murley et al., eds., *Law and Philosophy,* 2:774–818. See as well Anastaplo, "Justice Antonin Scalia's Constitutionalism," *Blackacre* (Loyola

2) We need a reassertion of the rights, powers, and duty of the community to shape character and provide education—and, indeed, to serve the general welfare. It should be recalled that the Confederate Convention—meeting in Montgomery, Alabama in March 1861 to write a new constitution—took as its "first draft" the Constitution of 1787 with its (by then) twelve amendments. Particularly instructive, especially for would-be originalists today, is the fact that that Convention removed both of the "general Welfare" phrases in the Constitution of 1787. Those Secessionists recognized that the General Welfare Clause may be potent.[22] This bears, for instance, upon what may be done by Congress about the nationwide crime problem in the United States, including the grim state of affairs that we have let ourselves in for by permitting the almost unbelievable amount of privately-held weaponry we do.[23]

3) We need a reassertion of those fundamental principles of the regime that citizens (and especially lawyers) should be concerned with. A proper education, which would encourage law students to expect to rely more upon politicians (or, if you will, statesmen) than upon judges, is harder to provide because of various consequences among us of the Cold War and of television.[24]

I should not leave my three proposals without recognizing the defensible aspects of the "systems" I have questioned. We have avoided, for a half-century now, a nuclear war (as well as a nuclear-free Third World War) and have lowered perhaps the status of tyranny in the world, however endangered we may still be by the condition in which Russia has been left and by the "perpetual" lethal nuclear wastes we have generated. Television does seem to have contributed to better race relations in the United States, troublesome

University of Chicago School of Law), 18:4 (May 6, 1997); note 26 below. Here, as elsewhere, the work of William W. Crosskey remains invaluable. See note 18 above. Compare Michael Conant, *The Constitution and the Economy: Objective Theory and Critical Commentary* (Norman: University of Oklahoma Press, 1991); Leonard R. Sorenson, *Madison on the "General Welfare" of America* (Lanham, MD: Rowman & Littlefield, 1995). Also instructive, especially as we contemplate a future without the Great [Bolshevik] Satan around which to "organize" our fears and energy, is Constantine P. Cavafy, "Waiting for the Barbarians." See Murley et al., eds., *Law and Philosophy*, 2:1048–49.

[22] See Anastaplo, *The Amendments to the Constitution*, 132–33, 344, 349, 442.

[23] See, for example, Fox Butterfield, "Survey Finds That Crimes Cost $450 Billion a Year," *New York Times*, April 23, 1996, A8. This suggests why *United States v. Lopez*, 115 S.Ct. 1624 (1995), should be of limited application.

[24] See, for additional education reforms, Anastaplo, "Law & Politics," *Political Science Reviewer* 25 (1996): 127–50. See also Anastaplo, *The American Moralist*, 454–68.

though it may be to turn African-American athletes into our recognized gladiators. And, however troubled our educational undertakings may be, we still have, by and large, a decent people capable of self-government to a remarkable extent. We also have, here and there, opportunities for students to secure a sound education, if they (or their parents) should chance to be so inclined.

VII.

It may be useful for me to add (as a liberal) that the conservative/liberal dichotomy should not be controlling with respect to the matters I have touched upon in this essay. I return here to what I said at the outset about our *polis*: thoughtful conservatives and thoughtful liberals have much in common, sharing (or, at least, being equipped to consider sharing) both fundamental principles and long-run objectives. Prudence and a political sense should be promoted by a proper education; mechanical solutions are hardly likely to suffice for deep-rooted problems. Affirmative action, I dare add, has much to be said for it, especially if deliberately used (*and* terminated in a timely fashion) in the spirit of Section 5 of the Fourteenth Amendment. (I, for one, cannot forget the disproportionate Vietnam War casualties we were *willing* to exact of our minorities, our uneducated, and our depressed classes, whatever the actual figures may have been. We did not hear much about the iniquity of special privileges in those days from the quarters now protesting affirmative action.[25])

A proper education helps us not only to be prudent as citizens but also to be happy as human beings. At the core of the *Don Quixote* novel, after all, is the insistence that we very much need to face up to our mortality. The masquerade of death, Cervantes shows us, has to be dealt with.

Still, in our circumstances, a single warrior, whether Don Quixote or the Lone Ranger, should not be relied upon to right all wrongs. One might even wonder whether Don Quixote, who can sometimes be reckless in what he does, may stand for a questionable individualism.

Individualism is still, at least for us, a problem to be reckoned with as well as a trait to be cherished. Particularly useful for us could be a revival of confidence in our right and power as a community to

---

[25] Consider, for example, Speaker Jim Wright's report: "Olin 'Tiger' Teague and I, so far as I was aware, were the only congressional parents with sons [in the Vietnam War]." Wright, *Balance of Power*, 148. See also Stone, ed., *Essays on The Closing of the American Mind*, 223–34, 272–75. See as well notes 3 and 11 above.

take control of our lives. Citizens, especially our younger citizens, should be taught that attempts at such control need not be either oppressive or improperly "judgmental."

In most of our public controversies the role of the courts should be subordinated to the guidance provided by legislatures, those bodies in which competing interests have their say and in which critical differences can be resolved (often by way of compromise) rather than repeatedly litigated with a view to determining winners and losers, which tends to have what is called a "polarizing" effect. In short, jurisprudence should be subordinated to political philosophy. Political philosophy, in turn, is properly guided by that Idea of the Good which instructs us how to achieve as much of perfection as is possible in our circumstances. What perfection can mean is usefully suggested in lines given to Heracles (a different kind of Don Quixote figure) in one of Euripides' tragedies, lines that the Socrates of Plato's *Republic* could endorse: "If God is truly God, He is perfect, lacking nothing."[26]

[26] Euripides, *Heracles*, 1345. See, on Plato's *Republic* and the Idea of the Good, Anastaplo, *The Thinker as Artist: From Homer to Plato & Aristotle* (Athens: Ohio University Press, 1997), 182–91, 303–17; Anastaplo, *The Constitutionalist*, 278–81. See also Anastaplo, "Natural Law or Natural Right?" *Loyola of New Orleans Law Review* 38 (1993): 915–30. See, on the tension between the noble and the just, Anastaplo, *The Thinker as Artist*, 182–91. An overarching sense of the good should be relied upon in dealing with this tension. Various of the matters touched upon in this essay are examined in Anastaplo, *Campus Hate-Speech Codes, Natural Right, and Twentieth Century Atrocities* (Lewiston, N.Y.: Edwin Mellen Press, 1997) (second printing). See also Anastaplo, *Abraham Lincoln's Constitutionalism* (Dallas: Spence Publishing Company, forthcoming).

Part II

THE SUPREME COURT AND CONSTITUTIONAL POLITICS

The Future of Constitutional Criminal Procedure

Akhil Reed Amar

WE LIVE IN interesting times, and the times are especially interesting for those of us who work in the field of constitutional criminal procedure. In a series of essays, I have sought to explore the foundations of the field—to lay bare, and elaborate upon, the "first principles" of the Fourth, Fifth and Sixth Amendments.[1] These essays have already begun to provoke heated controversy over some of my specific doctrinal claims.[2] (As I said, we live in interesting times.) In this brief review essay, I shall try to pull the camera back, highlighting some of the general features of my "first principles" project. In the process, I hope to say a few words about the past and present of constitutional criminal procedure, and a few more words about its future—in courts, in Congress, in classrooms, and in conversations everywhere in between.

I. WHERE ARE WE, AND HOW DID WE GET HERE?

A. *The Past*

As a subfield of constitutional law, constitutional criminal procedure stands as an anomaly. In many other areas of constitutional law,

---

[1] These essays, as well as a version of this one, have been collected in my book, *The Constitution and Criminal Procedure* (New Haven: Yale University Press, 1997). The reader interested in more elaboration of any of my claims here about the Fourth, Fifth, and Sixth Amendments is urged to consult the relevant essays in that volume.

[2] See, e.g., Donald A. Dripps, "Akhil Amar On Criminal Procedure and Constitutional Law: 'Here I Go Down That Wrong Road Again,' " *North Carolina Law Review* 74 (1996): 1559–639; Yale Kamisar, "On the 'Fruits' of Miranda Viola-

major Marshall Court opinions stand out, and continue to frame debate both in courts and beyond. In thinking about judicial review and executive power, we still look to *Marbury v. Madison*;[3] in pondering the puzzle of jurisdiction-stripping, we go back to *Martin v. Hunter's Lessee*;[4] in reflecting on the scope of Congress' enumerated powers, and related issues of federalism, we re-examine *McCulloch v. Maryland*;[5] in considering vested property rights, we return to *Fletcher v. Peck*[6] and *Dartmouth College v. Woodward*;[7] and so on. But no comparable Marshall Court landmarks dot the plain of constitutional criminal procedure.

It is often thought that the explanation for this anomaly lies in another Marshall Court landmark, *Barron v. Baltimore.*[8] Most criminal law, the argument goes, is state law: murder, rape, robbery, and the like are generally not federal crimes. Under *Barron*, the constitutional criminal procedure rules of the Bill of Rights did not apply against states, and so the Marshall Court predictably heard few cases raising issues of constitutional criminal procedure.

Barron is indeed part of the story, but only part. For the federal government was very much in the crime-fighting business in the first century of the Bill of Rights. For constitutional scholars, perhaps the most vivid example of early federal criminal law comes from the infamous Sedition Act of 1798; but we must also not forget the territories. Perhaps *the* most central and sustained project of the federal government in its first century was the "Americanization" of this continent

tions, Coerced Confessions, and Compelled Testimony," *Michigan Law Review* 93 (1995): 929–1010; Tracey Maclin, "When the Cure for the Fourth Amendment is Worse than the Disease," *Southern California Law Review* 68 (1994): 1–72; Carole S. Steiker, "Second Thoughts About First Principles," *Harvard Law Review* 107 (1994): 820–57.

[3] 5 U.S. (1 Cranch) 137 (1803). See generally Akhil Reed Amar, "Marbury, Section 13, and the Original Jurisdiction of the Supreme Court," *University of Chicago Law Review* 56 (1989): 445–53.

[4] 14 U.S. (1 Wheat.) 304 (1816). See generally Akhil Reed Amar, "The Two-Tiered Structure of the Judiciary Act of 1789," *University of Pennsylvania Law Review* 138 (1990): 1499–1505; Akhil Reed Amar, "A Neo-federalist View of Article III: Separating the Two Tiers of Federal Jurisdiction," *Boston University Law Review* 65 (1985): 205–19.

[5] 17 U.S. (4 Wheat.) 316 (1819). See generally Akhil Reed Amar, "Of Sovereignty and Federalism," *Yale Law Journal* 96 (1987): 1451–55, 1512–17.

[6] 10 U.S. (6 Cranch) 87 (1810). See Akhil Reed Amar, "The Bill of Rights and the Fourteenth Amendment," *Yale Law Journal* 101 (1992): 1198 n.21.

[7] 17 U.S. (4 Wheat.) 518 (1819). See generally Akhil Reed Amar, *The Creation and Reconstruction of the Bill of Rights*, ch. 7 (forthcoming 1998).

[8] 32 U.S. (7 Pet.) 243 (1833). For discussion of *Barron*, see Amar, "Bill of Rights," 1198–1203.

through territorial expansion, organization of territorial governments, and eventual admission to statehood of these territories.[9] In the territories, the federal government did indeed enforce garden-variety criminal laws against murder, rape, robbery, and so on. And the Bill of Rights very much applied to these criminal cases, even under *Barron*. Territorial law was, constitutionally speaking, federal law.

But—and this is the key point—for virtually the entire first century of the Bill of Rights, the United States Supreme Court lacked general appellate jurisdiction over federal criminal cases.[10] This little-known fact helps explain why, for example, the Sedition Act prosecutions in the late 1790s—which raised the most important and far-reaching constitutional issues of their day—never reached the Supreme Court for ultimate judicial resolution.[11]

By the time Congress decided to give the High Court general appellate review over federal criminal cases in 1891, the sun was already setting on the territorial era. Thus, the criminal cases the Supreme Court heard under the new jurisdictional regime were indeed a skewed lot, with disproportionately more federal customs violations, tax evasions, and bootlegging than murders, rapes, and robberies. And this was the era, of course, that gave birth to the controversial exclusionary rule.

Then came the Warren Court, which overruled *Barron* and began applying the Fourth, Fifth and Sixth Amendments directly against states. With many, many more state criminal cases fueling its docket, the Warren Court proceeded to build up, in short order, a remarkable doctrinal edifice of Fourth Amendment, Fifth Amendment, and Sixth Amendment rules—the foundations of modern constitutional criminal procedure.

But these foundations were none too sure. On a jurisprudential level, some of the Warren Court's most important criminal procedure pronouncements lacked firm grounding in constitutional text and structure. Key rulings ran counter to early case law in lower federal

---

[9] See Akhil Reed Amar, "Some New World Lessons for the Old World," *University of Chicago Law Review* 58 (1991): 483–91; Denis P. Duffey, "The Northwest Ordinance as a Constitutional Document," *Columbia Law Review* 95 (1995): 942–44, 949–66.

[10] See Amar, "A Neo-federalist View," 222 n.63; Lawrence Gene Sager, "The Supreme Court 1980 Term—Foreword: Constitutional Limitations on Congress' Authority to Regulate the Jurisdiction of the Federal Courts," *Harvard Law Review* 95 (1981): 53 n.105.

[11] Akhil Reed Amar, "Reports of My Death Are Greatly Exaggerated: A Reply," *University of Pennsylvania Law Review* 138 (1990): 1670.

courts, and in state courts construing analogous provisions of state constitutions. (Precisely because so few Marshall Court cases existed, this break with founding-era understandings was less visible.) On key issues, the Warren Court seemed to contradict itself, laying down sweeping rules in some cases that it could not quite live by in other cases. On a political level, many of the Warren Court's constitutional criminal procedure pronouncements did not sit well with the American electorate. The guilty too often seemed to spring free without good reason—and by this time the guilty regularly included murderers, rapists, and robbers and not just federal income tax frauds and customs cheats. In a constitutional democracy, the People, in the long run, usually prevail. Federal judges may be, at times, "insulated" and "countermajoritarian," but majorities elect presidents, and presidents (with the advice and consent of senators) pick federal judges.

And so, with Earl Warren's retirement, and Richard Nixon's election on a "law and order" platform, the counter-revolution began. But the foundations of this counter-revolution are also none too sure. Like the Warren Court, the Burger and Rehnquist Courts have at times paid little heed to constitutional text, history and structure and have mouthed rules one day only to ignore them the next. If the Warren Court at times was too easy on the guilty, the Burger and Rehnquist Courts at times have been too hard on the innocent.

B. The Present

Where does all this leave us today? At a crossroads. On at least four different levels, I submit, the present is a particularly ripe moment for a fundamental rethinking of constitutional criminal procedure, and for a choice among competing visions.

Consider first the level of *Supreme Court doctrine*. At this level, constitutional criminal procedure is a mess. For more than a quarter of a century, the Burger and Rehnquist Courts have busily reshaped Warren Court doctrine in this field. But often, the Court has chosen to proceed by indirection. Warren Court landmarks are distinguished away rather than overruled; old cases are hollowed out from within, but the facade remains—or does it? And so *United States Reports* now swells with language bulging this way and that, at virtually every level of generality and specificity.

But the problem runs even deeper. For starters, many of the contradictions came from the Warren Court itself. The Warren Court told us that the Fourth Amendment requires warrants and probable cause for all searches and seizures.[12] But in *Terry v. Ohio*, Chief Justice Warren himself, writing at the peak of his reign, told us that frisking is a "search" that does *not* require warrants *or* probable cause.[13] Indeed, *Terry* quoted the amendment as simply banning *unreasonable* searches and seizures, and declined even to recite the amendment's language about warrants and probable cause.[14] The Warren Court told us that the Constitution requires exclusion of illegally-obtained evidence.[15] But in *Terry*, the Court warned against a "rigid and unthinking application of the exclusionary rule."[16] The Warren Court told us that the exclusionary rule derived from a synergy between the Fourth Amendment and the Fifth Amendment Self-Incrimination Clause.[17] But in *Schmerber v. California*, Justice Brennan—the play making guard of Earl Warren's team—sharply separated the Fourth and Fifth Amendments.[18] In so doing, Justice Brennan and the Court clearly held that a man could indeed be obliged to furnish evidence—his very blood, no less—against himself in a criminal case. And the logic of that clear holding, as I have explained elsewhere,[19] left both the exclusionary rule and broad theories of self-incrimination exclusion dangling in midair, with no principled support, constitutionally speaking.

So too, the Burger and Rehnquist Courts have failed to live up to their articulated principles. The post-Warren Court has admitted that the exclusionary rule lacks constitutional footing,[20] but has kept the rule nonetheless. The Court has failed to build up alternative remedial schemes that would protect innocent people from outrageous searches and seizures, and would also deter future government abuse. In the *Lyons* case, during the heyday of the Burger era, the Court simply looked the other way when Los Angeles police officers engaged in obviously brutal, possibly racist, and at times deadly choke holds of presumptively innocent citizens.[21] The post-Warren Court

[12] See, e.g., *Chimel v. California*, 395 U.S. 752, 760–62 (1969); *Katz v. United States*, 389 U.S. 347, 357–59 (1967).

[13] 392 U.S. 1, 16–20 (1968).

[14] Id. at 8.

[15] See *Mapp v. Ohio*, 367 U.S. 643 (1961).

[16] 392 U.S. at 15.

[17] See, e.g., *Malloy v. Hogan*, 378 U.S. 1, 8–9 (1964); *Murphy v. Waterfront Commission*, 378 U.S. 52, 74 (1964); *Ker v. California*, 374 U.S. 23, 30 (1963); *Mapp*, 367 U.S. at 646–47, 646 n.5, 656–57; id. at 661–66 (Black, J., concurring).

[18] 384 U.S. 757, 760–65, 766–72 (1966).

[19] See Amar, *The Constitution and Criminal Procedure*, chaps. 1, 2; see also Akhil Reed Amar & Renée B. Lettow, "Self-Incrimination and the Constitution: A Brief Rejoinder to Professor Kamisar," *Michigan Law Review* 93 (1995): 1012 n.5.

[20] See *United States v. Leon*, 468 U.S. 897, 905–06 (1984).

[21] *Los Angeles v. Lyons*, 461 U.S. 95 (1983).

has (at times) admitted that warrants are not the ultimate Fourth Amendment touchstone; reasonableness is.[22] But in *Zurcher v. Stanford Daily News*, the Court worshipped the warrant and blessed the most constitutionally unreasonable of searches—paper searches of anti-government newspapers.[23] The *Stanford Daily News* was not even alleged to have been engaged in criminal wrongdoing, and yet it, too, got the back of the judicial hand.

When judges either must strain against dominant doctrine to explain easy cases (like *Terry* and *Schmerber*), or actually get easy cases wrong (like *Lyons* and *Zurcher*), they have obviously taken a wrong turn somewhere. Hence a desperate need for returning to, and rethinking, first principles.

Consider next the level of *Supreme Court personnel.* We now stand at a generational changing of the guard. With the retirements of Justices Brennan, Marshall and White in the early 1990s, none of those who shared the bench with Chief Justice Earl Warren now sits. Two-thirds of the current High Court never even sat with Chief Justice Warren Burger.[24] Very few of the current justices have much of a *personal* stake—as an author or dissenter—in the elaborate doctrinal structures that have been built up and then whittled down in constitutional criminal procedure. The swing justices today are highly intelligent and relatively nonideological. They just want to do what is right—and so here again, there is a desperate need for a clear statement of what are, or should be, the first principles in the field. Again, precedent alone cannot guide the way—even for those justices who steer by precedent as their polestar—because precedent in this field is so regularly contradictory or perverse.

Now turn to the level of *congressional and national political conversation.* Here too, we are in the midst, it seems, of a generational changing of the guard. After a half-century of democratic domination, the House now sits in republican hands. At first, it might seem implausible that a bare majority of the House and Senate could radically rewrite criminal procedure policy. Intra-branch filters like the committee system and the filibuster rule can slow things down, and force slim majorities to yield to strong minorities; and of course, there is always the possible presidential veto to consider. But even if a mere majority cannot unilaterally prevail in enacting law, it can often uni-

---

[22] See, e.g., *New Jersey v. T.L.O.*, 469 U.S. 325, 340–41 (1985); *Zurcher v. Stanford Daily*, 436 U.S. 547, 559–60 (1978).

[23] 436 U.S. at 565.

[24] The post-Burger members are, in order of seniority, Justices Scalia, Kennedy, Souter, Thomas, Ginsburg, and Breyer.

laterally define a national agenda—holding hearings to shine a national spotlight on certain issues while pushing other issues off the stage. When the Democrats controlled, they did not schedule lots of hearings on affirmative action or on the exclusionary rule—wedge issues that might have splintered the democratic coalition of minorities, liberal elites, and the working class. But with Republicans in charge, the exclusionary rule and other issues of criminal procedure have indeed leaped onto the agenda, and many different proposals now jostle for attention. But which, if any, of the various proposed reforms now swirling about would actually move America in the right direction? Yet again, we see the need for an overall framework of analysis and vision of proper first principles.

Finally, let us consider the level of *academic scholarship*. On this level, too, we stand near a generational changing of the guard in constitutional criminal procedure. Those who in their youth led cheers for the Warren Court are moving towards, or have already passed into, their retirement years. Dramatic trends are at work in the academy generally. In constitutional law, textualism and originalism have staged a come-back; economic analysis has reconfigured many curricular fields; critical race theory and feminism insistently urge us to ask "the race question" and "the gender question" everywhere; and so on. How will a new generation of constitutional criminal procedure scholars reshape the academic orthodoxies we have inherited?

In a series of "first principles" essays, I have put forth my vision of how constitutional criminal procedure must be reshaped. In what follows, I shall try to summarize and explain some of the key elements of this vision.

II. Where Should We Go From Here?

A. *Constitutional Methodology*

To begin with, we must distinguish *constitutional* criminal procedure from criminal procedure generally. Not all sensible rules of criminal procedure can or should be constitutionalized.[25] The Constitution may simply not speak to some issues when read in light of its text, history, and structure, its doctrinal elaboration in precedent, the need for principled judicial standards, and so on. This is, of course,

---

[25] Here I echo the plea of the great Henry Friendly. See Henry J. Friendly, "The Bill of Rights as a Code of Criminal Procedure," *California Law Review* 53 (1965): 929–56.

one of the purposes of the legislature—to make sensible policy where the Constitution permits choice. Legislative solutions can be adjusted in the face of new facts or changing values far more easily than can rules that have been read into the Constitution.

Consider, for example, the so-called exclusionary rule. I have attacked this as a rule of *constitutional* criminal procedure. This rule is, quite simply, not in our Constitution. I have not claimed that the Constitution prohibits exclusion, only that it does not require it. In some times, and in some places, a legislative scheme of exclusion might be sensible—a two-by-four between the eyes to get the attention of mulish police. I have emphasized the costs to innocent victims of such exclusion schemes, but a legislature certainly could decide that the benefits outweigh the costs for now. If the facts change over time—if, say, police are now generally more sensitive to Fourth Amendment issues than they were in 1961—a legislature is free without embarrassment to change the law. A court, however, is not likewise free to rule one day that the Constitution requires exclusion as a matter of principle, and then to disregard that very principle the next day.

A critic might object that the Supreme Court has never really said that the Constitution requires exclusion as a matter of principle, but only that exclusion is one apt remedy and deterrent. And, the critic might argue, a court is free to fashion flexible remedies one day and adjust them the next. Such a critic, however, would be wrong both about Supreme Court case law and constitutional remedial theory. In about twenty cases, decided over almost a century, the Supreme Court practiced exclusion in the name of a *requirement* of the Fifth Amendment Self-Incrimination Clause, in tandem with the Fourth Amendment.[26] Exclusion was not merely a judicially-fash-

---

[26] See, e.g., *Malloy*, 378 U.S. at 8–9; *Murphy*, 378 U.S. at 74; *Ker*, 374 U.S. at 30; *Mapp*, 367 U.S. at 646–47, 646 n.5, 655–57 (1961); id. at 661–66 (Black, J., concurring); *Feldman v. United States*, 322 U.S. 487, 489–90 (1944); *United States v. Lefkowitz*, 285 U.S. 452, 466–67 (1932); *Olmsted v. United States*, 277 U.S. 438, 462 (1928); id. at 477–78 (Brandeis, J., dissenting); *Gambino v. United States*, 275 U.S. 310, 316 (1927); *Marron v. United States*, 275 U.S. 192, 194 (1927); *Agnello v. United States*, 269 U.S. 20, 33–35 (1925); *Carroll v. United States*, 267 U.S. 132, 147–48 (1925); id. at 169 (McReynolds and Sutherland, JJ., dissenting); *Hester v. United States*, 265 U.S. 57, 57–58 (1924); *Amos v. United States*, 255 U.S. 313, 315–16 (1921); *Burdeau v. McDowell*, 256 U.S. 465, 474–76 (1921); *Gouled v. United States*, 255 U.S. 298, 306, 311 (1921); *Perlman v. United States*, 247 U.S. 7, 13 (1918); *Weeks v. United States*, 232 U.S. 383, 393, 395 (1914); *Adams v. New York*, 192 U.S. 585, 594, 597–98 (1904); *Boyd v. United States*, 116 U.S. 616, 630, 633–35 (1886). See generally Edward S. Corwin, "The Supreme Court's Construction of the Self-Incrimination Clause," *Michigan Law Review* 29 (1930): 1–2, 13–16, 203–04.

ioned, empirical and deterrence-based *remedy* for an antecedent Fourth Amendment violation. It was also, and more importantly, a *right* under the Self-Incrimination Clause: introducing illegally-obtained evidence at trial would *itself* violate the Fifth Amendment. Only this argument from principle explains some of the most basic features of the Supreme Court's case law. Only this explains where exclusion comes from, as a constitutional mandate. Only this explains why exclusion applies in criminal cases, but not civil cases. Only this explains why illegal arrests are different from illegal searches. Only this explains so-called "standing" rules.[27]

I have argued that this argument from principle rested on an incorrect reading of the Constitution. Today, the Supreme Court agrees.[28] But if so, then exclusion must fall. The critic's deterrence/remedy idea fails as a matter of *constitutional* law. Once we admit—as the Supreme Court now does[29]—that a Fourth Amendment violation is complete at the time of the search, and that no new violation occurs when evidence is admitted at trial, we are admitting that exclusion is not logically linked to the scope of the violation. Judicial remedies must fit the scope of the right. For example, a court is not free, as a matter of constitutional law, to play the "Leavenworth lottery": because the government violated the Constitution in case A, judges spin the wheel and spring some lucky (but unrelated) convict B from Leavenworth. This scheme might indeed deter—and a legislature might have power to enact this into law—but courts have no such

The only major Supreme Court exclusion case that does not invoke the Fifth Amendment is *Silverthorne Lumber Co. v. United States*, 251 U.S. 385 (1920). The government stressed the Fifth Amendment issue at length: under *Hale v. Henkel*, 201 U.S. 43, 75 (1906), corporations lacked Self-Incrimination Clause rights, therefore they could not demand exclusion. See 251 U.S. at 385–90 (argument of the United States). Holmes's three-page opinion for the Court never carefully addresses this argument, but instead offers us an epigram: illegal evidence and its fruits "shall not be used at all," 251 U.S. at 392. But epigram is not analysis—even when (I would say, especially when) it comes from Holmes. Analytically, Holmes's statement is simply false. Government has always been allowed to use illegally-obtained evidence in civil cases, in criminal cases against others, in keeping contraband, in returning stolen goods to their rightful owners, and so forth. Perhaps *Silverthorne*'s technical disposition could be upheld nevertheless on the narrow theory that the case, in effect, did not exclude evidence in a criminal case on the basis of a constitutional mandate but simply quashed a subpoena in a collateral proceeding on supervisory power grounds.

[27] For my elaboration of these points, see Amar, *The Constitution and Criminal Procedure*, 23–25.

[28] See, e.g., *Leon*, 468 U.S. at 905–06; *Fisher v. United States*, 425 U.S. 391, 405–14 (1976).

[29] See *United States v. Leon*, 468 U.S. at 905–06 (1984); *United States v. Calandra*, 414 U.S. 338, 354 (1974).

power, as a matter of traditional remedial theory. And without the Fourth-Fifth fusion argument shattered by *Schmerber, Fisher* and *Leon,* exclusion is analytically indistinguishable from the "Leavenworth lottery."

As these last points suggest, the Constitution is not some ventriloquist's dummy that can be made to say anything the puppeteer likes. Yet it is remarkable how little attention many leading scholars and distinguished judges have paid to the text of the Constitution while busily making criminal procedure pronouncements in its name. Perhaps this is because so much of the debate, both academic and judicial, took shape in the early to mid-1960s, when textual argument in constitutional law often drew smirks from "sophisticated" lawyers. But most of the major Warren Court pronouncements did draw, at least in part, on text, and stood on the shoulders of that giant of constitutional textualism, Justice Hugo Black. Exclusion in *Mapp* was required by the words and spirit of the Fourth *and* Fifth Amendments, said Justice Black in providing the critical fifth vote[30]— echoing repeated invocations in Justice Clark's opinion for the Court.[31] Application of the Bill of Rights to the states, reminded Justice Black in *Duncan,* simply followed the words and spirit of the Fourteenth Amendment as a whole, including its Privileges or Immunities Clause.[32] Warrants and probable cause, said the Warren Court, were required because the text of the Fourth Amendment implicitly said so; its words made no sense otherwise.[33] Florida could not try Gideon without a lawyer, Justice Black wrote for the Court, because the Sixth Amendment's words provided for a "right of counsel" and the Fourteenth Amendment's words incorporated fundamental rights against states.[34] Miranda must go free, said the Court, because he was in effect compelled to be a witness against himself in a criminal case in violation of the words and spirit of the Fifth Amendment.[35]

What is more, sophisticated constitutional lawyers today no longer scoff at textual argument. Unlike Coach Lombardi on winning, we do not consider text "the *only* thing," but we do think it is relevant—it is *something*—that the Fourth Amendment's text fails to require warrants and probable cause for all searches and seizures;

[30] *Mapp,* 367 U.S. at 661–66 (Black, J., concurring).
[31] Id. at 646–47, 646 n.5, 655–57.
[32] *Duncan v. Louisiana,* 391 U.S. 145, 165–67 & n.1 (1968) (Black, J., concurring).
[33] See, e.g., *Chimel,* 395 U.S. at 760–62; *Chapman v. United States,* 365 U.S. 610, 613–15 (1961).
[34] *Gideon v. Wainwright,* 372 U.S. 335, 339–40, 341 (1963).
[35] *Miranda v. Arizona,* 384 U.S. 436, 439, 442, 457–62, 467 (1966).

and that this failure makes lots of sense. Surely it is relevant that the Fourth Amendment says nothing about exclusion, and that if it did, it surely doesn't distinguish between civil and criminal cases. Surely it is relevant that the Fourth Amendment's words about the people's right to be secure in "their persons, houses, papers and effects" conjures up tort law, which does protect these interests. Surely it is relevant that when Colonel Oliver North is forced to testify before Congress and his words are never admitted against him in his criminal trial, but testimonial fruits do come in, Colonel North has never been *compelled to be a witness against himself in a criminal case.* Surely it is relevant that the Sixth Amendment speaks only to rights of the "accused." Surely it is relevant that, if I testify about what my mom told me one day, my mom is not in any ordinary-language sense a "witness" within the wording of the Confrontation Clause. Surely it is relevant that in other clauses featuring the word "witness"—such as the Treason Clause[36]—the Constitution uses the word in its plain-meaning sense.

Textual argument is, as I have said, a proper starting point for proper constitutional analysis. Sometimes, plain-meaning textual arguments in the end must yield to the weight of other proper constitutional arguments—from history, structure, precedent, practicality, and so on.[37] And so the astonishing thing is not that someone might find the above-catalogued textual points to be outweighed at times by other arguments. Rather, the astonishing thing to me is that these textual points are almost never weighed in the first place. This is true even when they explain most or all of the leading cases in a given area, or when they resonate with obvious common sense. In virtually every other area of constitutional law, such a state of affairs is unimaginable. I think it cannot last much longer in the area of constitutional criminal procedure. The field may have evolved as an insular ecosystem unto itself, but global changes in constitutional law discourse must soon affect the atmosphere here, too.

Similar points can be made about constitutional history and structure. English common-law antecedents of the Fourth, Fifth, and Sixth Amendments, as well as early state and federal cases, certainly

---

[36] U.S. Constitution, art. III, § 3.

[37] See generally Richard H. Fallon, Jr., "A Constructivist Coherence Theory of Constitutional Interpretation," *Harvard Law Review* 100 (1987): 1189–286. For other powerful and illuminating accounts of interpretive methodology in constitutional law, see Phillip Bobbitt, *Constitutional Interpretation* (Oxford: B. Blackwell, 1991); Phillip Bobbitt, *Constitutional Fate* (New York: Oxford University Press, 1982); Jed Rubenfeld, "Reading the Constitution as Spoken," *Yale Law Journal* 104 (1995): 1119–85.

belong in a proper conversation about *constitutional* criminal procedure. The fact that English courts have *never* excluded evidence on Fourth-Amendment-like grounds, and that *no* American court, state or federal, *ever* did so during the first century after Independence surely deserves some mention. So too with the fact that England has never excluded "fruits" of immunized testimony or coerced confessions, and that the English rule reigned as the dominant one in Congress and in American courts prior to the Supreme Court's 1892 *Counselman*[38] case for testimonial immunity, and until the 1960s for coerced confessions. Similarly, it must matter that early courts never claimed that the "only" remedy for speedy trial violations was dismissal with prejudice.

Structurally, we must pay close attention to how different parts of our Constitution fit together, textually and practically. Textually, should not "reasonableness" under the Fourth Amendment be read in light of other constitutional values—of property, privacy, equality, due process, free speech, democratic participation, and the like— affirmed in other amendments? Should not Seventh Amendment juries play some role in determining Fourth Amendment reasonableness, just as they play a role in determining reasonableness generally in tort law? Why should preclusive *ex parte* warrants be worshipped in the Fourth Amendment when they so obviously present genuine Fifth Amendment due process problems of notice and opportunity to be heard? Would not it be nice if the word "witness" could have the same meaning in the Treason Clause, the Self-Incrimination Clause, the Confrontation Clause, and the Compulsory Process Clause? Practically, has not an overbroad reading of the Fifth Amendment's Self-Incrimination Clause betrayed the accused's explicit Sixth Amendment right to compel witnesses in his favor? Has not that overbroad reading also obstructed the defendant's explicit Sixth Amendment right to a speedy trial? Thus, has not our Fifth Amendment doctrine ended up helping guilty defendants while hurting innocent ones?

As these last points make clear, proper methodology of constitutional criminal procedure does not blind itself to practical effects. Indeed, though my "first principles" essays have always sought to respect text, history, and structure, they have also sought to make good common sense, motivated by the simple idea that constitutional criminal procedure should protect the innocent, and not needlessly advantage the guilty.

[38] *Counselman v. Hitchcock*, 142 U.S. 547 (1892).

B. The Substance of Process

This commonsensical point, I submit, is the essence of our Constitution's rules about criminal procedure and so I shall repeat it: the Constitution seeks to protect the innocent. The guilty, in general, receive procedural protection only as an incidental and unavoidable byproduct of protecting the innocent *because* of their innocence. Law breaking, *as such*, is entitled to no legitimate expectation of privacy, and so if a search can detect only law breaking as such, it poses little threat to Fourth Amendment values.[39] By the same token, the exclusionary rule is wrong, as a constitutional rule, precisely because it creates huge windfalls for guilty defendants but gives no direct remedy to the innocent woman wrongly searched. The guiltier you are, the more evidence the police find, the bigger the exclusionary rule windfall; but if the police know you are innocent, and just want to hassle you (because of your race, or politics, or whatever) the exclusionary rule offers exactly zero compensation or deterrence.

Truth and accuracy are vital values. A procedural system that cannot sort the innocent from the guilty will confound any set of substantive laws, however just. And so to throw out highly reliable evidence that can indeed help us separate the innocent from the guilty—and to throw it out by pointing to the Constitution, no less—is constitutional madness. A Constitution proclaimed in the name of We the People should be rooted in enduring values that Americans can recognize as *our* values. Truth and the protection of innocence are such values. Virtually everything in the Fourth, Fifth, and Sixth Amendment, properly read, promotes, or at least does not betray, these values.

If anyone believes that other nice-sounding, albeit less intuitive, ideas are also in the Constitution, the burden of proof should be on him. Here are two examples: (1) "The Constitution requires that government must never profit from its own wrong. Hence, illegally-obtained evidence must be excluded." (2) "No man should be compelled to be an instrument of his own destruction. Hence, reliable physical fruits of immunized testimony should be excluded." These sound nice, but where does the Constitution say *that*? Furthermore, are we truly willing to live by these as constitutional rules? The first would require that the government return stolen goods to thieves, and illegal drugs to drug-dealers. But this has *never* been the law. The second would prevent coerced fingerprinting and DNA sampling.

[39] See *United States v. Jacobsen*, 466 U.S. 109, 122–23 & nn. 22–23 (1984); Arnold H. Loewy, "The Fourth Amendment as a Device for Protecting the Innocent," *Michigan Law Review* 81 (1983): 1229–72.

This, too, is almost impossible to imagine in practice. By contrast, the innocence-protection rock on which I stand, and the specific Fourth, Fifth and Sixth Amendment derivations therefrom, are things that we can all live by, without cheating.

C. *Light From Afar*

My vision of constitutional criminal procedure borrows from and builds on insights elaborated in other scholarly fields. Consider, for example, how much we constitutional criminal proceduralists can learn from what might at first seem a most unlikely source: tax scholarship. In developing a now-classic framework of analysis, Professor Stanley Surrey brought into view the "upside-down" effect of certain tax subsidies: by subsidizing certain private activity via tax deductions rather than direct governmental outlays, the federal government effectively gave greater subsidies to high-bracket taxpayers than to low-bracket taxpayers. In light of the purposes underlying some subsidies, argued Professor Surrey, this distributional pattern of benefits was perverse—"upside down" in Professor Surrey's famous phrase.[40]

Professor Surrey understood that both direct expenditures and tax deductions could subsidize and create incentives, but with very different distributional consequences. A similar focus on distribution helps explain one of the many ways in which the exclusionary rule is so perverse—"upside down," if you will. Both tort law and evidentiary exclusion seek to create incentives for deterrence, but with very different distributional patterns. Under proper tort law, the guilty man never recovers a windfall simply because he is guilty;[41] but the exclusionary rule rewards the guilty man, and only the guilty man, precisely

[40] See generally Stanley S. Surrey, *Pathways to Tax Reform: The Concept of Tax Expenditures* (Cambridge: Harvard University Press, 1973); Stanley S. Surrey, "Federal Income Tax Reform: The Varied Approaches Necessary to Replace Tax Expenditures with Direct Government Assistance," *Harvard Law Review* 84 (1970): 352–408; Stanley S. Surrey, "Tax Incentives as a Device for Implementing Governmental Policy: A Comparison With Direct Government Expenditures," *Harvard Law Review* 83 (1970): 705–38.

Although Professor Surrey's specific approach is controversial in tax circles, no serious tax scholar can avoid thinking about, and confronting head-on, Professor Surrey's argument about "upside-down" effects. Yet many major scholars in constitutional criminal procedure seem to have spent their entire careers without ever seriously confronting the upside-down effect of various exclusion rules.

[41] See Douglas Laycock, *Modern American Remedies: Cases and Materials*, 2d ed. (New York: Little, Brown, & Co., 1994), 143; Daniel J. Meltzer, "Deterring Constitutional Violations by Law Enforcement Officials: Plaintiffs and Defendants as Private Attorneys General," *Columbia Law Review* 88 (1988): 270.

because he is guilty. (That is the "bite" of the rule, the lever by which it moves the police to repent and reform.) Under the Self-Incrimination Clause, fruits-immunity similarly rewards the guilty without helping the innocent. Indeed, it rewards the guilty in ways that hurt the innocent. Constitutional criminal procedure must cleanse itself of these and other similarly perverse "upside down" rules.

It is often claimed that the exclusionary rule and fruits-immunity never truly "reward" the guilty. Had the government not searched illegally, or compelled the testimony, the argument goes, the government would not have the fruit, and so exclusion of the fruit never creates a windfall for guilty defendants, but only restores the status quo ante.[42] But this glib argument ignores what I have called the "causation gap," encompassing all the possible ways in which the fruit might very well have come to light anyway. Courts have given too little rein to anti-exclusionary doctrines such as inevitable discovery; and where eventual fruits discovery is only probable, or possible, rather than inevitable, permanent exclusion creates huge windfalls for many guilty defendants.

With issues of incentives, deterrence, distribution of reward, and causation so obviously important, it should be plain that criminal procedure scholars can also learn important lessons from tort law scholarship. The text of the Fourth Amendment presupposes tort law, and the Founders repeatedly invoked the idea of punitive damages to "deter"—their word—unreasonable searches and seizures. Originalism and functionalism converge here, for the Founders understood deterrence far better than many sophisticated modern-day scholars. Consider, for example, the following passage from Professor Bill Stuntz in favor of the exclusionary rule:

> Thus, the difficulty with [tort] damages boils down to this: no one knows how to value damages for illegal searches with any accuracy. . . . Overdeterrence is a special concern. . . . Underdeterrence, however, is also a serious problem. . . .[43]

Now, Professor Stuntz is a friend of mine—and there is no one in the field whose work I respect more—but there are so many things

[42] See, e.g., Yale Kamisar, "Remembering the 'Old World' of Criminal Procedure: A Reply to Professor Grano," *University of Michigan Journal of Law Reform* 23 (1990): 568–69; Yale Kamisar, " 'Comparative Reprehensibility' and the Fourth Amendment Exclusionary Rule," *Michigan Law Review* 86 (1987): 36 n.151, 47–48.

[43] See William J. Stuntz, "Warrants and Fourth Amendment Remedies," *Virginia Law Review* 77 (1991): 905.

wrong with his pseudo-functionalist defense of the exclusionary rule that it is hard to know where to start. Here, and elsewhere, Professor Stuntz acts as if the choice is tort law *or* exclusion—but nobody (and surely not Professor Stuntz) really thinks so. No one proposes that tort and tort-like remedies be abolished. To do so would be insane—like declaring open season on those whom the police know to be innocent, but do not like, and want to hassle. Exclusion alone could never be sufficient.

But if so, the wrinkles of tort law must be ironed out regardless of whether we keep or scrap exclusion. For the Webster Bivenses of the world—innocent citizens, hassled by government—it will always be "damages or nothing"[44] and courts will need to fashion sensible rules about damage remedies here just as they do everywhere else in tort law. And if at the end of the day there is, as Professor Stuntz believes, a real risk of overdeterrence, how does that argue for *adding*—not, I repeat, substituting—whatever additional deterrence comes from exclusion?

But Professor Stuntz's problems are only beginning. Suppose that we really did have to choose between tort law and exclusion. Tort law risks overdeterrence and underdeterrence—but so does the exclusionary rule! (So does *any* solution.) The underdeterrence of exclusion is obvious. For starters, it has no bite—no bark, even—when police want to hassle someone they know to be innocent, from whom they expect to find no evidence. But even when police expect to and do find evidence, the exclusionary rule underdeters by allowing government to get the drugs off the street or return the stolen goods to their rightful owner, to use the evidence in a civil suit against the searchee, or to use the evidence in a criminal suit against anyone else. Exclusion can also exceedingly overdeter, as we have seen, by preventing government from *ever* using critical evidence (or its fruit) against the searchee, even though that evidence (or its fruit) might otherwise have come to light anyway.

Perhaps Professor Stuntz thinks that the exclusionary rule's unavoidable overdeterrence and underdeterrence will somehow cancel each other out, leaving us with something that Goldilocks would call "just right." But like the story of the three bears, this is pure fantasy. Tort law, by contrast, is logical and realistic—tort law remedies can be squarely tailored to fit the tortious wrong of unreasonable search and seizure. Unlike exclusion, tort law is thus not inherently mis-

[44] See *Bivens v. Six Unknown Federal Agents*, 403 U.S. 388, 410 (1971) (Harlan, J., concurring).

matched, and is far more likely to reach the right amount of overall deterrence. Punitive-damage multipliers can always be cranked up or down to achieve a given overall level of deterrence, whereas exclusion cannot be adjusted at the margins without raising serious "Leavenworth lottery" issues.

Let us now summarize, on purely functional grounds, the contrast between tort law and exclusion. The "upside-down" exclusionary rule skews benefits towards the guilty; tort law is "right-side up." The precise amount of deterrence from exclusion turns on a whole range of accidental contingencies: whether a search uncovers evidence, whether that evidence may be used in other ways (civilly, or against other criminal defendants), whether other evidence will suffice to convict the target, and whether the unavoidable causation gap will be big or small. Tort law, by contrast, focuses on the invasion of the search itself—its intrusiveness, its outrageousness, its violence, etc. Put a different way, exclusion is simply not linked, analytically speaking, to the scope of the violation, which occurs before a criminal trial, not during it. Tort law focuses precisely on the scope of the violation. (Professor Stuntz thinks that Fourth Amendment doctrine should focus more on police violence.[45] I agree—but the exclusionary rule simply does not work here; whether the police punched me in the nose is almost never analytically—or even causally—linked to whether they found evidence in my house.)[46] Exclusion would thus achieve the right amount of overall deterrence only by the wildest of coincidences, like the broken watch that tells the correct time twice a day. Finally, tort law payment comes from the wrongdoing government, whereas the visible sight of grinning criminals freed by exclusion localizes savage "demoralization costs" on identifiable crime

---

[45] See William J. Stuntz, "Privacy's Problem and the Law of Criminal Procedure," *Michigan Law Review* 93 (1995): 1060–77.

[46] Professor Stuntz seems to recognize this problem, see id. at 1072, but then breezes by it in a way that would make "Leavenworth lottery" fans cheer, and traditional remedies scholars wince. [His approach has also been squarely rejected in case law, see *Frisbee v. Collins*, 342 U.S. 519 (1952); *Maryland v. Macon*, 472 U.S. 463, 471 (1985). Cf. id. at 475–76 (dissenting opinion by Brennan and Marshall arguing for Stuntz-like approach while conceding that the Court's contrary approach was "following precedent").] A bit later in his discussion, Professor Stuntz again seems to miss the obvious ways that exclusion can over deter because of causation gaps—gaps his approach two pages earlier would of course dramatically widen. "Privacy's Problem," 1074 n. 210. And he continues to reveal real confusion about how damage remedies fit into his world. Compare ibid., 1072, n. 201 with 1073 and n. 203. Some of this confusion may stem from an uncharacteristic inattention to the Coase Theorem.

victims. This last phrase, of course, comes from Professor Michelman's classic analysis of the Just Compensation Clause,[47] a clause that, as I have shown, resembles the Fourth Amendment in some ways.[48]

The "demoralization costs" concept reminds us that beyond tort law, narrowly defined, lies the broad field of law and economics generally. Here too, constitutional criminal proceduralists have much to learn. Perhaps the biggest lesson is the importance of *ex ante* incentive effects.[49] Overprotection of some rights may trigger strategic reactions that will lead to predictable underprotections elsewhere. The exclusionary rule tempts judges to deny that Fourth Amendment violations occurred; so too do dismissals with prejudice and the Sixth Amendment remedies. If all searches really do require warrants and probable cause, judges will strain to deny that some intrusions really are "searches." If we prevent the government from freezing a suspect's story in place early on in a civilized deposition, we may drive interrogation underground into far more potentially abusive fora; we will also encourage surprise searches, sting operations, and other serious intrusions. Precisely because courts overprotect the guilty by excluding testimonial fruit, they undermine other defendants' explicit right to compel incriminating testimony from third-party witnesses—a right of surpassing importance to *innocent* defendants. More generally, if doctrine creates an overly intricate matrix of trial rights, the government may react by trying to hold fewer trials, thereby forcing defendants into harsher plea bargains. And in general, plea bargaining may tend to punish guilty and innocent alike—or to advantage those with powerful lawyers—rather than to sift the innocent from the guilty. For many innocent defendants, less may be more: less trial procedure may mean more trials, and thus more chance to prove their innocence.

Just as "less" can sometimes be "more," "different" can at times be the "same": some of the Founders' basic vision must be "translated" into our legal culture.[50] Entity liability is one example; since the locus of government decision making has shifted over 200 years

[47] See Frank I. Michelman, "Property, Utility, and Fairness: Comments on the Ethical Foundations of 'Just Compensation' Law," *Harvard Law Review* 80 (1967): 1214.

[48] On the similarities, see Amar, *The Constitution and Criminal Procedure*, chap. 1. On the differences, see ibid., chap. 3.

[49] See generally Frank Easterbrook, "The Supreme Court, 1983 Term—Foreword: The Court and the Economic System," *Harvard Law Review* 98 (1984): 10–12.

[50] See generally Lawrence Lessig, "Fidelity in Translation," *Texas Law Review* 71 (1993): 1165–1268.

from the individual constable to the police department, so should the locus of de jure liability for constitutional torts. By contrast, various exclusionary rules are bad "translations" because they impose "upside-down" effects that were anathema to the framing generation, and are hateful to the general citizenry even today.

Administrative law is in some ways a modern-day translation of tort law—with workers' compensation boards and OSHA rules displacing common-law negligence suits. Similar translations may make sense in constitutional criminal procedure. Administrative compensation schemes with "right-side up" recovery patterns may sensibly supplement, and perhaps in places supplant, individual (and more cumbersome) tort suits. Citizen review panels within police departments can serve functions akin to common-law style juries. Speedy trial framework statutes can regularize pretrial process. The list could go on. Because some of those schemes are distinctly subconstitutional, whereas I have emphasized *constitutional* criminal procedure, I have perhaps devoted less attention to administrative schemes than they deserve. Nevertheless, my relative de-emphasis must not be mistaken for hostility.

If *constitutional criminal procedure* must attend to *constitutional* law, it also must attend to *criminal* law and *procedural* law. Criminal procedure must work to vindicate rather than undermine sensible norms of substantive criminal law. At one specific level, my framework links up the criminal procedural rule against compelled self-incrimination based on a fear of false confession, and the sensible substantive criminal law doctrine of corpus delicti. At a more general level, my procedural vision seeks to vindicate substantive norms by emphasizing accuracy and truth-finding in adjudication. Process should be arranged to separate those who did violate the substantive law from those who did not. If some substantive criminal laws—drug laws, perhaps—are bad policy, then let us change them directly rather than trying to offset or neutralize them with procedural gimmicks that will also obstruct our efforts to enforce uncontroversially sensible criminal laws, like laws against murder, rape, and robbery. At times, however, some procedural rules will have a differential impact on different crimes.[51] For example, a rule excluding compelled testimony but admitting compelled fruit casts a happy substantive shadow: it will help political and religious dissenters without giving much aid and comfort to murderers. Blasphemy and libel tend not to generate physical fruit, but murder results in dead bodies, bloody knives, and

---

[51] See generally William J. Stuntz, "The Substantive Origins of Criminal Procedure," *Yale Law Journal* 105 (1995): 393–447.

the like. Criminal proceduralists must carefully attend to the ways that procedure can affect substantive enforcement policy for good or for ill. At the most general level, things do not "cancel out" if we exclude half the evidence, catch half the truly bad guys, and then simply double the punishment for those unlucky enough to get caught. The social norms underlying sensible substantive laws are best reinforced with high detection, and quick (though not necessarily severe) punishment. "War on crime" rhetoric needs to be channelled away from savage penal policies, towards strategies that lead to high detection and quick, reliable adjudication.

Laws against murder, rape and robbery remind us of the importance of *victims*. Feminist theory is especially important here, given that women are more likely to be victims than to be criminal defendants.[52] And in asking the "race question" we must also remember that racial minorities are often the victims of crime, too. In thinking about feminism and critical race theory more generally, we should also ask about the race and gender of those doing the searching, seizing, questioning, and adjudicating: the police, prosecutors, judges and juries. All of these issues, I submit, are central to the idea of a truly *constitutional* criminal procedure.

III. Conclusion

Will judges, scholars, lawmakers, and citizens hearken to my call for a reconceptualization of the field? It is far too early to tell, but I am optimistic. Some will no doubt oppose my vision—but others, I hope, will rally behind me. Debate will be vigorous—perhaps even heated—but vigorous debate is healthy in a vibrant democracy. As I said, we live in interesting times.

[52] In a recent essay, Professor Schulhofer seems to tiptoe up to, but not quite admit, the many and profound ways that feminism may call into question the generally pro-defendant stance of now-orthodox criminal procedure scholarship (including Schulhofer's own oeuvre). See Stephen J. Schulhofer, "The Feminist Challenge in Criminal Law," *University of Pennsylvania Law Review* 143 (1995): 2151–2207.

Fundamental Rights, the Supreme Court and American Constitutionalism: The Lessons of the Civil Rights Act of 1866

Michael Zuckert

> Roses have thorns, and silver fountains mud;
> Clouds and eclipses stain both moon and sun,
> And loathsome canker lives in sweetest bud.
>
> Shakespeare, Sonnet 35

I.

The Supreme Court was originally intended to be the crown jewel of American constitutionalism. As the voice of the Constitution and constitutionalism, it would uphold the separation of powers and checks and balances by pronouncing on the legitimate scope of the powers exercised by the other branches; it would enforce the various limitations contained in the Constitution on behalf of the states and of citizens; it would serve as a pacific and orderly umpire of the federal system, painlessly preventing encroachments by the states on each other or on the general government.[1]

Nonetheless, the topic "The Supreme Court and American Constitutionalism" is not raised today in a simply celebratory mode, be-

---

[1] See Michael Zuckert, "Epistemology and Hermeneutics in the Constitutional Jurisprudence of John Marshall," in Thomas Shevory, ed., *The Achievement of John Marshall* (Greenwood Press, Westport, CT: 1989).

cause it names a problem as well as a solution. The Court is not only the crown jewel, but, in the eyes of many, the canker of American constitutionalism. To its critics, the Supreme Court poses three inter-related problems for American constitutionalism. First, the Supreme Court has made numerous decisions with which many people dis-agree, and which are seen by many as harmful to the fabric of Ameri-can life. The Court, for example, disrupted the accommodation between public institutions and religion that had (healthily, many think) prevailed throughout most of American history.[2] The Court developed a far more libertarian approach to freedom of speech is-sues than we had seen in the past so that now communities find them-selves nearly helpless in efforts to keep pornography off the streets and, with recent decisions about cable television and the internet, out of homes.[3] And, of course, probably most offensive to many was the abortion decision.

Given the place of the Constitution in American public life, a Supreme Court that persuasively shows its decisions to be genuinely compelled by the Constitution can gain legitimacy even for disliked results. But in so many of these controversial areas the Court was proceeding on the basis of novel constitutional theories, theories that did not seem evidently compelled by the text or known history of the Constitution. When the Court made as important an intrusion into American life as it did in *Roe v. Wade* on the basis of a rights-claim to be found only in "penumbras and emanations" of the Bill of Rights, it was no wonder that many who were not inclined to support the result (and even some who were) did not find the constitutional ra-tionale persuasive, or even plausible.[4] Not merely do individual decisions seem improvised, but only a small amount of historical knowledge makes it clear that the Court has no pipe line to constitu-tional truth. At one time, the Court assured us, racial segregation was perfectly acceptable under the Fourteenth Amendment; later it was pronounced unacceptable.[5] In 1872 the Supreme Court insisted that states could, even should, prohibit women from pursuing many of the ordinary occupations of life, like the practice of law, but in 1996

[2] See, e.g., Stephen Carter, *The Culture of Disbelief* (New York, NY: Anchor, Dou-bleday, 1993).
[3] See, e.g., Harry Clor, *Obscenity and Public Morality* (Chicago: University of Chi-cago Press, 1969).
[4] See *Roe v. Wade*, 410 U.S. 113 (1973); *Griswold v. Connecticut*, 381 U.S. 479 (1965). See, e.g., John Hart Ely, "The Wages of Crying Wolf: A Comment on *Roe v. Wade*," *Yale Law Journal* 82 (1973): 920–49.
[5] See, e..g., *Plessy v. Ferguson*, 163 U.S. 537 (1896); *Loving v. Virginia*, 388 U.S. 1 (1967).

it insists that states may not withhold opportunities from women (much less prohibit them from the pursuit) for occupations far from ordinary, like the military life.[6] For fifty years the Supreme Court had not seen an exercise of the commerce power it didn't like, but all of a sudden in 1995 it discerns there are limitations on congressional power after all.[7] The Constitution cannot equally mean all these different things. Is the Court really the voice of the Constitution within the government? Or is it the voice of the political interests, the moral sensibilities or policy preferences of the Justices and those who appoint them?

The highly politicized character of the appointment process these days suggests the answer increasingly being given to these questions. In our hermeneutically sophisticated age, it is easy to generalize from the observations about current and past Supreme Court practice to the conclusion that the very idea of "a voice of the Constitution," of something like "objective interpretation," is an illusion, a myth, like the tooth fairy, the Easter bunny, and George Washington's cherry tree.[8] One of our theoretical sophisticates asked in one of his famous essays, "Is there a text in this class?"[9] Slightly transposed, that question now becomes, "Is there a constitution in constitutional law?" We now have an impressive array of clever theories of interpretation assuring us that original intention is a hopeless muddle, that constitutional text is intractably indeterminate, that time ineluctably changes meanings.

To these general problems we must add the specific problem arising under the Fourteenth Amendment. Although the Court's difficulties do not begin—or end—with the Fourteenth Amendment, yet that provision certainly has been a center of difficulty. Under its aegis, the Court has intruded regularly, deeply, and controversially in American life—liberty of contract, mandatory school busing, incorporation of the Bill of Rights, legislative reapportionment—these are only a few of the very controversial judicial interventions rooted in the Fourteenth Amendment.[10]

---

[6] *Bradwell v. Illinois,* 83 U.S. 130 (1872); *United States v. Virginia,* 116 S.Ct. 2263 (1996).

[7] *United States v. Lopez,* 115 S.Ct. 1624 (1995).

[8] A good selection of hermeneutically sophisticated writings as applied to legal interpretation is Sanford Levinson and Steven Mailloux, eds., *Interpreting Law and Literature: A Hermeneutic Reader* (Evanston, IL: Northwestern University Press, 1988).

[9] Stanley Fish, *Is There a Text in this Class?* (Cambridge, MA: Harvard University Press: 1980).

[10] See William E. Nelson, *The Fourteenth Amendment: From Political Principle to Judicial Doctrine* (Cambridge, MA: Harvard University Press, 1988), 1, 2.

Much of the opposition results, of course, from resistance to the results reached in these cases, but much follows from the amendment itself.[11] Robert Bork has called it an ink blot on the Constitution, meaning either a text of such opaque language that its meaning is no more discernible than if its framers had spilt ink on their text, or a text of such open-endedness that it, like the Rorschach ink-blot test, can only give back the meaning the interpreter projects into it.[12] The language of the amendment is notoriously broad and apparently ill defined. States are forbidden from abridging the privileges or immunities of citizens of the United States, but the amendment gives little explicit guidance on what these are. It requires equal protection of the laws, but this too is so general as to be suggestive at best. The same might perhaps be said for the due process clause, although this at least has the advantage of having been part of the original constitution and of many state constitutions before the Civil War.

These several problems converge in one larger problem—a crisis of legitimacy both for the Supreme Court and American constitutionalism. It isn't merely that the Court is looking (to many, even of its friends when they think about it) like a usurper. If the Court does not give answers to constitutional questions based on the Constitution, then what business has it got countering the judgments of elected officials? Why should the Supreme Court, any more than any nine randomly chosen citizens, possess this awesome power? The problem goes yet deeper, however. It is not just a problem of the Court (willfully or otherwise) making variable or faulty decisions; it is a problem of the silence, or polysemousness (to use a favorite term of our hermeneuticists), of the Constitution itself. The problem lurking in the problem of "The Supreme Court and American Constitutionalism" is the problem of constitutionalism as such. This is far more challenging than the purported fall from constitutional fidelity by the Supreme Court in one or another case. Abraham Lincoln, for example, believed the Supreme Court profoundly mistaken in its decision in *Dred Scott v. Sanford*, but he did not doubt for a moment that there was a standard of constitutional truth to hold up to the errant Taney Court. It is the questionability of that kind of faith that our topic now brings to the fore. "The Supreme Court and American Constitutionalism" names this dual problem then: an "errant" court and a silent "constitution."

[11] Ibid., 5.
[12] Robert Bork, *The Tempting of America* (New York: The Free Press, 1990), 166. See also Philip A. Hamburger, "Natural Rights, Natural Law, and American Constitutions," *Yale Law Journal* 102 (1993): 922.

II.

I wish to address this dual problem via a reexamination of a now largely forgotten law stemming from the Reconstruction Era. This law, the Civil Rights Act of 1866, was part of the astonishing surge of fundamental reform legislation promulgated in the wake of the Civil War. The Civil Rights Act emerged directly between two other exceedingly important acts of the Reconstruction Congress: the Thirteenth Amendment, banishing slavery, and the Fourteenth Amendment, redefining citizenship in the American federal republic and securing a series of important rights against state abridgment and deprivation.

It might seem that a relatively obscure piece of legislation passed in 1866 could have little to say to our topic, the Supreme Court and American Constitutionalism. Yet it does. Its relation to the Fourteenth Amendment helps us understand that most important and controversial addition to the Constitution. Moreover, the Civil Rights Act helps us understand the doctrine of rights that underlies the original constitution, as well as the Fourteenth Amendment.

The act followed hard on the heels of the Thirteenth Amendment, which in January of 1865, finally mustered the two-thirds vote it needed in the House of Representatives to begin its march through the states toward ratification, accomplished in just under a year, so that it became an official part of the Constitution on December 18, 1865. The drafters of the Thirteenth Amendment did not see it as the first stage in a larger constitutional reform, as we now tend to with the hindsight afforded by the Fourteenth and Fifteenth Amendments.[13] The immediate impetus to further action came from the enactment in the former slave states of Black Codes, which subjected the freedmen to special disabilities and restraints that did not apply to other persons within the states—limitations, for example, on the right to own property or make contracts, to bear arms, or to walk the streets after dark. One such law, quoted during congressional debates of the time, provided that any "freedman, free negro or mulatto" who shall "quit the service of his employer before the expiration of his term of service . . . shall forfeit his wages for that year, up to the time of quitting." Any such person was subject to arrest (a duty laid on all "civil officers" in the state) and return to "his of her legal employer," the costs of arrest and return to be charged against the

---

[13] Harold Hyman and William Wiecek, *Equal Justice Under Law* (New York: Harper and Row, 1982), 389. Also see Herman Belz, *A New Birth of Freedom* (Westport, CT: Greenwood Press, 1976), 150; Belz, *Emancipation and Equal Rights: Politics and Constitutionalism in the Civil War Era* (New York: W.W. Norton and Co., 1978), 113.

wages of the "employee."[14] As the saying goes, one does not need to be a rocket scientist to see this law as an effort to maintain the reality of slavery beneath the veneer of formal freedom. Rumors of these laws and other forms of ill treatment of the freedmen led to the Schurz Mission, a fact-finding tour of the South. Particularly striking was the observation by one of Schurz's informants that white Southerners had more or less come to terms with the abolition of slavery as a relationship between individual masters and slaves, but retained an "ingrained feeling that the blacks at large belong to the whites at large, and whenever opportunity serves, they treat the colored people just as their profit, caprice, or passion may dictate."[15]

This information promoted a flurry of congressional responses, the two most important of which were the introduction in December 1865 of a proposal for a new constitutional amendment by John Bingham, congressman from Ohio, and the introduction in early January 1866 of a Civil Rights bill by Sen. Lyman Trumbull of Illinois. Bingham's proposal, modified in some important respects, eventually became the Fourteenth Amendment, and Trumbull's the Civil Rights Act of 1866.

Although both proposals eventually passed both houses by large majorities, neither had an altogether smooth path. In February the Joint Committee on Reconstruction adopted Bingham's draft amendment, but after a sharp debate at the end of that month it was postponed indefinitely in the House of Representatives. The Civil Rights bill had a similar fate—recommitted to the House Judiciary Committee in early March. By mid-March, however, a revised Civil Rights bill passed both houses of Congress and by early April it had been repassed by Congress over a presidential veto.

The Bingham amendment, meanwhile, had languished while congressional attention focused on the Civil Rights bill. After the passage of the Civil Rights Act all eyes returned to the now revised draft amendment, which passed both houses in early June. Although the Fourteenth Amendment was introduced first and at first was considered more or less independently of the Civil Rights bill, in its latter phase the draft amendment became much entangled with the Civil Rights bill. Thence arose the common view that the amendment postdated the Civil Rights Act and was somehow derivative from it.

[14] *Congressional Globe,* 39th Cong., 1st sess. (Sen.), 13 December 1865, 39 (Wilson).
[15] See *Congressional Globe,* 39th Cong., 1st sess. (Sen.), 19 December 1865, 21. Cf. Belz, *Emancipation,* 114; Steven J. Heyman, "The First Duty of Governments," *Duke Law Journal* 41 (1991): 547–50.

Although the amendment preceded the Civil Rights bill and had independent point, the two came to be inextricably intertwined in the minds of the congressmen who adopted both. Almost all participants in the discussions voiced the view that the two proposals overlapped a great deal. For participants in those debates and most modern scholars, that overlap is important, because the Civil Rights Act speaks in quite precise and defined terms, while the amendment speaks in very general, some think overly vague, terms. Thus the Civil Rights Act, then as now, can be taken as a guide to the interpretation of the Fourteenth Amendment.

III.

A telling instance of the pitfalls that await those who pay insufficient attention to the link between the act and the amendment is William Nelson's fine but flawed recent study of the Fourteenth Amendment. Nelson almost totally ignores the Civil Rights Act, choosing to treat the amendment as an aspirational statement directly linked to ante-bellum political rhetoric. The amendment was thus not meant in any full sense to be "a legal document."

> Those who adopted the Fourteenth Amendment did not design it to provide judges with a determinative text for resolving [conflicts] in a narrow doctrinal fashion. They wrote the amendment for a very different audience and purpose: to reaffirm the lay public's long-standing rhetorical commitment to general principles of equality, individual rights, and local self-rule.[16]

They succeeded "in elaborating and incorporating important moral principles such as equality and rationality in the constitution," but "they made only slight headway in the task of applying those principles to specific cases." Most importantly, the framers of the amendment had in mind no "specification of the fundamental rights" to be protected; when asked, they were unwilling "to be pinned down." The "most common characteristic" of their discussion of rights "was its vagueness and imprecision. Users of the rhetoric [of rights] made it clear that citizens possessed rights guaranteed by the Constitution, but they never specified the precise content of those rights."[17] The jobs of specification and application, the transforming of an aspirational and rhetorical text into a proper legal text, was a task for courts

[16] Nelson, *Fourteenth Amendment*, 8, 110; cf. 143.
[17] Ibid., 71, 123–23, 146–47; cf. Hyman and Wiecek, *Equal Justice*, 418–19, for a parallel reading of the Civil Rights Act.

and others who were to come later. Thus the subtitle of Nelson's book: "From Political Principle to Judicial Doctrine."

Nelson's approach to the Fourteenth Amendment both justifies, in a sense, the judicial discovery of new fundamental rights in areas like the right to privacy and, if correct, also helps explain how the Fourteenth Amendment contributes to our current crisis of legitimacy. Yet Nelson's approach is largely circular. The framers of the Fourteenth Amendment regularly pointed to the Civil Rights Act of 1866 as an exemplar of (at least some of) the rights contained in the amendment, but Nelson ignores the Civil Rights Act and therefore sees no "specification" of rights in their thinking. If he had paid attention to the Civil Rights Act he would have found much evidence about how they thought about fundamental rights.

The debates on the Civil Rights bill reveal on their face their deep relevance to understanding the framers' views on rights. Officially named "An act to protect all persons in the United States in their civil rights and furnish the means of their protection," the list of rights in the bill obviously intended to specify (at least some of) the civil rights of persons. Lyman Trumbull, Chair of the Senate Judiciary Committee (which had the bill in charge), affirmed that "the first section of the bill defines what I understand to be civil rights."[18] Henry Wilson, Republican Senator from Massachusetts and the first to introduce the legislation from which the Civil Rights bill evolved, spoke in much the same way: the bill provides for equality of citizens in the enjoyment of "civil rights and immunities."[19] James Wilson, a representative from Iowa, echoes the point: the bill in its first section aims to protect "the great fundamental civil rights," or just "the great civil rights."[20]

Congressmen also spoke of the bill as protecting "fundamental rights," which they understood to be the same as "civil rights." According to Trumbull the rights enumerated in the first section are "civil rights, fundamental rights belonging to every man as a free man."[21] Martin Thayer, Republican from Pennsylvania, repeatedly described the rights of the bill's first section as "the fundamental rights of citizenship."[22] Ohio's William Lawrence also was among those who

[18] *Congressional Globe*, 39th Cong., 1st sess. (Sen.), 29 January 1866, 375; ibid., 2 February 1866, 599.
[19] Ibid., 1 March 1866, 1117.
[20] *Congressional Globe*, 39th Cong., 1st Sess. (House), 8 March 1866, 157 (Appendix); ibid., 9 March 1866, 1294.
[21] Ibid. (Senate), 29 January 1866, 476.
[22] Ibid. (House), 2 March 1866, 1151.

spoke interchangeably of the rights protected by the bill as both "fundamental rights" and "civil rights."[23]

The drafters also identified the rights in the bill as "natural rights," or as "absolute rights which pertain to every citizen," rights which are "inherent and indestructible."[24] More than a few identified the bill directly with the greatest American statement of natural rights: according to Minnesota's William Windom, the Civil Rights Act "is one of the first efforts made since the formation of the government to give practical effect to the principles of the Declaration of Independence."[25] Wilson of Iowa clarifies the content of "civil rights" simply by explaining that 'civil rights are the natural rights of man."[26] Senator John Sherman of Ohio, a particularly important person in the drafting of the bill, urged passage because "it is the duty of Congress to give to the freedmen of the southern states ample protection in all their natural rights."[27]

The identity of "civil rights," "fundamental rights," and "natural rights" seems to have been the consensus view of the framers. Of course, matters are a bit more complex than this simple formula makes them sound, as we will see. But it is most significant that the framers of the Civil Rights bill, the same men who adopted the Fourteenth Amendment, did not consider these kinds of rights to be vague and uncertain, as Nelson and so many others do. Rather they had a quite precise list of specific rights to which they attached these more general terms. If we wish to know what the glittering generalities of the Fourteenth Amendment are about, we must pay close attention to the treatment of rights in the Civil Rights Act.

Section one of the bill begins by defining who are citizens of the United States and then throwing around them the following protection:

> Such citizens, of every race and color, without regard to any previous condition of slavery or involuntary servitude, except as a punishment for a crime whereof the party shall have been duly convicted, shall have the same right, in every State and Territory in the United States, to make and enforce contracts, to sue, be parties, and give evidence, to inherit, purchase, lease, sell, hold, and convey real and personal property, and to full and equal benefit of

[23] Ibid., 7 April 1866, 1832, 1835–36.
[24] Ibid., 7 April 1866, 1833.
[25] Ibid., 2 March 1866, 1157; cf. ibid., 29 January 1866, 474 (Trumbull); ibid., 22 January 1866, 344 (Wilson).
[26] Ibid., 1 March 1866, 1117.
[27] Ibid. (Senate), 13 December 1865, 41.

all laws and proceedings for the security of persons and property,
as is enjoyed by white citizens, and shall be subject to like punishment, pains, and penalties, and to none other, any law, statute,
ordinance, regulation, or custom, to the contrary notwithstanding.

Our task is to understand this list of rights, to grasp its principle
of construction. It is sometimes speculated that the list of rights was
constructed by perusing the Black Codes and inducing from them
the protections that were required. Neither the character of the list
nor the record of the deliberation that produced the bill support that
approach, however.

IV.

Just as President Johnson was forwarding to the Senate the
Schurz Report, Henry Wilson (Rep., Mass.) attempted to introduce
directly onto the floor of the Senate a bill aimed to nullify the new
Black Codes. Unlike the Civil Rights bill that would ultimately emerge
from Congress, the operation of Wilson's bill is originally limited to
the 'insurrectionary states." It thus raises quite different constitutional issues than will the Civil Rights bill since the war powers remain
relevant for it. Wilson wanted the Senate to enact that "all laws . . . of
any description whatsoever . . . whereby . . . any inequality of civil
rights and immunities among inhabitants" of the rebellious states "is
recognized, authorized, established or maintained, by reason . . . of
any distinctions or differences of color, race or descent, or by reason
of previous condition or status of slavery . . . are hereby declared null
and void." And, he would add, all efforts to enact such legislation in
the future would be "unlawful."

Wilson burns with the fire of holy outrage against efforts in the
old Confederacy to "make the freedmen the slaves of society"—he
even thinks it "far better to be the slave of one man than to be the
slave of arbitrary law."[28] He feels the special urgency of the occasion:
"We ought not to adjourn over Christmas until we have declared such
laws null and void. . . . We ought to pass, and pass instantly, as a
matter of justice and humanity . . . a measure of this character." Then
as now, however, the Senate rarely gives same day service. While most
Senators, even those who ultimately line up on the conservative side
of the reconstruction legislative battles, express sympathy with Wilson's aim, there is general consensus that delay in the form of com-
mittal to the Senate Judiciary Committee is appropriate.

[28] Ibid.

Two of the grounds voiced in favor of Judiciary Committee consideration are particularly pertinent to the evolution of Wilson's proposal into the Civil Rights Act. Wilson himself points to the possibility of broader coverage than his bill provides because under the Thirteenth Amendment (about to become an official part of the Constitution in a mere three days) Congress will be able to "pass not only a bill that shall apply these provisions to the rebel states, but also to Kentucky, to Maryland, to Delaware" (slave states that had remained in the Union), and, Wilson continues, "to all the loyal states. But this bill is confined entirely to the [rebel] states." When the bill later emerges from Committee the coverage will be expanded as Wilson suggests to transform it into the Civil Rights Act, and the Committee will report out a separate bill aimed to protect the freedmen only in the rebel states.

John Sherman of Ohio (years later the author of the famous Anti-Trust Act) makes a yet more significant intervention. He strongly favors the broader coverage Wilson had suggested and thus urges delay until the Thirteenth Amendment supplies constitutional authority for that. He also objects to "the manner" in which Wilson has cast the protections he seeks to secure in his bill. "I do not wish it to be left to the uncertain and ambiguous language of this bill. I think the rights which we desire to secure to the freedmen of the South should be distinctly specified."[29] Wilson's text did not do that. It forbids state legal provision of "any inequality of civil rights and immunities" on the basis of race or previous condition of servitude. But, as Sherman points out, most or all of the states "make distinctions on account of color." His own state of Ohio, for example, allows lighter skinned negroes to vote, but not darker skinned ones. "Is it the purpose of this bill to wipe out all these distinctions?" Sherman asks.[30]

Sherman is uncertain, with good reason, because Wilson's draft is, as Sherman says, "uncertain and ambiguous" in key respects. The bill does not, for example, forbid all distinction by states on the basis of race or previous servitude, but only such that establishes or maintains "inequality of civil rights and immunities." Wilson does not seem to set colorblind law *per se* as the standard at which he aims, and thus Sherman's hesitation to accept that standard seems congruent with Wilson's original intent. Yet Wilson's language remains ambiguous in two different senses. First, although it does not in terms set legal colorblindness *per se* as its standard, the language used might be taken to be its equivalent. The phrase "civil rights and immunities"

[29] Ibid., 42.
[30] Ibid.

can be taken to apply to any legally defined right or immunity, i.e., a civil right is any right established or defined by law. Sherman clearly does not understand civil rights in that way—they are some specifiable subset of legally defined or definable rights.

Even if one reads "civil rights" in the Sherman-like restrictive manner (which Wilson in fact seems to do), Wilson's language is ambiguous, because it is at least somewhat unclear, or debatable, just what rights belong in this subset. As later stages of the debate on the Civil Rights Act make clear, there is a core of agreement among most members of Congress (and of the American legal community) as to what rights are civil rights, yet there remains a peripheral area of disagreement and uncertainty. The broad agreement is not so great but that there may well be "dispute or controversy," especially when one recalls that the bill is meant to correct actions of those who are hostile to the freedmen and thus likely to attempt to exploit any ambiguities in the law.[31] Sherman's "distinct specification of the rights" to be secured would remove all that uncertainty and ambiguity.

Sherman has a related and, I think, even more important additional point in mind. It is in part a constitutional point, in part a response to the inherent ambiguity of the notion of civil rights, and most centrally an attempt to elucidate the underlying moral and political principle that governs the kinds of rights protections that persons, in effect, have a right to. "I believe," Sherman says, "it is the duty of Congress to give to the freedmen . . . ample protection in all their natural rights." Congress possesses this duty (or is about to) under the Thirteenth Amendment, which is "not only a guarantee of liberty . . . but an express grant of power . . . to secure this liberty." A freeman is a man who has his natural rights secured by law. For example, "to say that a man is a freeman and yet not able to assert and maintain his right in a court of justice, is a negation of terms." So, Sherman concludes, Congress has the power "to secure the rights of freedmen by appropriate legislation."[32]

Sherman wants a list, because not all the matters the law might touch on are genuinely matters of natural right, or of the rights of freedom. Sherman seems inclined to think, for example, that the right to vote is not such a right, while the right "to acquire and hold property" is. He also believes that beginning with the idea of natural rights or the rights of freedom will give a constitutionally secure and theoretically complete, satisfying and pellucid table of fundamental rights. The premise of Sherman's intervention, then, is that one can

[31] Ibid.
[32] Ibid.

specify with relative precision what the legal rights of freedom are, what civil rights protections are required for the security of natural rights. This, he believes, is both more reliable and more perspicuous than the use of such a vague term as "civil rights and immunities."[33] Sherman's idea then is very far from Nelson's, both as to what the drafters were attempting (or should attempt) to do, and as to the basic meaning of general notions like natural or fundamental or civil rights.[34]

Sherman is not so foolish as to attempt to rewrite the bill on the floor of the Senate, although he does provide several examples of the specific rights he thinks should be included. He obviously hits the correct note, for Trumbull, chairman of the Judiciary Committee, promises to "introduce a bill . . . that will secure" to the freedmen "every one of those rights" in a lengthy list he recites very like the list Sherman has provided.[35] A few days later Wilson himself endorses the list approach by submitting one of his own, a list again remarkably close in content to those offered by Sherman and Trumbull.[36] The ease with which Senators accepted the idea of a list of specific rights and the consensus they achieve on the items to be included on that list confirm Herman Belz's conclusion that the content of the list of civil rights is not a matter of great uncertainty for them.[37]

On January 12, 1866, Trumbull initiates the second stage of the gestation of the Civil Rights Act when he reports two bills from the Judiciary Committee, both descendants of the original Wilson proposal of December 13. The first is a bill "to enlarge the power of the Freedman's Bureau," which, like Wilson's earlier initiative, applies to the rebel states only, and only until such states are "fully restored" to their normal constitutional position. The second bill extends much further, however, for it is an attempt "to protect all persons in the United States in their Civil Rights" and has no expiration date.[38] Both bills embody Sherman's wish for a precise delineation of the rights to be protected; indeed the list of rights in the bill introduced on Janu-

[33] Sherman's position and the definitive role it had in shaping the Civil Rights Act show how far off base Hyman and Wiecek are in their assessment of what was happening in this legislation. "Congress," they claim, "made judges the potential creators and particular guardians of some unknowable catalog of organic rights." Sherman would be stunned and dismayed to see his effort to incorporate a fixed and definite list of fixed fundamental rights taken in this way. Hyman and Wiecek, *Equality Under Law,* 419.

[34] *Congressional Globe,* 39th Cong., 1st sess. (Senate), 13 December 1865, 43.
[35] Ibid., 21 December 1865, 111.
[36] Belz, *New Birth,* 162; Belz, *Emancipation and Equal Rights,* 116.
[37] *Congressional Globe,* 39th Cong., 1st sess. (Senate), 12 January 1866, 209–11.
[38] Ibid., 29 January 1866, 476.

ary 12 is nearly identical to that in the final version of the Civil Rights Act's section one, with two important differences. First, the January 12 draft applies to all "inhabitants of any state or territory of the United States"; the bill as enacted applies to citizens of the United States. Secondly, in addition to the list of specifics to which all persons are guaranteed "the same right" without regard to race or previous condition of servitude, which is in both versions, the January 12 draft contains the following general provision: "there shall be no discrimination in civil rights or immunities" on account of race or previous condition. The January 12 draft is a hybrid of the Wilson and Sherman approaches of December.

Debate on Trumbull's proposal is heated, but significantly, very little of that heat is roused by the list of rights to be protected. Most opposition to the bill centers rather on the assertion of congressional power to protect the rights. That there should be a list or that these particular rights are on it is not contested at all—further evidence of the general consensus on the content or nature of the rights to be protected in 1866.

Even though the bill carries over the more general language Wilson originally suggested, it now appears to give few senators any difficulty. Late in the debate, James McDougall, a Democrat of California, does ask Trumbull "how he interprets the term 'civil rights' in the bill." Trumbull's reply indicates both how he understands the hybrid bill he has introduced and, again, the amount of consensus there is on the concept of civil rights: "The first section of the bill defines what I understand to be civil rights. [He lists those in the bill.] These I understand to be civil rights, fundamental rights belonging to every man as a free man."[39] Trumbull does not appear to understand the general Wilson-inspired language to add anything to the more specific enumeration of protected rights: the list of rights is an exhaustive specification of civil rights. Most remarkably, perhaps, McDougall, no friend to the bill, accepts Trumbull's statement: "Allow me to remark," he comments, "that I think all those rights should be conceded." His concern, and that of a few other senators, is that the Wilson language could be taken to have broader bearing than this, for example, that it might be taken "to involve questions of political rights" (especially the vote), in addition to "giving protection to the enjoyment of life and liberty and the pursuit of happiness and the protection of the Courts, and to have justice administered to all."[40] Trumbull explicitly assures him that "this bill has nothing to do with

[39] Ibid.
[40] Ibid., 29 January 1866, 478.

the political rights or status of parties. It is confined exclusively to their civil rights, such rights as appertain to every free man." The premise of the bill, and of Trumbull's thinking about rights, is the distinction, common in the nineteenth century, between civil and political rights, the latter concerning one's share in political power in the community.[41]

Trumbull's assurances seem to settle the minds of his fellow senators, for the bill finally passes the Senate in this hybrid form. (The House will be more troubled by the hybrid language and will insist that Wilson's part be excised.) The important part of the Senate debate centers on the question of the constitutional warrant for the bill, a debate that leads Trumbull to propose an amendment on January 29. He would now open with an assertion "that all persons of African descent born in the United States, are hereby declared to be citizens of the United States." The main point of this revision is to open up additional sources of constitutional power for the bill (in addition to the Thirteenth Amendment). Not all are persuaded of the validity of the Republican constitutional arguments—Sen. Willard Saulsbury (D, Del.) pleads with Trumbull towards the end of the debate: "Sir, stop, stop; the mangled, bleeding body of the Constitution of your country lies in your path; you are treading upon its bleeding body, when you pass these laws." The Republicans are undeterred, and by a large majority (33–12–5) the bill as amended passes the Senate on February 2.

The debate in the House echoes the debate in the Senate, although some of the common issues are pressed harder in the lower house and produce two further revisions in the bill. The most important modification involves a restatement of the parties to be protected in the bill; Rep. James Wilson for the House Judiciary Committee proposes on March 1 to substitute "citizens" for "inhabitants." This carries forward the change already made in the Senate when a definition of U.S. citizenship was added to the bill, and relates to continuing questions about the constitutional basis for the bill.

The House also takes more seriously the potential ambiguity introduced by the hybrid form of the bill. Members are less easily assuaged by assurances that the general language regarding "civil rights and immunities" has no meaning in addition to the list of more specific rights that follows it. The Wilsonian language either is superfluous or it is potentially mischief-making. Accordingly, after the bill is

---

[41] See especially the important discussion in William Blackstone, *Commentaries on the Laws of England* (Chicago: University of Chicago Press, 1979), vol. 1, bk. 1, chap. 1, esp. 125.

recommitted in early March the other Wilson (of Iowa) recommends on March 13 that the clause regarding "civil rights and immunities" be dropped. The House readily concurs and immediately passes (111–38–34) the amended bill, which the Senate accepts two days later.

No more than the Senate does the House raise questions about the idea of an enumeration of rights or of what rights were to be protected. If anything, the House's action in dropping the Wilsonian language indicates an even firmer rejection of an open-ended bill, or of a vague and merely general notion of rights.

V.

The drafting of the Civil Rights Act of 1866 shows that in 1866, at the time of the drafting of the Fourteenth Amendment, there was a firm consensus and a well-articulated understanding of those recurrent "ghosts" of American constitutional law—fundamental, or civil, or natural rights. One of the more remarkable features of the entire process of the drafting of the Civil Rights bill is the fact that despite the centrality of the definition of protected rights to the whole enterprise, there was remarkably little discussion of the particular rights to be included, and only a little more of those to be excluded. This fact follows, however, from that other remarkable fact we have noted repeatedly—how much agreement there was among the drafters about fundamental rights. What was not contested was not debated.

This consensus presents us with a serious difficulty, however, in our efforts to come to understand what they understand about fundamental rights. They readily list off the rights but say little in explanation of why just this table of rights. To some degree, this makes their thoughts and deeds opaque to us, but I think not entirely so. At least one of the lists, the most important one, the list contained in section one of both the Civil Rights and Freedman's Bureau bills appears to have been put together with uncommon thoughtfulness. Careful examination of that list, of its elements and most importantly of its structure and organization will allow us to reconstruct the understanding that went into its initial construction. Surprisingly, given the importance most scholars attach to the Civil Rights Act for understanding the Fourteenth Amendment, very little attention has been paid to the actual contents of the act's first section.

Despite appearances to the contrary, section one is tightly and carefully organized. It contains two broad classes of protections for "the citizens of the United States" defined in its opening clause. A schematic presentation allows the structure to stand out clearly.

> "Citizens of every race and color:
>> (A.) "Shall have the same right . . . as white persons:"
>>> (1) "To make and enforce contracts."
>>> (2) "to sue, be parties, and give evidence."
>>> (3) "to inherit, purchase, lease, sell, hold, and convey real and personal property."
>>> (4) "to full and equal benefit of all laws and proceedings for the security of person and property."
>> (B.) "Shall be subject to like punishment, pains, and penalties, and to none others."

The first and chief division in the law corresponds to what citizens "shall have" equally ("rights"), and what they "shall be subject to" equally ("punishments, pains, and penalties"). This division seems to correspond perfectly to the two sides of the state as that is conceived in natural rights/social contract theory. The state exists, as the Declaration of Independence puts it, "to secure these [natural] rights." Its "first duty," then, is to provide protection of the law for these rights; its next duty is not to deny rights itself. As James Madison puts the general point in *Federalist* 51, "In framing a government which is to be administered by men over men, the great difficulty lies in this: you must first enable the government to control the governed; and in the next place oblige it to control itself." The state exists to secure rights, and it does so in part by using its monopoly of legitimate coercive authority to punish those who would violate rights. Yet, the Civil Rights Act is first and foremost an act to secure rights from violation not by other citizens but by the states themselves. A state may be a rights violator in either of two ways. It may violate rights when it misuses its coercive powers of punishment, when, for example, it punishes innocent people, or, as is of special concern here, when it does not punish people equally for the same crimes, or makes one act a crime for some persons that is not a crime for others. These last were among the abuses that caught Republican attention in the Black Codes. In any case, the last part of section one is perfectly clear in meaning: when the state acts against citizens it must do so equally, meaning in this context that it must act without making distinctions based on race, color or previous condition of servitude.

A state may also fail in its rights-protecting function when it fails to supply protection of the laws, or supplies such protection imperfectly. The other part of section one sets standards for state actions on behalf of citizens rather than against them. In our post welfare state era we must note that state action on behalf of citizens is not conceived here in terms of what we would think of as public benefits, e.g., the provision (or distribution) of material goods and services of one sort or another, but rather is defined exclusively in terms of "rights." The state acts on behalf of persons when it recognizes "rights." As the debates makes clear, the background theory out of which this set of provisions arises is natural rights theory, but the provisions of the law may seem puzzling in light of that theory. According to the theory, persons acquire rights not from the state but from "the creator," that is, from God or nature, and possess these rights prior to the existence of the state. But the law is clearly referring to rights under state, not natural, law. That is why the law is properly named the Civil Rights Act—these are civil not natural rights.

Civil rights, according to natural rights theory, are in the ideal case intimately tied to natural rights. Civil rights are, as is said in the debates on the act, the civil embodiments of natural rights.[42] The state exists in order to "secure rights," which it does in part by using or threatening coercion against those who violate the rights of others, but also by "granting rights," such as the rights to "make and enforce contracts." The state is not the original source of the right, however, The right is, in William Blackstone's term, a "residuum of natural liberty"—part of natural liberty is the right to enter into agreements with others. The state becomes relevant because its coercive powers exist in part in order to provide enforcement for those agreements. The state in effect defines or even grants a civil right to contract, however, when it defines what sorts of agreement it will recognize as objects on which it will apply its enforcement machinery. This is not, strictly speaking, a natural right at all, for the state does not exist in the pre-political situation where natural rights are defined. States, for example, typically refuse to recognize a right to make contracts to murder others (or, in general, to commit a crime). The state must also specify who may or may not be valid contractors, i.e., whose agreements it will consider legally binding and enforceable. So, for instance, states typically refuse to acknowledge children or the mentally incompetent as valid contractors. Slave law had treated slaves as unable to contract, and the Black Codes set stringent limitations on the rights of freedmen to contract. Again, to say that someone has a right to make a certain sort of contract is to say that the state will recognize as valid and place its coercive authority behind the enforcement of that contract. In such cases, the state benefits or acts on be-

[42] See Hamburger, "Natural Rights," 908–09.

half of its citizens—it recognizes their capacity to be rights holders or generators, and acts to vindicate these rights.

With respect to the two sides of state action toward citizens— state action on behalf of individuals (rights), and state action against individuals (pains and penalties)—the Civil Rights Act has but a limited aim. It does not attempt to legislate a complete code governing contract or property rights, nor does it lay out a complete code regarding criminal law or criminal procedure. These matters were then, as they for the most part remain, matters for the individual states rather than for Congress. The act anticipates that the states will continue to recognize and protect rights, and to punish those who violate rights, but it sets an important boundary around the way states may do this. States must supply "the same right" to persons of different races or colors as it does to white citizens. It must impose "like" punishments when it acts against its citizens.

Congressional intervention is intentionally modest: the states are to continue to set the basic terms in which they benefit and harm citizens, but Congress insists that civil rights and punishments be the same for all without regard to race, that is, the same as they are for the most favored class in the community on the dimension of race or color—the whites. Thus states may continue to disqualify minors from making contracts, but they may not treat African-American or Chinese American citizens *per se* differently from white citizens with respect to the specified rights.

As becomes clear in the debates Congress is not mandating colorblind state legislation. In the first instance, the law covers only the benefits and harms specified, not all the possible benefits and harms a state might make available. Unequal rights based on race in other spheres are acceptable under the act. Likewise, even in the sphere of the specified rights, the requirement that all possess "the same right" can be satisfied (in some instances at least) by color-conscious legislation. The example frequently given in the debates is anti-miscegenation legislation. Although there was some disagreement on the matter, the consensus view, emphatically endorsed by Trumbull himself, was that such laws would remain acceptable under the act, for the law equally limits the rights of blacks and whites to enter into marriage contracts with each other.

Congress attempts only a modest intervention into areas normally entrusted to the states in the American constitutional order for reasons of both constitutional and political scruple. Many doubt that Congress has the constitutional power to intervene too much further into these matters, and believe that it is desirable that it not do so. The framers of the bill value federalism only slightly less than equal rights. Nonetheless, Congress intervenes, in effect, to establish and attempt to maintain a right to equal (in the particular sense of the bill) civil rights. A right to equal (non-racially differentiated) civil rights is itself a civil right, and one of sufficiently different constitutional status, the framers believe, that Congress is justified in guaranteeing it, even if not justified in establishing and maintaining the full panoply of civil rights citizens do or should enjoy. The constitutional issue is not of interest here, but the broader rights claim is, i.e., that there is a civil right to equal civil rights. It was that civil right that the Black Codes denied or violated, and that the act attempts to vindicate. But, why, we must ask, do citizens have a right to equal civil rights?

As do the drafters of the act, we must return to the basics of the natural rights theory in order to answer that question. Trumbull, Sherman, the two Wilsons and the others do not premise their rejection of the Black Codes merely on the view that these unequal laws disadvantage the freedmen. Surely the laws do that and the act's sponsors react to that, but their point is not the essentially utilitarian one that the Black Codes have disadvantageous consequences for those against whom they are aimed. They are concerned more with the issue of rights: the Black Codes violate the rights of the freedmen, most generally the right to equal civil rights. The most perspicuous view of the natural rights grounding of equal civil rights arises on the punishment side of rights. The state does indeed possess rightful coercive power, but state coercion (punishment) is legitimate only when used as duly authorized in the rational social contract, that is, when used for the protection of rights and "the publick good."[43] State coercion against private individuals for any other purposes is not different in principle from unjust private coercion. Individuals can call down on themselves rightful coercion (i.e. punishment) through doing or in some cases threatening to commit some action against the rights of others or the common good. Nonetheless majorities who control the state apparatus may be tempted to deploy coercion for other, illegitimate purposes, for example, to rob others of their rights for their own advantage, or to express vicious prejudices and hatred against members of some identifiably different group, or both. Criminal law that differentiates on the basis of race or color on its face indicates its character as doing one or the other of these forbidden things. The key point is that the state may not punish individuals on the basis of status *per se*, but only on the basis of actions.

---

[43] John Locke, *Two Treatises of Government*, ed. Peter Laslett (Cambridge: Cambridge University Press, 1988), II, § 3.

Thus the framers of the act rightly conclude, the natural rights origin of civil government implies a civil right to be treated by the criminal law as equal individuals, with status figuring neither in the definition of crime nor in the severity of punishment.

A similar argument holds for the public benefits called civil rights. All rights bearers are equal as rights bearers; that is, none is inherently or *per se* the possessor of a greater quantity or more extensive set of natural rights. Every rights possessor has the same right to life, no more no less. Now this does not mean that the state must treat all persons identically. The mentally incompetent may rightfully be granted lesser civil rights (e.g., to contract) because they are not full blown rights bearers. More to the point, the state may even discriminate in various ways among the full rights bearers. Consider the simple case of drivers' licenses. The state surely may rightfully deny drivers' licenses to those who are unable to pass a test showing them capable of operating an automobile safely. A law that discriminates between the capable and the incapable in this way and grants rights differentially accordingly violates no rights. The standard here is just the same as the standard regarding punishment. Discriminations are permissible when they are in the service of rights protection (e.g., only safe drivers allowed) and the public good. Exercise of state power not in the service of these ends is not legitimate. The framers operate with a presupposition that they render conclusory by writing it into the law, that race classification *per se* does not in fact serve these legitimate ends. Differentiating according to racial status again is either an expression of prejudice or an effort to provide less than full civil rights to some. So, again, equal civil rights, as defined in the act, follow as prima facie rights from the premises of the natural rights philosophy.

VI.

The first major division in the list of rights makes evident sense: the state can fail to secure rights either by acting against individuals in such a way as to itself abridge rights or it can fail to recognize and protect rights adequately. It can do so absolutely—a government that threatens in a general and widespread way the rights of its citizen is oppressive or tyrannous, a government that fails to protect rights in a general and widespread way is incompetent or "imbecile." It can also do so relatively in that it can act appropriately in general but fail in either or both ways with respect to some recognizable element of the community. The Civil Rights Act was drafted to remedy the relative kind of failure only.

We must now turn our attention to the first subdivision, the civil rights or benefits that the act requires states to vest or protect equally. Here, too, appears a list of uncertain meaning and coverage. Why these particular rights? The act protects four clusters of such rights and, unlike the distinction between state action on behalf and state action against individuals, the list here does not seem so well constructed, for the rights appear to overlap and thus to lack a clear principle of organization or articulation. For example, the first cluster guarantees "the same right . . . to make and enforce contracts" whereas the second cluster establishes "the same right . . . to sue." Yet suing is one of the chief devices by which one would enforce contracts and therefore those two rights, if not identical, certainly are not mutually exclusive.

Nonetheless, there is a definite principle of order to the list of rights in section one of the act. Grammatically and conceptually there is a difference in kind between the first three clusters of rights and the last. A schematic representation again aids in making the situation manifest:

> "Citizens of every race and color shall have the same right . . . as white persons:
>   (A'):
>   (1) "To make and enforce contracts."
>   (2) "to sue, be parties, and give evidence."
>   (3) "to inherit, purchase, lease, sell, hold, and convey real and personal property."
>   (B'): "to full and equal benefit of all laws and proceedings for the security of persons and property."

Both clusters of rights involve areas where the state acts on behalf of citizen rights, but the two broad divisions represent two different ways in which the state does so. The rights listed under (B') are the most straightforward: the state supplies "laws and proceedings for the security of person and property." For example, it has laws against murder or assault, or laws against robbery. The act mandates that the state make these laws and proceedings fully equal and available to all without regard to race, so that, for example, an assault against a black man is equally defined and enforced as a crime by the authorities as an assault against a white. The right granted here is a right to equal security, or in the later language of the Fourteenth Amendment, to equal protection of the laws of rights already possessed by the rights bearers. Better is to say that the rights the protection of which is established in the act are in a real sense already property in the sense of possessed objects. Laws for security of property refer to protection of possessed property; laws for security of person treat the person as the equivalent of a possessor of property in the person. The laws for security of person and property are directed against their violation by private individuals. The threat to rights (or property) comes in the first instance from persons who invade the property of others, and in the second from states who do not act appropriately (equally and fully) to prevent or punish invasions. The act forbids the states from failing to do their part in preventing or responding to these private invasions of property.

The three clusters of rights gathered together as (A′) above are different: The addressee is the state, but these rights differ from those in (B′) in two ways. First, the rights protection failure forbidden in these cases is not in the first instance due to an invasion by private persons. Second, the rights have less the character of property, i.e., already held and acquired, or vested possession, but rather have the character of rights to vest, i.e. to engage in actions that vest, divest, change the status of property. The right to make contracts is a right to enter agreements through which rights can vest. The right to contract or the right to acquire and sell property are rights, in effect, to acquire rights. The rights under (A′) are thus dynamic, dealing with the rights of gaining and giving up, and not like (B′) static, dealing with "security" of what is already held.

The two differentia of the rights in (A′) from those in (B′) are related. The party who violates one's right, e.g., to security of one's person, is another person who, say, commits an assault. The party who fails to honor one's right to contract is not a private person, but the state, if it refuses either to recognize one's agreements as capable of generating contractual rights, or to make its governmental machinery available to enforce one's contractual rights. A private individual cannot deny one's right to contract; only the state can do so by refusing to recognize this right. An example may help. Under the Black Codes the freedmen suffered different rules from whites as to labor contracts they could enter into. Thus the states refused to recognize many kinds of potential contracts (e.g. for day labor) that blacks might enter into that it would recognize for whites. So if a black did make an agreement with a white outside the allowed sphere, the state refused to accept it as a contract able to vest rights. A law like this fell afoul of (A′)(1), because it involved the way the state defined or extended rights to contract.

We can summarize the difference between (A′) and (B′) by saying that (A′) protects a cluster of equal rights to vest (or in the broad Lockean sense, to acquire property), and (B′) protects the cluster of equal rights to the security of vested rights, or, again, in the broad Lockean sense, to acquired property. That is, (A') and (B') are as logically and legally complementary as (A) and (B): just as under (A) and (B) citizens are protected in their equal right to rights when the state acts on their behalf and when it acts against them, so under (A') and (B') they are recognized in their equal rights to vest and to security in what is vested.

Under (A') appear three clusters of rights: (1) "to make and enforce contracts"; (2) "to sue, be parties, and give evidence"; and (3) "to inherit, purchase, lease, sell, hold, and convey real and personal property." We have already noticed some overlap among the items: the right to sue may be part of the right to enforce contracts; the right to contract may be part of the right to acquire or convey property. Despite the probably unavoidable overlap there are distinct contributions each item makes to filling in a complete or comprehensive set of modes by which one may acquire or vest rights. Through contract one may acquire or vest rights in "real or personal property," but also in far more intangible things, such as in the service of others. Likewise, property may transfer via contract, but also through a variety of other ways, e.g., gift or outright purchase or exchange. Thus (A')(1) and (A')(3) demand that states recognize, without regard to race, etc., that citizens may become vested with the rights to the tangibles we call property in the narrow sense, or to the intangible rights that can also vest through contract.

Although this way of grasping the clusters of rights under (A') is illuminating, it does not yet appear to get to the heart of (A'), as witnessed by its failure to give a clear place to (A')(2), the rights to sue, be parties, and give evidence. We must go deeper. In making contracts George gains rights and obligations in interaction with the will of others. To recognize the right to contract is to recognize the rights holder as a person possessing the ability, character, power of being able to generate such rights and obligations vis-à-vis the wills of individual others.

To possess the right to sue, be party and give evidence is to possess the right to acquire rights and duties, to affect legal rights and duties in general via interaction not with private others, but with the public other, the state itself in the form of its judicial machinery. To recognize the rights to participation in the judicial system is to recognize the rights holder as a person possessing the ability, character, power of generating and affecting such rights and obligations vis-à-vis the public will or the public entity, the state.

Although property may arise and transfer via contract, the third cluster of rights concerns less the means of acquisition than it constitutes an insistence that the rights bearers be recognized as the sort of being capable of having the relations we call property (ownership, sovereignty, control) with nonhuman objects, i.e., with objects that possess neither individual (private) will as contracting partners, nor public will, as the states. Understood in this way the items in (A′) contain the same completeness, mutual exclusivity and categorical perfection as the rest of the Civil Rights Act.

The last set of rights we have discussed are most revealing of all of the theory of rights underlying the act as a whole. The table of rights laid out in (A′) indicates clearly what the basis and point of the act is—to recognize the freedmen as beings equally possessing the kind of will that can generate sets of rights and obligations vis-à-vis other human and nonhuman entities. As Trumbull (and others) insisted from the first to the last discussion of the bill, these are the rights of freedom—free human beings are the beings with the sorts of wills that generate these rights and obligations. To protect these rights is, in the full and most significant sense, to recognize them as that sort of free being. The rights thus recognized may be useful to the empirical ends of human beings; no doubt the rights to property or to contract help one to survive, but the consequences of these rights is less their point than their power to express status. In contemporary philosophic language, the rights theory embodied in the act is an ontological one in that it expresses the nature of being of the agents cognized by the law, and it is deontological in that it identifies rights in terms other than their consequences. This rights theory is clearly a product of the long ante-bellum period of intense reflection on slavery and freedom. The republicans had come to a very clear conception of what the legal implications of being a free human being were and these they attempted to write into their postwar legislation.[44]

In light of this grasp of the theory of the act we may now redescribe slightly the relation between the clusters of rights in (A′) and (B′). As we have seen, the defining term for the different categories of rights in (A′) is the person or object vis-à-vis the rights holder—individual will, public will, willess object. We might extend that analysis to (B′) as well. The affirmation of the right to full and equal benefit of laws and proceedings for security of person and property introduces a new type of actor vis-à-vis the rights bearer—the poten-

---

[44]For the application of a similar theory of rights to the problem of freedom of speech, see Heyman, "Hate Speech and the Theory of Free Expression," in *Hate Speech and the Constitution*, ed. S. Heyman (New York, NY: Garland Publishing Co., 1996), 1:xlii–xliii.

tial rights violators or the negator of rights. According to the mandate of (B′), the negator's will cannot divest the rights bearer of his or her rights but the latter will continue to be recognized and protected in them by the state. To summarize the main categories of rights protection in the act, we may deploy a slightly different schematization.

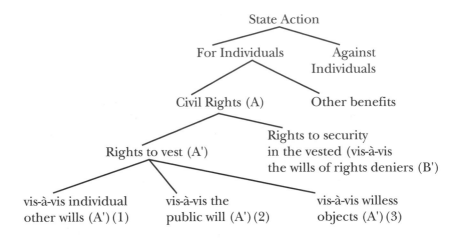

VII.

What then does an understanding of the theory of rights contained within the Civil Rights Act of 1866 contribute to the resolution of our problem, the Supreme Court and American Constitutionalism? In one respect, all conclusions must be tentative, because the rights theory of the Reconstruction Congress becomes especially relevant when it comes to be embodied in the Fourteenth Amendment. Nonetheless, one might briefly identify conclusions in three areas that are relevant to our topic. First, contrary to what Nelson and others have said about the draftsmen of the amendment or to what many contemporary jurisprudes and scholars say about fundamental rights in general, behind the drafting of the Civil Rights Act lay a precise, theoretically satisfying theory of rights. Fundamental rights do not appear to be a merely subjective set of "important values" as they are so often treated today by the Court and commentators both. So far as the Supreme Court requires a clear conception of fundamental rights in order to play its role in the constitutional system adequately, the Civil Rights Act appears to contain such a theory, coherent, precise, and profound beyond the reflections on rights we are accustomed to from Court and commentators in the post-New Deal period.

Before we systematically study the Fourteenth Amendment in this context it is impossible to say with precision to what degree the amendment in fact embodies that theory of rights and thus gives it constitutional status, and to what degree that theory helps give precision and definiteness to what many take to be the vague contours of the Fourteenth Amendment. Brief concluding comments are not the place for a statement on such large topics, but the findings of the above study are suggestive. At many places along the way we found conceptions embedded in the Civil Rights Act that seem to translate quite readily into the somewhat different (certainly more general) language of the amendment. Particularly striking is the way the act's major division into rights regarding state action against and state action on behalf of the individual appears to relate readily to two very important clauses of the Amendment, the due process and equal protection clauses respectively. Absent a more detailed analysis, I believe there are prima facie grounds for concluding that the act, and especially its theory of rights, does supply a valid hermeneutic tool for interpreting and applying the amendment.

So far as that is true, the act gives some insight into how an originalist court might have dealt with various areas of Fourteenth Amendment jurisprudence. This is, again, too large a topic for a brief conclusion, but some suggestive conclusions emerge. One area of constitutional law that rose to prominence within a generation of the adoption of the Fourteenth Amendment was the so-called doctrine of substantive due process. Since the New Deal it has generally been held to have been a mistake to find in the amendment substantive protection of rights like liberty of contract, rights that, for example, placed limitations on the kinds of regulations states could put on the labor contracts people would be free to make, or set limitations on the kinds of regulations to which property could be subjected.

The testimony of the Civil Rights Act is not decisive until we can relate it more precisely to the Fourteenth Amendment. The act clearly does not itself justify a substantive due process jurisprudence, for it is concerned only to prevent discrimination states make on the basis of race, color, or previous condition of servitude. But the act does indicate that the underlying theory of rights is concerned with the kinds of rights the Supreme Court took under its wing, including active and forward looking rights—the rights to acquire, the right to vest rights. That underlying theory of rights unquestionably has implications for the issues taken up under substantive due process, and points to, if it does not yet quite compel, a somewhat more favorable judgment on the courts of that era. The act certainly does not support the extreme positivism regarding economic rights that has mostly dominated the Supreme Court since the New Deal.

Another area where the evidence from the act is relatively clear is reapportionment. The theory of rights in the act and presumably in the amendment does not support the Supreme Court's use of the Fourteenth Amendment in the reapportionment cases. The civil rights protected do not include political rights involving the suffrage.

Perhaps the two areas of application of the act and its theory of rights of most interest to us are race and inexplicit fundamental rights like the right to privacy. The issues here are so complex that it would be best, given the shortage of space, not to attempt an answer.

Necessary and Proper

Randy E. Barnett

IT SHOULD GO without saying, but often does not, that the framers of the U.S. Constitution believed in "the pre-existent rights of nature,"[1] by which they meant those rights that "are essential to secure the liberty of the people"[2] from abuses by either minority or majority "factions"[3] operating through representative government. What divided the founding generation was not *whether* such rights existed, but *how* these rights are best protected.

Some, perhaps most Federalists, thought that the structures embodied in the Constitution would adequately protect rights. These structures included the separation of powers, limited and enumerated powers, and the fact that direct democracy played a role, but only a limited one, in each branch of government. Opponents of the Constitution—dubbed "Antifederalists" by its supporters—argued that more explicit protection of these rights in the form of a bill of rights was needed. Taken together, the constitutional strategy of limited powers (structurally reinforced by separation of powers and federalism) and protected rights was supposed to enable an energetic

---

[1] *The Debates and Proceedings in the Congress of the United States*, ed. Joseph Gales (Washington: Gales & Seaton, 1834), 1:454 (hereinafter cited as *Annals of Congress*) (statement of James Madison).

[2] Ibid. In the passage from which these phrases are taken, Madison is arguing that the right of trial by jury enumerated in the proposed amendments, though a "positive right," is as essential to secure the liberty of the people as any natural right. See also "Roger Sherman's Draft of the Bill of Rights," reprinted in Randy E. Barnett, ed., *The Rights Retained by the People: The History and Meaning of the Ninth Amendment* (Fairfax, VA: George Mason University Press, 1993), 1:351: "The people have certain natural rights which are retained by them when they enter into Society. . . ."

[3] See *The Federalist*, no. 10, 54 (James Madison) (Mod. Lib. ed. 1937): "By a faction I understand a number of citizens, whether amounting to a majority or minority of the whole, who are united by some common impulse of passion, or of interest, adverse to the *rights of other citizens*, or to the permanent and aggregate interests of the community." Emphasis added.

national government to accomplish certain ends, while ensuring that the liberty of the people would be protected.

The rise in this century of a powerful administrative state at the national level has put a strain on this theory of constitutionalism and the role of the judiciary. Though not every act of the federal administrative state constrains the exercise of liberty, the breadth of its ambitions increases the likelihood of clashes between the will of the government and the liberties of the citizenry. When the powers of the federal administrative state are used to restrict citizens' exercise of their liberty, there are really only three responses the judiciary may make.

First, the judiciary could completely acquiesce to the assumption of power by the other two branches of the national government. This option, though appealing to "judicial conservatives" who advocate "judicial restraint," would amount to a unilateral surrender by the judiciary—supposedly a co-equal branch of the federal government—of its powers of judicial review. With this surrender, enumerated powers and enumerated (or unenumerated) rights would no longer provide any constraints on the size and scope of the administrative state. This would represent a profound change in our theory of constitutionalism from one in which powers are retained by the people unless granted to government to one in which all powers are held by two branches of the national government and it is solely for these branches to decide when and how they should exercise them, subject only to the constraints of democratic electoral processes.

Second, whether the national government is operating within or beyond its enumerated powers, the judiciary could scrutinize legislative restrictions on liberty to ensure that they do not violate the rights retained by the people. This option is the one that the judiciary has all-too-tepidly been pursuing these past sixty years. Elsewhere I have argued that, given its refusal to hold the federal government within its enumerated powers, the judiciary has been far too timid in protecting both enumerated and unenumerated individual rights from infringement by the administrative state.[4]

Third, courts could try to confine the national government to operating within its enumerated powers and thus reduce its opportunity to restrict the liberties of the people. Until the 1995 Supreme Court decision of *United States v. Lopez,*[5] this option was considered

---

[4] See Randy E. Barnett, "Getting Normative: The Role of Natural Rights in Constitutional Adjudication," *Constitutional Commentary* 12 (1995): 93–122; Randy E. Barnett, "Reconceiving the Ninth Amendment," *Cornell Law Review* 74 (1988): 1–42.

[5] 115 S.Ct. 1624 (1995).

antiquated and beyond the bounds of respectable academic discussion. In *Lopez*, the Court struck down a federal statute mandating Gun-Free School Zones around local public schools on the ground that such legislation did not lie within the enumerated powers of Congress, in particular, its Commerce Power. Significantly, by enforcing this limitation on the scope of federal power in this way, the Court never had to address the question of whether this statute violated the Second Amendment. In this case, stopping the Congress from exceeding its enumerated powers also deprived it of the chance to infringe upon the retained enumerated right to keep and bear arms.[6]

In this essay, I shall maintain that, if the courts are to hold Congress to the exercise of its enumerated powers, then they must come to grips with the congressional power "To make all Laws which shall be necessary and proper for carrying into Execution the foregoing Powers, and all other Powers vested by this Constitution in the Government of the United States, or in any Department or Officer thereof."[7] While the Necessary and Proper Clause has long been used to greatly expand congressional power, I argue that, to the contrary, it provides a two-part standard against which all national legislation should be judged: such laws shall be "necessary *and* proper." According to this standard, laws which are either unnecessary or improper are beyond the powers of Congress to enact.

In Part I, I consider the meaning of this requirement. First, I identify what I shall call the Madisonian and Marshallian conceptions of necessity. Then I discuss the meaning of "proper," the other half of the standard that all laws enacted by Congress must meet, and discuss how propriety is distinct from necessity. Finally, in Part II, I consider a doctrinal means of implementing the Necessary and Proper Clause. I conclude that a rigorous application of the necessary and proper standard would serve to protect both the enumerated and, especially, the unenumerated rights retained by the people.

I. THE MEANINGS OF "NECESSARY" AND "PROPER"

It is beyond serious question that, by the time of ratification, the framers contemplated judicial review that would nullify unconstitu-

---

[6] This is not to say that the statute in *Lopez* did infringe the right to keep an bear arms. I am of the opinion (reflected in an *amicus brief* to which I was a signatory) that, as applied to minors carrying guns in or near public schools, it did not violate the Second Amendment. See Amicus Curiae Brief of Academics for the Second Amendment, *United States v. Lopez*, 115 S. Ct. 1624 (1995) (no. 93–1260). As applied to adults transporting guns on public streets, perhaps in their vehicles, within 1000 feet of a public school, however, I have serious qualms about its constitutionality under the Second Amendment.

[7] U.S. Constitution, art. 1, sec. 8, emphasis added.

tional legislation[8]—including whatever amendments might be ratified in the future.[9] While a vigorous scholarly debate continues as to whether judicial review was intended also to protect other unenumerated rights "retained by the people,"[10] in any event, *neither* enumerated nor unenumerated rights received much, if any, consideration

[8] See, e.g., *Federalist* no. 78 (Alexander Hamilton), 507–08: "[W]henever a particular statute contravenes the Constitution, it will be the duty of the judicial tribunals to adhere to the latter and disregard the former. . . . [T]he courts of justice are to be considered as the bulwarks of a limited Constitution against legislative encroachments. . . ." Hamilton also answered the charge that this would be to advocate judicial supremacy:

> Nor does this conclusion by any means suppose a superiority of the judicial to the legislative power. It only supposes that the power of the people is superior to both; and that where the will of the legislature, declared in its statutes, stands in opposition to that of the people, declared in the Constitution, the judges ought to be governed by the latter rather than the former. They ought to regulate their decisions by the fundamental laws, rather than by those which are not fundamental.

Ibid., 506.

[9] See *Annals of Congress*, 1:457 (statement of Rep. James Madison): "If they are incorporated into the constitution, independent tribunals will consider themselves in a peculiar manner the guardian of those rights; they will be an impenetrable bulwark against every assumption of power in the legislative or executive; they will naturally be led to resist every encroachment upon rights expressly stipulated for in the constitution by the declaration of rights.

[10] For those who say nay, see, e.g., Raoul Berger, "The Ninth Amendment, as Perceived by Randy Barnett," *Northwestern University Law Review* 88 (1994): 1508–36; Raoul Berger, "Natural Law and Judicial Review: Reflections of an Earthbound Lawyer," *University of Cincinnati Law Review* 61 (1992): 5–28; Philip A. Hamburger, "Natural Rights, Natural Law, and American Constitutions," *Yale Law Journal* 102 (1993): 907–60; Thomas B. McAffee, "The Original Meaning of the Ninth Amendment," *Columbia Law Review* 90 (1990): 1215–1320; Thomas B. McAffee, "The Bill of Rights, Social Contract Theory, and the Rights 'Retained' by the People," *Southern Illinois University Law Journal* 16 (1992): 267–325; Thomas B. McAffee, "Prolegomena to a Meaningful Debate of the 'Unwritten Constitution' Thesis," *University of Cincinnati Law Review* 61 (1992): 107–69; Helen K. Michael, "The Role of Natural Law in Early American Constitutionalism: Did the Founders Contemplate Judicial Enforcement of 'Unwritten' Individual Rights?" *North Carolina Law Review* 69 (1991): 421–90.

For those who say aye, see, e.g., Calvin R. Massey, *Silent Rights: The Ninth Amendment and the Constitution's Unenumerated Rights* (Philadelphia: Temple University Press, 1995); Randy E. Barnett, "Introduction: Implementing the Ninth Amendment," in *Rights Retained by the People*, 2:1–46; Steven J. Heyman, "Natural Rights, Positivism and the Ninth Amendment: A Response to McAffee," *Southern Illinois University Law Journal* 16 (1992): 327–36; Calvin R. Massey, "The Natural Law Component of the Ninth Amendment," *University of Cincinnati Law Review* 61 (1992): 49–105; David N. Mayer, "The Natural Rights Basis of the Ninth Amendment: A Reply to Professor McAffee," *Southern Illinois University Law Journal* 16

from the courts during the first several decades of the United States. Indeed, the first time a federal statute was held to be an unconstitutional violation of the natural right of freedom of speech enumerated in the First Amendment[11] was in the 1965 case of *Lamont v. Postmaster General.*[12]

The courts' early willingness to defer to legislative judgment was the central focus of James Thayer's classic 1893 *Harvard Law Review* article, "The Origin and Scope of the American Doctrine of Constitutional Law."[13] There he reproduced a goodly number of examples of judicial unwillingness to second-guess legislative judgment, beginning with the 1811 opinion of Chief Justice Tilghman, of Pennsylvania:

> For weighty reasons, it has been assumed as a principle in constitutional construction by the Supreme Court of the United States, by this court, and every other court of reputation in the United States, that an Act of the legislature is not to be declared void unless the violation of the constitution is so manifest as to leave no room for reasonable doubt.[14]

What are these "weighty reasons" to which Justice Tilghman alluded? It is not enough to assert separation of powers concerns, since the courts are themselves a separate and co-equal branch of govern-

(1992): 313–26; Suzanna Sherry, "The Founders' Unwritten Constitution," *University of Chicago Law Review* 54 (1987): 1127–77; Suzanna Sherry, "Natural Law in the States," *University of Cincinnati Law Review* 61 (1992): 171–222; Bruce N. Morton, "John Locke, Robert Bork, Natural Rights and the Interpretation of the Constitution," *Seton Hall Law Review* 22 (1992): 709–88.

[11] That the freedom speech was considered a natural right is evidenced by James Madison's notes for his congressional speech in which he introduced and explained his proposed amendments to the Constitution. These notes are reprinted in Barnett, ed., *Rights Retained by the People,* 1:64–65. In the section discussing "Contents of Bill of Rhts," the following appears: "3. natural rights retained as speach [sic]." Ibid., 64.

[12] 381 U.S. 301 (1965). See Laurence H. Tribe, *American Constitutional Law,* 2d ed. (Mineola, NY: Foundation Press, 1988), 327 n. 18: "The federal statute struck down in *Lamont* [was] the first federal law the Supreme Court ever held to be violative of the first amendment."

[13] James Thayer, "The Origin and Scope of the American Doctrine of Constitutional Law," *Harvard Law Review* 7 (1893): 129–56. Recently, on the one-hundredth anniversary of its publication, an entire symposium was devoted to the legacy of this one article. See "One Hundred Years of Judicial Review: The Thayer Centennial Symposium," *Northwestern University Law Review* 88 (1993): 1–468.

[14] *Commonwealth v. Smith,* 4 Bin. 117 (1811), as it appears in Thayer, "Origin and Scope," 140.

ment whose judgment concerning constitutionality presumably merits a weight at least equal to that of the other branches. Giving courts a genuinely equal voice to that of legislatures means giving no presumption to legislative judgment. Still, judicial deference might have rested upon a factual assumption that the representatives of the people were conscientious enough to consider the constitutional implications of their legislative acts. To question the judgment of the legislature was to question the good faith of a co-equal branch, an accusation that should not lightly be made.

Then there was the reason offered by Thayer himself:

> This rule recognizes that, having regard to the great, complex, ever-unfolding exigencies of government, much which will seem unconstitutional to one man, or body of men, may reasonably not seem so to another; that the constitution often admits of different interpretations; that there is often a range of choice and judgment; that in such cases the constitution does not impose upon the legislature any one specific opinion, but leaves open this range of choice; and that whatever choice is rational is constitutional. This is the principle which the rule that I have been illustrating supports.[15]

According to Thayer, constitutional judgments were sufficiently uncertain that a judgment by a legislature that it was acting within its proper powers should be respected unless it was clearly wrong.

Thayer's argument for judicial deference to legislatures on the grounds that exigency requires and the Constitution permits a range of legislative choices arises most tellingly when interpreting the clause that gives Congress the power "To make all Laws which shall be necessary and proper for carrying into Execution the foregoing Powers, and all other Powers vested by this Constitution in the Government of the United States, or in any Department or Officer thereof."[16] With every enactment, the Necessary and Proper Clause raises the question of how much deference courts owe to a legislative judgment that an act is both necessary and proper. In the next section I shall suggest that whether an assessment of a statute's necessity is too uncertain to be decided by courts depends, in important part, on how this constitutionally-supplied standard is conceived.

A. *The Meaning of "Necessary"*

The term "necessary" in the Necessary and Proper Clause immediately raises two questions: (1) how *necessary* is "necessary," and

[15] Ibid., 144.
[16] U.S. Constitution, art. 1, sec. 8, emphasis added.

(2) who decides what is and is not necessary? I shall contend that the answer to the second of these questions depends, at least in part, on how one answers the first.

Madisonian v. Marshallian Conceptions of "Necessary"

When the Constitution says that a law passed by Congress *"shall be . . . necessary,"* what does this require? It might mean *really* necessary in the sense that the end cannot be performed in some manner that does not infringe the retained liberties of the people, as Madison argued in his speech to the first House of Representatives opposing the creation of a national bank:

> But the proposed bank could not even be called necessary to the Government; at most it could be but convenient. Its uses to the Government could be supplied by keeping the taxes a little in advance; by loans from individuals; by the other Banks, over which the Government would have equal command; nay greater, as it might grant or refuse to these the privilege (a free and irrevocable gift to the proposed Bank) of using their notes in the Federal revenues.[17]

While he was speaking here in his capacity as a legislator, Madison was not at this point in his speech arguing the "policy" issues raised by a national bank, but rather its constitutionality. He had previously addressed the policy issues when, at the start of his speech, he "began with a general review of the advantages and disadvantages of Banks."[18] However, "in making these remarks on the merits of the bill, he had reserved to himself the right to deny the authority of Congress to pass it."[19]

> Madison was primary concerned with the meaning of the Necessary and Proper Clause:
>
> Whatever meaning this clause may have, none can be admitted, that would give an unlimited discretion to Congress.
>
> Its meaning must, according to the natural and obvious force of the terms and the context, be limited to means necessary to the end, and incident to the nature of the specified powers. . . .
>
> The essential characteristic of the Government, as composed of limited and enumerated powers, would be destroyed, if, instead of direct and incidental means, any means could be used, which,

[17] *Annals of Congress*, 2:1901 (statement of Rep. James Madison).
[18] Ibid., 1894.
[19] Ibid., 1896.

in the language of the preamble to the bill, "might be conceived
to be conducive to the successful conducting of the finances, or
might be conceived to tend to give facility to the obtaining of
loans."[20]

Madison thought trying to justify the constitutionality of a national bank as necessary for carrying into execution an enumerated
power (in this case the Borrowing Power) required too great a
stretch:

> Mark the reasoning on which the validity of the bill depends! To
> borrow money is made the end, and the accumulation of capitals
> is made the means. The accumulation of capitals is then the end,
> and a Bank implied as the means. The Bank is then the end, and
> a charter of incorporation, a monopoly, capital punishments, &c.
> implied as the means.
>
> If implications, thus remote and thus multiplied, can be
> linked together, a chain may be formed that will reach every object
> of legislation, every object within the whole compass of political
> economy.

In defense of this interpretation of the Necessary and Proper
Clause, Madison gave several examples of enumerated powers that
were not left to implication, though if a latitudinarian interpretation
of the Necessary and Proper Clause were correct, they surely could
have been:

> Congress have the power "to regulate the value of money,"
> yet it is expressly added, not left to be implied, that counterfeiters
> may be punished.
>
> They have the power "to declare war," to which armies are
> more incident than incorporated banks to borrowing; yet the
> power "to raise and support armies" is expressly added; and to this
> again, the express power "to make rules and regulations for the
> government of armies"; a like remark is applicable to the powers
> as to the navy.
>
> The regulation and calling out of the militia are more apper-
> tinent to war than the proposed Bank to borrowing; yet the former
> is not left to construction.
>
> The very power to borrow money is a less remote implication
> from the power of war, than an incorporated monpoly [sic] Bank
> from the power of borrowing; yet, the power to borrow is not left
> to implication.

[20] Ibid., 1898.

Madison did not mean to exaggerate the significance of these sorts of drafting decisions: "It is not pretended that every insertion or omission in the Constitution is the effect of systematic attention. This is not the character of any human work, particularly the work of a body of men." Yet he thought these examples "with others that might be added, sufficiently inculcate, nevertheless, a rule of interpretation very different from that on which the bill rests. They condemn the exercise of any power, particularly a great and important power, which is not evidently and necessarily involved in an express power."[21]

Perhaps most importantly to those, like me, who wish to draw a connection between the Necessary and Proper Clause and the protection of the rights and powers retained by the people, Madison also cited in support of this "rule of interpretation," the Ninth[22] and Tenth[23] Amendments. Of course, in February of 1791, these had yet to be ratified and on that date were the eleventh and twelfth on the list of amendments then pending before the states. Perhaps because he referred to them by these numbers, Madison's only known use of the Ninth Amendment in a constitutional argument had, until recently, largely been ignored.[24]

> The *latitude of interpretation* required by the bill is condemned by the rule furnished by the Constitution itself. . . .
>
> The explanatory amendments proposed by Congress themselves, at least, would be good authority with them; all those renunciations of power proceeded on a rule of construction, excluding the latitude now contended for. . . . He read several of the articles proposed, remarking particularly on the 11th [the Ninth Amendment] and the 12th [the Tenth Amendment], *the former, as guarding against a latitude of interpretation*; the latter, as excluding every source of power not within the Constitution itself.[25]

[21] Ibid., 1899.

[22] See U.S. Constitution, amend. 9: "The enumeration in the Constitution of certain rights shall not be construed to deny or disparage others retained by the people."

[23] See U.S. Constitution, amend. 10: "The powers not delegated to the United States by the Constitution, nor prohibited by it to the States, are reserved to the States respectively, or to the people."

[24] Prior to my discussions of this speech (and reactions thereto), the only reference to it that I had found in the entire corpus of Ninth Amendment scholarship was Eugene M. Van Loan III, "Natural Rights and the Ninth Amendment," *Boston University Law Review* 49 (1968): 15: "As evidence that the federal government was restricted to delegated powers and that even the necessary and proper clause was not unlimited, [Madison] pointed to, among other things, the ninth amendment."

[25] *Annals of Congress*, 2:1901.

Thus, for Madison, whether or not a proposed action of government that restricted the liberty of the people was necessary and therefore within the powers of Congress to enact, required some assessment of whether the means chosen were essential to the pursuit of an enumerated end. Without this assessment, the scheme of limited enumerated powers would unravel.

True, Madison was speaking here as a legislator, not a judge. But he was speaking about the constitutionality, not the wisdom, of a national bank, and other statements by him make it clear that he desired this issue to be justiciable. A few days after his bank speech, Madison replied to those who asserted that necessary meant merely expedient as follows: "[W]e are told, for our comfort, that the Judges will rectify our mistakes. How are the Judges to determine in the case; are they to be guided in their decisions by the rules of expediency?"[26] This statement should not be interpreted as a rejection of judicial review, but as a rejection of a standard of constitutionality that would preclude judicial review. As will be seen below, Madison later made clear that he objected to equating "necessary" with mere expedience or convenience because such a standard would place the issue of necessity outside the competence of courts.

It is true as well that Madison did not address in *this* speech whether any benefit of the doubt should be attached to legislative judgment, but, as shall be seen below, Madison himself later argued that whether judicial deference is due legislative judgment depends, at least in part, on one's view of necessity. Moreover, in his speech replying to those who took issue with his initial remarks, Madison denied that the House should "respect" the judgment of the Senate concerning constitutionality, or that the president should "sanction their joint proceedings." Madison "then enlarged on the exact balance or equipoise contemplated by the Constitution, to be observed and maintained between the several branches of Government; and showed, that except this idea was preserved, the advantages of different independent branches would be lost, and their separate deliberations and determinations be entirely useless."[27]

Although I call this conception of necessity Madisonian, I do not contend that it was original to him, nor that he stood alone in asserting it. Secretary of State Thomas Jefferson, for example drew the same distinction between necessity and convenience:

> [T]he constitution allows only the means which are "necessary," not those which are merely convenient for effecting the enumer-

26 Ibid., 1958.
27 Ibid., 1956.

ated powers. If such a latitude of construction be allowed to this phrase, as to give any non enumerated power, it will go to every one; for there is no one, which ingenuity may not torture into a *convenience, in some way or other, to some one* of so long a list of enumerated powers: it would swallow up all the delegated powers. . . . Therefore it was that the constitution restrained them to the *necessary* means; that is to say, to those means, without which the grant of power would be nugatory.[28]

In Congress, Madison was joined by Representative Stone, who argued that the Necessary and Proper Clause "was intended to defeat those loose and proud principles of legislation which had been contended for. It was meant to reduce legislation to some rule."[29] Representative Jackson observed that "If the sweeping clause, as it is called, extends to vesting Congress with such powers, and *necessary* and *proper* means are an indispensable implication in the sense advanced by the advocates of the bill, we shall soon be in possession of all possible powers, and the charter under which we sit will be nothing but a name."[30] And Representative Giles defined necessary as "that mean without which the end could not be produced." He rejected the suggestion that "'*necessary*,' as applicable to a mean to produce an end, should be construed so as

to produce the greatest quantum of public utility." That definition, if pursued, will be found to teem with dangerous effects, and would justify the assumption of any given authority whatever. Terms are to be so construed as to produce the greatest degree of public utility. Congress are to be the judges of this degree of utility. This utility, when decided on, will be the ground of Constitutionality. Hence *any measure may be proved Constitutional which Congress may judge to be useful.* These deductions would suborn the Constitution itself, and blot out the great distinguishing characteristic of the free Constitutions of America, as compared with the despotic Governments of Europe, which consist in having the boundaries of governmental authority clearly marked out and ascertained.[31]

[28] "Opinion of Thomas Jefferson, Secretary of State," in M. St. Clair Clarke and D. A. Hall, *Legislative and Documentary History of the Bank of the United States* (Washington, DC: Gales & Seaton, 1832), 91, 93; see also ibid.: "Perhaps, indeed, bank bills may be a more *convenient* vehicle than treasury orders; but a little *difference* in the degree of *convenience* cannot constitute the *necessity*, which the constitution makes the ground for assuming any non enumerated power."

[29] *Annals of Congress*, 2:1933.

[30] Ibid., 1916–17, emphasis added.

[31] Ibid., 1941, emphasis added.

In contrast with Madison's treatment, we might view "necessary" to mean merely *convenient* or useful, as John Marshall argued in his opinion in *McCulloch v. Maryland*[32] upholding the constitutionality of the national bank. Maryland had asserted the Madisonian conception of necessity in challenging the constitutionality of the bank:

> But the laws which they are authorized to make, are to be such as are necessary and proper for this purpose. No terms could be found in the language, more absolutely excluding a general and unlimited discretion than these. It is not 'necessary or proper,' but 'necessary and proper.' The means used must have both these qualities. It must be, not merely convenient—fit—adapted—proper, to the accomplishment of the end in view; it must likewise be necessary for the accomplishment of that end. Many means may be proper, which are not necessary; because the end may be attained without them. The word 'necessary,' is said to be a synonyme of 'needful.' But both these words are defined 'indispensably requisite;' and, most certainly, this is the sense in which the word 'necessary' is used in the constitution. To give it a more lax sense, would be to alter the whole character of the government as a sovereignty of limited powers. This is not a purpose for which violence should be done to the obvious and natural sense of any terms, used in an instrument drawn up with great simplicity, and with extraordinary precision.[33]

Marshall rejected the Madisonian conception of necessity in favor of the position that both Madison and Maryland posed as its opposite—"necessary" means convenient:

> If reference be had to its use, in the common affairs of the world, or in approved authors, we find that [the word "necessary"] frequently imports no more than that one thing is convenient, or useful, or essential to another. To employ the means necessary to an end, is generally understood as employing any means calculated to produce the end, and not as being confined to those single means, without which the end would be entirely unattainable.[34]

Although Marshall's textual and functional defense of this interpretation of "necessary" is both well known and more readily available than Madison's bank speech, I shall briefly summarize it here.

Textually, Marshall contrasted the use of the term "necessary"

[32] 17 (4 Wheat.) U.S. 316 (1819).
[33] 17 U.S. at 366–67.
[34] 17 U.S. at 413–14.

in this clause with the term "absolutely necessary" used in Article I, sec. 10,[35] arguing that it is "impossible to compare the[se] sentence[s] . . . without feeling a conviction, that the convention understood itself to change materially the meaning of the word 'necessary,' by prefixing the word 'absolutely.' "[36] Thus it is a mistake, as a textual matter, to equate the term necessary with the term absolutely necessary, as the State of Maryland purportedly did.[37]

Functionally, he argued that

> It must have been the intention of those who gave these powers, to insure, so far as human prudence could insure, their beneficial execution. This could not be done, by confiding the choice of means to such narrow limits as not to leave it in the power of congress to adopt any which might be appropriate, and which were conducive to the end. . . . To have declared, that the best means shall not be used, but those alone, without which the power given would be nugatory, would have been to deprive the legislature of the capacity to avail itself of experience, to exercise its reason, and to accommodate its legislation to circumstances.[38]

Marshall dismissed, almost casually, concerns about how such an open-ended grant of discretionary power squared with the theory of limited and enumerated powers.

> This government is acknowledged by all, to be one of enumerated powers. The principle, that it can exercise only the powers granted to it, would seem too apparent, to have required to be enforced by all those arguments, which its enlightened friends, while it was pending before the people, found it necessary to urge; that principle is now universally admitted. But the question respecting the extent of the powers actually granted, is perpetually arising, and will probably continue to arise, so long as our system shall exist.[39]

And, just as Madison gave examples of enumerated powers that were not left to implication, Marshall offered three examples of unenumerated powers that had already been implied, even though they were arguably not "indispensably necessary" to the accomplishment

[35] See U.S. Constitution, art. 1, sec. 10: "No State shall, without the Consent of the Congress, lay any Imports or Exports, except what may be absolutely necessary for executing its inspection Laws. . . ."

[36] *McCulloch*, 17 U.S. at 414–15.

[37] In its brief, the State of Maryland did not use this phrase, though it did use the phrase "indispensably requisite." See text accompanying note 33 above.

[38] Id. at 415.

[39] Id. at 405.

of some enumerated purpose: the implied powers to carry mail between post offices and along post roads,[40] to punish any violations of its laws,[41] and to require congressional oaths of office.[42]

There are any number of quite plausible responses to these examples that a person employing a Madisonian conception of necessity could make. The power to carry mail can surely be considered, in Madison's words, both requisite to and "incident to the nature"[43] of the postal power. And, for many, a legislative enactment with no sanctions for disobedience can hardly be called a law. Once again, this power is clearly incident, if not identical, to the nature of the lawmaking power. In contrast, the power to require congressional oaths of office may well be inessential to the performance of government;[44] let candidates for office challenge their opponents to take such an oath or suffer the electoral consequences. If the inability to require congressional oaths be the price for holding Congress to its enumerated powers, a Madisonian might contend, Justice Marshall's opinion notwithstanding, it is a price well worth paying.[45]

We may summarize Marshall's argument in *McCulloch* as follows: *Because it is absolutely necessary that "necessary" not mean absolutely necessary, and because the word "necessary" does not necessarily mean absolutely necessary, of necessity it does not.* Marshall's functional argument depends upon the fear that the national government will fail without the sort of discretionary powers that his interpretation allows. As im-

[40] Id. at 417: "It may be said, with some plausibility, that the right to carry the mail, and to punish those who rob it, is not indispensably necessary to the establishment of a post-office and post-road."

[41] Ibid. "The several powers of congress may exist, in a very imperfect state, to be sure, but they may exist and be carried into execution, although no punishment should be inflicted, in cases where the right to punish is not expressly given."

[42] Id. at 416: "The power to exact this security for the faithful performance of duty, is not given, nor is it indispensably necessary."

[43] *Annals of Congress*, 1:1898 (statement of Rep. Madison).

[44] A mandatory congressional oath might be considered a qualification for holding office in addition to those mandated by Article 1, secs. 2 and 3, and thus beyond the powers of Congress to impose. See *Powell v. McCormack*, 395 U.S. 486 (1969), limiting Congress to judging only the qualifications for membership enumerated in article 1, section 2. On the other hand, an oath requirement might be considered a procedural rule within the powers of each house to determine for itself rather than a law. On either theory, an oath requirement is either permissible or impermissible independent of the Necessary and Proper Clause.

[45] Assuming Marshall was correct in claiming that a Madisonian conception of necessity would mean that a mandatory congressional oath to preserve, protect and defend the Constitution lies outside the powers of Congress, a Madisonian might respond that a Congress that imposed such a requirement would be violating the terms of such an oath.

portant, it assumes that this open-ended grant of discretionary powers will not eventually undermine the enumerated powers scheme as Madison feared.

Although as president Madison had actually signed into law the bill establishing the national bank that Marshall upheld as constitutional,[46] Madison took immediate exception to Marshall's opinion in *McCulloch*, renewing the argument he had made as a congressman nearly thirty years before:

> [O]f most importance is the high sanction given to a latitude in expounding the Constitution, which seems to break down the landmarks intended by a specification of the powers of Congress, and to substitute, for a definite connection between means and ends, a legislative discretion as to the former, to which no practical limit can be assigned. In the great system of political economy, having for its general object the national welfare, everything is related immediately or remotely to every other thing; and consequently, a power over any one thing, if not limited by some obvious and precise affinity, may amount to a power over every other thing. Ends and means may shift their character at the will and according to the ingenuity of the legislative body. . . .
>
> Is there a legislative power, in fact, not expressly prohibited by the Constitution, which might not, according to the doctrine of the court, be exercised as a means of carrying into effect some specified power?[47]

Notice that Madison both acknowledges the supposedly modern insight that the national economy is interconnected and rejects this as a basis for a latitudinarian interpretation of "necessary".

Perhaps most importantly for those who would deny that such issues ought to be justiciable, in the same letter, President Madison makes crystal clear his objection to removing the constitutional determination of necessity from the province of the courts: "Does not the court also relinquish, by their doctrine, all control on the legislative exercise of unconstitutional powers?" Madison objected to interpreting necessary as merely expedient or convenient, in part, because

---

[46] Madison later justified his decision by citing the precedent established by the longstanding acquiescence to the claimed power as well as by the expediency of the bank: "A veto from the Executive under these circumstances, with an admission of the expediency and *almost necessity* of the measure, would have been in defiance of all the obligations derived from a course of precedents amounting to the requisite evidence of the national judgment and intention." James Madison, "Letter to Mr. Ingersoll" (June 25, 1831), in *Letters and Other Writings of James Madison* (1867), 4:186, emphasis added [hereinafter cited as *Works*].

[47] Madison, "Letter to Judge Roane" (September 2, 1819), in *Works*, 4:143–44.

doing so would place the matter "beyond the reach of judicial cognizance. . . . [B]y what handle could the court take hold of the case?"[48]

This view of the judiciary was not limited to Madison; nor was it a view that developed only later when Madison was president. Back during the 1791 bank debate in Congress an interesting exchange occurred between Representatives Stone and Smith. Stone accused Smith of holding the view that "all our laws proceeded upon the principle of expediency—as soon as we gave it as our opinion that a thing was expedient, it became constitutional."[49] To this, Representative Smith replied:

> He had never been so absurd as to contend, as the gentleman had stated, that whatever the Legislature thought expedient, was therefore Constitutional. He had only argued that, in cases where the question was, whether a law was necessary and proper to carry a given power into effect, the members of the Legislature had no other guide but their own judgment, from which alone they were to determine whether the measure proposed was necessary and proper. . . . That, nevertheless, it was still within the province of the Judiciary to annul the law, if it should be by them deemed not to result by fair construction from the powers vested by the Constitution.[50]

In sum, Representative Smith rejected the "absurd" accusation that Congress was the sole judge of a measure's necessity and propriety.

Of course, it was the opinion of Marshall the Supreme Court Chief Justice, not Madison, that prevailed on this question of how to interpret "necessary." Notwithstanding that Marshall's opinion in

[48] Ibid., 144.

[49] *Annals of Congress,* 2:1932.

[50] Ibid., 1936–37. Smith also asserted that members should determine "that the measure was not prohibited by any part of the Constitution, *was not a violation of the rights of any State or individual,* and was peculiarly necessary and proper to carry into operation certain essential powers of Government." This statement is interesting for three reasons. First, it refers to individual not collective rights. Second, it was made before the ratification of the Bill of Rights and therefore presumably refers to unenumerated individual rights that constrain the powers of Congress. Finally, by distinguishing between prohibitions in the Constitution and violations of unenumerated individual rights, Smith assumed that unenumerated rights were not, as some have alleged, simply defined "residually" by those powers. See, e.g., McAffee, "Original Meaning," 1221. Having said this, I should concede that, by distinguishing between a violation of individual rights and a measure's propriety, this statement appears somewhat inconsistent with the theory endorsed below that a law is "improper" if it violates the background rights retained by the people.

McCulloch was lambasted at the time as a usurpation,[51] it became, as Stephen Gardbaum has observed,

> one of the handful of foundational decisions of the Supreme Court that are automatically cited as original sources for the propositions of constitutional law that they contain. But *McCulloch* has the further (and even rarer) distinction of being treated as providing a full and complete interpretation of a particular clause of the Constitution. Analysis of the Necessary and Proper Clause has historically begun and ended with *McCulloch.* . . .[52]

Marshall's latitudinarian conception of necessity survives to this day, largely unchallenged. Yet, while Marshall's fear of impotent government remains a matter of speculation (because he got his way), history seems to have borne out Madison's expressed concern for the integrity of the enumerated powers scheme. With rare exception, such as *Lopez*, the enumeration of powers has largely been vitiated as a limitation on the scope of the national government, due in no small measure to the influence of Chief Justice Marshall's opinion in *McCulloch*.

The term "necessary" also raises a second question: *who is to decide the issue of a measure's necessity?* Although it is clear that Marshall's decision in *Marbury v. Madison*[53] was correct in its holding that legislative decisions are not immune from judicial assessment of constitutionality and nullification,[54] the crucial question is how much deference do the courts owe to legislatures. While the degree of deference depends on the perceived competency and good faith of the legislative process to reach knowledgeable, as opposed to merely rent-seeking, decisions, it also depends on how you resolve the first question concerning the requirement of necessity.

For if you take the Madisonian view that "necessary" means *really* necessary, then courts are quite capable of assessing the government's claim that Congress had no way to accomplish this legitimate end other than by restricting the liberties of the people. If, on the other hand, you take the Marshallian view of necessary as merely *convenient*, then making a choice among competing means of accomp-

---

[51] See G. Edward White, *The History of the Supreme Court of the United States,* (New York: Macmillan Publishing Co., 1988), 8:552–62 (describing contemporary criticisms of Marshall's opinion in *McCulloch*); Francis N. Stites, *John Marshall: Defender of the Constitution* (Boston: Little, Brown, & Co., 1981), 132–34 (same).

[52] Stephen Gardbaum, "Rethinking Constitutional Federalism," *Texas Law Review* 74 (1996): 814.

[53] 1 Cranch (5 U.S.) 137 (1803).

[54] See, e.g., authorities cited in notes 8–9 above.

lishing a legitimate end appears to be a matter of discretion properly left to legislative processes. As Madison himself wrote,

> [T]he expediency and constitutionality of means for carrying into effect a specified power are controvertible terms; and Congress are admitted to be judges of the expediency. The court certainly cannot be so; a question, the moment it assumes the character of mere expediency or policy, being evidently beyond the reach of judicial cognizance.[55]

In sum, a Madisonian or *strict* conception of necessity is a matter of constitutional *principle* and *within* the purview of judicial review, whereas a Marshallian or *loose* conception of necessity is a matter of legislative *policy* and *outside* the purview of courts.[56] Thus, the proper role of the courts in protecting the rights retained by the people from unnecessary infringement by government depends *both* on an assessment of legislative competence to assess the constitutionality of its enactments—in particular their necessity (and propriety)—and on which view of necessity one adopts.

Whatever the views of the ratifying generation, by the time of the 1819 Marshall Court, the loose conception of necessity prevailed. From then until today, we can understand the two major swings of attitude concerning judicial deference—the *Lochner* and post-New Deal eras—as reflecting an alternation between a more Madisonian and more Marshallian view of necessity.

The Rise and Fall of Means-End Scrutiny of Necessity

Notwithstanding the triumph of the Marshallian conception of necessity, the assumptions on which early judicial deference to legislatures rested began to be undermined at exactly the time it reached its ascendance. The antebellum concern over slavery eroded the widespread belief that legislatures—in particular, state legislatures—were so likely to honor the rights of their citizens that they merited a presumption in their favor. After the civil war, the enactment of the Fourteenth Amendment was specifically intended to subject state legislation to federal scrutiny to determine whether it violated the privileges or immunities of citizenship or whether it deprived any person of life, liberty, or property without due process or law.[57]

[55] Madison, "Letter to Judge Roane," 144.
[56] Cf. Ronald Dworkin, *Taking Rights Seriously* (Cambridge, MA: Harvard University Press, 1977), 22, 90–94 (distinguishing between principles and policies).
[57] See generally Michael Kent Curtis, *No State Shall Abridge: The Fourteenth Amendment and the Bill of Rights* (Durham, NC: Duke University Press, 1986) (discussing the origins of the Fourteenth Amendment).

Although the 5–4 decision in the *Slaughter House Cases* precluded the use of the Privileges or Immunities Clause for this purpose, it failed to suppress the growing skepticism of legislatures as deserving of a presumption of acting in good faith. At first, the skepticism surrounded the treatment of racial minorities. That is, until *Slaughterhouse* cut off one avenue of scrutiny via the Privileges or Immunities Clause, lower courts were less willing to presume that statutes adversely affecting blacks were constitutional simply because they were properly enacted.

Later in the century, sympathy grew among intellectuals and the public for socialism and wealth redistribution grew. As a result, some among the judiciary became increasingly skeptical that state legislation infringing upon the liberties of the people was really being enacted as a necessary means to protect health, safety, and morals. On the national level, they suspected, instead, that arguments of necessity were merely pretexts for transforming the original constitutional scheme of limited and enumerated constitutional powers into one that would make possible the growth of what we now know as the administrative state.

This skepticism of legislative motive culminated in *Lochner v. New York*.[58] In *Lochner* and other such cases, the Court began to require proof that federal and state legislatures infringing the retained liberties of the people were *actually* pursuing a legitimate purpose rather than merely *purporting* to do so. Like Madison, they began requiring of legislation a showing of actual means-end fit, rather than merely deferring to legislative judgment. When judicial deference is based on trust and trust is eroded, increased scrutiny follows.[59]

---

[58] 198 U.S. 45 (1905).

[59] After evaluating each of the rationales proffered on behalf of a statute limiting the hours a baker could work, the Court in *Lochner* concluded:

> It is impossible for us to shut our eyes to the fact that many of the laws of this character, while passed under what is claimed to be the police power for the purpose of protecting the public health or welfare, are, in reality, passed from other motives. We are justified in saying so when, from the character of the law and the subject upon which it legislates, it is apparent that the public health or welfare bears but the most remote relation to the law. . . . It is manifest to us that the limitation of the hours of labor as provided for in this section of the statute under which the indictment was found, and the plaintiff in error convicted, has no such direct relation to, and no such substantial effect upon, the health of the employee as to justify us in regarding the section as really a health law. It seems to us that the real object and purpose were simply to regulate the hours of labor between the master and his employees (all being men *sui juris*) in a private business, not dangerous in any degree to morals or in any real and substantial degree to the health of the employees.

Id. at 64.

As we all know, this era of means-end scrutiny came to a close as the perceived legitimacy of legislative activism continued to grow and, with it, the administrative state. What is not well known today is that the vehicle by which the *Lochner*-era precedent was overturned was the renewal of the presumption of constitutionality—an innovation urged by James Thayer in his 1893 *Harvard Law Review*[60] article—and eventually accepted by the Supreme Court due in part to the efforts of Justice Louis Brandeis. Brandeis's opinion in *Gorman and Young v. Hartford Insurance Co.*[61] used the presumption of constitutionality to put the burden of proof on those challenging a statute:

> The statute here questioned deals with a subject clearly within the scope of the police power. We are asked to declare it void on the ground that the specific method of regulation prescribed is unreasonable and hence deprives the plaintiff of due process of law. As underlying questions of fact may condition the constitutionality of legislation of this character, the presumption of constitutionality must prevail in the absence of some factual foundation of record for overthrowing the statute.[62]

One contemporary of Brandeis, Walton Hamilton, writing glowingly in the *Columbia Law Review,* noted that the rejection of means-end scrutiny was accomplished merely by adopting a presumption in favor of the legislature:

> The demand is to find an escape from the recent holdings predicated upon "freedom of contract" as "the rule," from which a departure is to be allowed only in exceptional cases. The occasion calls not for the deft use of tactics, but for a larger strategy. The device of presumptions is almost as old as law; Brandeis revives the presumption that acts of a state legislature are valid and applies it to statutes regulating business activity. *The factual brief has many times been employed to make a case for social legislation;* Brandeis demands of the opponents of legislative acts a recitation of fact showing that the evil did not exist or that the remedy was inappropriate. He appeals from precedents to more venerable precedents, reverses the rules of presumption and proof in cases involving the control of industry; and sets up a realistic test of constitutionality. It is all done with such legal verisimilitude that a discussion of par-

---

[60] Thayer, "Origin and Scope," 144: "[T]here is often a range of choice and judgment [and] in such cases the constitution does not impose upon the legislature any one specific opinion, but leaves open this range of choice; and that whatever choice is rational is constitutional."

[61] *Gorman and Young v. Hartford Insurance Co.*, 282 U.S. 251 (1931).

[62] 282 U.S. at 257–58.

ticular cases is unnecessary; it all seems obvious—once Brandeis
has shown how the trick is done. It is attended with so little fanfare
of judicial trumpets that it might have passed almost unnoticed,
save for the dissenters, who usurp the office of the Greek tragedy
and comment upon the action. Yet the argument which degrades
"freedom of contract" to a constitutional doctrine of the second
magnitude is compressed into a single compelling paragraph.[63]

In the passage italicized, it is not clear whether Hamilton was
noting or simply missing the irony of the person lauded for bringing
"realism" to judicial proceedings via the "Brandeis Brief,"[64] adopting
a presumption that would fictitiously impute a rational basis to any
legislative decision. And who "realistically" is in the best position to
present to a court empirical information for or against the necessity
of a statute: Agencies of government or an affected individual or company? Those who have already succeeded in lobbying Congress to
enact legislation, or those who lost?

As Hamilton notes, the protests of the dissenters in *Gorman* make
it clear that the presumption of constitutionality was being used by
Brandeis to avoid the means-end scrutiny of the necessity of interfer-
ing with a citizen's liberty (albeit at the state level) that had previously
been required by the court. After rejecting the suggestion that "the
burden of establishing any underlying disputable fact rests upon the
appellant before it can successfully challenge the validity of the questioned enactment,"[65] the dissent argued that "[i]n order to justify
the denial of the right to make private contracts, some special circumstances sufficient to indicate the *necessity* therefor must be shown by
the party relying upon the denial."[66]

[63] Walton H. Hamilton, "The Jurist's Art," *Columbia Law Review* 31 (1931):
1074–75 (emphasis added).

[64] This term refers to the technique, pioneered by Brandeis as counsel in *Muller
v. Oregon* (208 U.S. 412 (1908)), of responding to the *Lochner*-era requirement to
show means-ends fit by presenting the courts with a variety of empirical evidence
purporting to show the necessity of economic legislation. The portion of Brandeis's famous brief in *Muller* devoted to this task ran some 95 pages. In light of
Hamilton's gushing praise for Brandeis' use of presumptions and the widespread
acceptance of the presumption of constitutionality ever since, it is tempting to
view the continuing veneration of Brandeis' "realist" tactics as a lawyer as merely
agreement with the outcome it was being used to promote, rather than as a sin-
cere endorsement of this method of evaluating the necessity of legislation. See
John W. Johnson, "Brandeis Brief," in Kermit L. Hall, ed., *The Oxford Companion
to the Supreme Court of the United States* (Oxford: Oxford University Press, 1992), 85
[hereinafter cited as *Oxford Companion*].

[65] 282 U.S. at 265.
[66] Id. at 269 (emphasis added).

We are accustomed to thinking that the issues raised by the *Lochner* era involve the Due Process Clause of the Fourteenth Amendment with regard to means-end scrutiny of state legislation, and the Commerce Clause with regard to the Congress' power to regulate commercial activity. However, Stephen Gardbaum has recently argued that, with respect to federal powers,

> the New Deal Court's own constitutional justification for its radical expansion of the scope of federal power over commerce was that the congressional measures in question were valid exercises of the power granted by the Necessary and Proper Clause and were not direct exercises of the power to regulate commerce among the several states. That is, the Court did not simply and directly enlarge the scope of the Commerce Clause itself, as is often believed. Rather, it upheld various federal enactments as necessary and proper means to achieve the legitimate objective of regulating interstate commerce.[67]

In this manner, the Court used the long-accepted Marshallian conception of necessity to expand its power to regulate commerce among the states.

Gardbaum offers several examples to support this claim. One is Justice Stone's opinion in the 1941 case of *United States v. Darby*,[68] in which *McCulloch v. Maryland* is cited by Stone in support of the following position:

> The power of Congress over interstate commerce is not confined to the regulation of commerce among the states. It extends to those activities intrastate which so affect interstate commerce . . . as to make regulation of them appropriate means to the attainment of a legitimate end, the exercise of the granted power of Congress to regulate interstate commerce. See McCulloch v. Maryland. . . .[69]

Later in this opinion Stone makes clear that he favors deference to Congress' judgment of a measure's necessity:

> Congress, having by the present Act adopted the policy of excluding from interstate commerce all goods produced for the commerce which do not conform to the specified labor standards, it

[67] Gardbaum, "Rethinking Constitutional Federalism," 807–08.
[68] 312 U.S. 100 (1941).
[69] Id. at 118, 118–19 [citing *McCulloch v. Maryland*, 17 U.S. (4 Wheat.) 316, 421 (1819)].

may choose the means reasonably adapted to the attainment of the permitted end, even though they involve control of intrastate activities. Such legislation has often been sustained with respect to powers, other than the commerce power granted to the national government, when the means chosen, although not themselves within the granted power, were nevertheless deemed appropriate aids to the accomplishment of some purpose within an admitted power of the national government.[70]

Gardbaum also notes that, among "the relatively few observers to acknowledge the basis on which the New Deal Court expanded federal power" was Justice O'Connor in her dissent in *Garcia v. San Antonio Metro. Transit Authority*:[71]

> The Court based the expansion [of the commerce power] on the authority of Congress, through the Necessary and Proper Clause, "to resort to all means for the exercise of a granted power which are appropriate and plainly adapted to the permitted end." It is through this reasoning that an intrastate activity "affecting" interstate commerce can be reached through the commerce power. . . . [A]nd the reasoning of these cases underlies every recent decision concerning the reach of Congress to activities affecting interstate commerce.[72]

The only thing Gardbaum fails to note (explicitly) is that using the Necessary and Proper Clause, as interpreted by Marshall's opinion in *McCulloch*, to expand federal power was also facilitated doctrinally by adopting a presumption of constitutionality in favor of congressional judgment.

The Limited Revival of Means-Ends Scrutiny via Footnote 4

When the Court in 1937 finally abandoned entirely the means-end scrutiny of regulation in the economic sphere by employing Brandeis' technique of shifting the presumption of constitutionality to one favoring all such legislation,[73] it immediately became necessary to establish some limits on this burden-shifting technique lest it swallow the entire constitutional practice of judicial review. This feat was accomplished one year later in the 1938 case of *United States v. Car-*

---

[70] Id. at 121.
[71] *Garcia v. San Antonio Metro. Transit Auth.*, 469 U.S. 528 (1985).
[72] Id. at 584–85 (O'Connor, J., dissenting).
[73] See *West Coast Hotels Co. v. Parrish*, 300 U.S. 379 (1937).

olene Products,[74] which concerned legislative restrictions on the sale of a milk substitute that competed with the product of dairy farmers. In the text of Justice Stone's opinion that immediately preceded the now-famous "Footnote Four,"[75] the court clearly asserted the presumption of constitutionality. "[T]he existence of facts supporting legislative judgment is to be presumed," it said,

> for regulatory legislation affecting ordinary commercial transactions is not to be pronounced unconstitutional unless in the light of the facts made known or generally assumed it is of such a character as to preclude the assumption that it rests upon some rational basis within the knowledge and experience of the legislators.[76]

With this in mind, we are now in a better position to appreciate fully the theory of Footnote 4 which began as follows:

> There may be a narrower scope for operation of the presumption of constitutionality when legislation appears on its face to be within a specific prohibition of the Constitution, such as those of the first ten amendments, which are deemed equally specific when held to be embraced within the Fourteenth.[77]

Thus, in Footnote 4 we have enunciated the modern theory of constitutional rights: adopt a Marshallian conception of necessity and presume all acts of legislatures to be valid, except when an enumerated right listed in the Bill of Rights is infringed (or when legislation affects the political process or discrete and insular minorities[78]), in which event the Court will employ a Madisonian conception of neces-

---

[74] 304 U.S. 144 (1938).
[75] The fame of this footnote is illustrated by the fact it merits its own entry in *The Oxford Companion to the Supreme Court of the United States*. See *Oxford Companion*, 306–07.
[76] *West Coast Hotels*, 304 U.S. at 152.
[77] Id. at 152 n.4.
[78] The rest of Footnote 4 adds:
It is unnecessary to consider no whether legislation which restricts those political processes which can ordinarily be expected to bring about repeal of undesirable legislation, is to be subjected to more exacting judicial scrutiny under the general prohibitions of the Fourteenth Amendment than are most other types of legislation.
   Nor need we enquire whether similar considerations enter into the review of statutes directed at particular religions, . . . or national, . . . or racial minorities . . . ; whether prejudice against discrete and insular minorities may be a special condition, which tends seriously to curtail the operation of those political processes ordinarily to be relied upon to protect minorities, and which may call for a correspondingly more searching judicial inquiry. . . .
Id. at 152–53 n.4.

sity and require of Congress a showing of means-ends fit. And subsequent cases have made the presumption in favor of legislation nearly irrebuttable, except when a fundamental enumerated right is at issue, in which event few statutes will withstand the "strict scrutiny" of both means and ends that will then be applied.

Indeed, the main reason why *Griswold v. Connecticut*[79] and *Roe v. Wade*[80] were so controversial among constitutional scholars when they were decided was because the right to privacy was the first right since *Carolene Products* to be protected as fundamental that was *not* "within a specific prohibition of the Constitution." Thus the right to privacy was controversial from the very first, not because it ran afoul of the original intent of either the initial Constitution or the Fourteenth Amendment, and not so much because it was used to protect contraceptives or abortion, but because it violated the post-New Deal jurisprudence of *Carolene Products* governing the presumption of constitutionality. And, ironically, no group has been more faithful to this twentieth century innovation than the modern judicial conservative proponents of original intent.[81]

Of course, the *Carolene Products* theory of constitutional rights neglects both the Ninth Amendment and the Privileges or Immunities Clause of the Fourteenth. Why is it that only the "specific prohibitions of the Constitution" may shift the presumption of constitutionality, when the Ninth Amendment declares that "The enumeration in the Constitution of certain rights shall not be construed to deny or disparage others retained by the people."[82] Disparaging the unenumerable liberties protected by the rights retained by the people by construing a Marshallian conception of necessity whenever government infringes upon them is *exactly* what Footnote 4 attempts to accomplish.

B. *The Meaning of "Proper"*

To this point, however, I have only addressed one portion of the Necessary and Proper Clause, the requirement of necessity. What

[79] 381 U.S. 479 (1965).

[80] 410 U.S. 113 (1973).

[81] See, e.g., Robert H. Bork, *The Tempting of America: The Political Seduction of the Law* (New York: The Free Press, 1990), 60:

One hardly knows what to make of the tentativeness with which Stone suggests that the Court might be less deferential to the legislature if the legislation appears to be specifically prohibited by the Constitution. Of course, review should be more stringent if the Constitution reads on a subject than if it does not. That distinction should spell the difference between review and no review.

[82] U.S. Constitution, amend. 9.

about the need to show that a measure is also proper? In what respect could a measure that was shown to be truly necessary to the effectuation of an enumerated purpose ever be *im*proper? Would a meaningful means-end scrutiny of the necessity of a restriction on the liberties of the people make an assessment of its propriety superfluous?

In Chief Justice Marshall's opinion in *McCulloch*, he purports to treat the issue of propriety as distinct from that of necessity: "Let the end be legitimate, let it be within the scope of the constitution, and all means *which are appropriate, which are plainly adapted to that end, which are not prohibited, but consist with the letter and spirit of the constitution,* are constitutional."[83] Gardbaum agrees with Justice O'Connor's opinion that this passage reflects a distinction between a determination of an act's necessity (which, according to Marshall, is a matter of legislative discretion) and its propriety (which presumably Marshall thought may be reviewable by a court): "It is not enough that the 'end be legitimate'; the means to that end chosen by Congress must not contravene the spirit of the Constitution."[84] Indeed, writing pseudononymously in a newspaper as "A Friend of the Union," Marshall defended his opinion in *McCulloch* by emphasizing this point:

> In no single instance does the court admit the unlimited power of congress to adopt any means whatever, and thus to pass the limits prescribed by the Constitution. Not only is the discretion claimed for the legislature in the selection of its means, always limited to such as are appropriate, but the court expressly says, "should congress under the pretext of executing its powers, pass laws for the accomplishment of objects, not entrusted to the government, it would become the painful duty of this tribunal . . . to say that such an act was not the law of the land.[85]

This leads to the question: *what could make a law that is necessary in the Madisonian sense nonetheless improper?* After an extensive examination of sources from the founding era, Gary Lawson and Patricia Granger proposed the following answer:

[83] *McCulloch*, 17 U.S. (4 Wheat.) at 421, emphasis added.
[84] *Garcia*, 469 U.S. at 585 (O'Connor, J. dissenting). See Gardbaum, "Rethinking Constitutional Federalism," 816.
[85] "A Friend of the Constitution" [Marshall], reprinted in Gerald Gunther, ed., *John Marshall's Defense of McCulloch v. Maryland* (Stanford, CA: Stanford University Press, 1969), 187. Madison doubted the effectiveness of this stated constraint: "But suppose Congress should, as would doubtless happen, pass unconstitutional laws, not to accomplish objects not specified in the Constitution, but the same laws as means expedient, convenient, or conducive to the accomplishment of objects entrusted to government; by what handle could the court take hold of the case?" Madison, "Letter to Judge Roane," 144.

In view of the limited character of the national government under the Constitution, Congress's choice of means to execute federal powers would be constrained in at least three ways: first, an executory law would have to conform to the "proper" allocation of authority within the federal government; second, such a law would have to be within the "proper" scope of the federal government's limited jurisdiction with respect to the retained prerogatives of the states; and third, the law would have to be within the "proper" scope of the federal government's limited jurisdiction with respect to the people's retained rights. In other words, . . . executory laws must be consistent with principles of separation of powers, principles of federalism, and individual rights.[86]

When Stephen Gardbaum considers the propriety of legislation, he focuses his attention on whether such laws are consistent with principles of federalism.[87] My concern here is instead with the last of these three ways by which, according to Lawson and Granger, laws could be improper: laws are improper if they violate the background rights retained by the people. If we adopt a Marshallian conception of necessity it is easy to see how the exercise of such a discretionary power might violate the background rights retained by the people— though this reintroduces under the rubric of propriety many of the difficulties Marshall argued attach to a strict construction of necessity.[88] Adopting a Madisonian conception of necessity, however, raises the following potential difficulty: If a restriction of liberty *is* shown to be truly necessary, in the Madisonian sense, to put into execution an enumerated power, in what way can it be considered an "improper" infringement on these background rights? Have not the people surrendered to the national government the powers that were enumerated in Article I and any right inconsistent with the exercise of such powers?[89]

---

[86] Gary Lawson and Patricia Granger, "The 'Proper' Scope of Federal Power: A Jurisdictional Interpretation of the Sweeping Clause," *Duke Law Journal* 43 (1993): 297.

[87] See Gardbaum, "Rethinking Constitutional Federalism."

[88] Using either an "originalist" or "constructive" method, we would have to devise a theory of unenumerated rights of sufficient specificity to identify improper exercises of government power, in the way that the First Amendment identifies as improper infringements on the freedom of speech. See Barnett, "Reconceiving the Ninth Amendment," 30–38 (describing the originalist, constructive, and presumptive methods of interpreting unenumerated rights and how they are not mutually exclusive).

[89] The answer to this rhetorical question is not as obvious as it may at first seem. For the appropriate legal construct is not the surrender of rights to a master, but the delegation of powers to an agent. See, e.g., "A Friend of the Constitution,"

To answer this we must look to the enumerated power that is most often linked to the Necessary and Proper Clause and used to justify the administrative state. This is the power found in the Commerce Clause, which reads: "Congress shall have Power . . . To regulate Commerce with foreign Nations, and among the several States, and with Indian Tribes. . . ."[90] Special attention needs to be given the words "to regulate." Congress was not given the power *to prohibit* commerce but to regulate it. Unfortunately the power "to regulate" liberty has for so long been used as a euphemism for the power to prohibit its exercise that we have lost the original sense of the term.

To regulate means literally "to make regular." For example, we would regulate the making of a will by requiring that there be two witnesses. One is too few and three are more than enough. Such a "regulation" of wills tells people how they may effectuate their purposes in such a way as to conform to the expectations of other people. It would defeat the intentions of testators and be very bad for heirs to find after it is too late that a will lacked enough witnesses to make it enforceable. But to regulate or make regular will-making in this way is not to prohibit the making of wills or to refuse to honor the intentions they manifest. A power to regulate wills does not imply, for example, a power to tax or confiscate all bequests above a certain amount.

In general usage, 18th and 19th century Americans often used

211–12: "It is the plain dictate of common sense, and the whole political system is founded upon the idea, that the departments of government are the agents of the nation, and will perform, within their respective spheres, the duties assigned to them." When a principal engages an agent, the agent can be empowered to act on behalf of and subject to the control of the principal, while the principal retains all his rights. So, for example, a principal can empower the agent to sell the principal's car, while retaining the right to sell it himself. And the fact that the principal retains the right to sell his car is one reason that agents can be sued for failing to act on the principal's behalf or refusing to conform her actions to the principal's exercise of control. In normal agency relationships, the fact that an agent is empowered to act on the principal's behalf does not make the agent the sole judge of whether or not she is acting within the scope of her agency, as the Marshallian discretionary conception of necessity seems to do. Moreover the fact that some rights are inalienable suggests that those who purport to exercise them on behalf of another need justify their assumption of such power. See Randy E. Barnett, "Squaring Undisclosed Agency Law with Contract Theory," *California Law Review* 75 (1981): 1969: "A principal who authorizes his agent to act 'on his behalf' consensually empowers the agent to exercise certain rights that the principal alone would normally exercise." See also Randy E. Barnett, "Contract Remedies and Inalienable Rights," *Social Philosophy & Policy* 4 (Autumn 1986): 179–202 (defining inalienable rights and providing four reasons why some rights are inalienable).

[90] U.S. Constitution, art. 1, sec. 8.

"regulate" not in the sense of legal prohibition but rather in the now less prominent uses given by Webster's:

> 2. to adjust to some standard or requirement, as amount, degree, etc.: *to regulate the temperature.* 3. to adjust so as to assure accuracy of operation: *to regulate a watch.* 4 to put in good order: *to regulate the digestion.*[91]

Consistent with this, President James Polk used "well-regulated" to mean operating in good order, correctly or properly, referring to "well-regulated self-government among men."[92]

For this reason it was not a contradiction for the Second Amendment to defend "the right of the people to keep and bear arms" as instrumental to securing the existence of "a *well-regulated* militia." "In eighteenth century military usage, 'well regulated' meant 'properly disciplined', not 'government controlled.' "[93] The 18th century usage of "regulate" had the more specialized meaning of "practiced in the use of arms, properly trained and/or disciplined." Thus we find Alexander Hamilton in *Federalist* no. 29 referring to "a well-regulated militia" as one that has been sufficiently drilled.[94] To empower the national government to see that the militia was "well-regulated" conferred upon it neither the power to prohibit the states from forming militias, nor the power to prohibit the private possession of firearms.[95]

So too with the Commerce Power. The power "to regulate" com-

---

[91] *Webster's Encyclopedic Unabridged Dictionary of the English Language* 1209 (1989) (italics in original).

[92] James Polk, "Inaugural Address" (1845) in Davis N. Lott, *The Presidents Speak: the Inaugural Addresses of American Presidents* (New York: Holt, Rinehart & Winston, 1961), 90.

[93] Nelson Lund, "The Second Amendment, Political Liberty and the Right to Self-Preservation," *Alabama Law Review* 39 (1987): 107 n.8.

[94] Hamilton assumes this meaning throughout Federalist 29, but it is made most explicit when he is discussing his reasons why Congress will not undertake to discipline "all the militia of the United States," pursuant to its powers under Art. I, sec. 8 ("to provide for organizing, arming, and disciplining the militia, and for governing such parts of them as may be employed in the service of the United States"):
> To oblige the great body of the yeomanry, and of the other classes of citizens, to be under arms for the purpose of going through military exercises and evolutions, *as often as might be necessary to acquire the degree of perfection which would entitle them to the character of a well-regulated militia,* would be a real grievance to the people, and a serious public inconvenience and loss.
Federalist no. 29, 78 (emphasis added).

[95] Citations to the extensive recent scholarship on the Second Amendment can be found in Randy E. Barnett & Don Kates, "Under Fire: The New Consensus on the Second Amendment," *Emory Law Journal* 45 (1996) 1139–1259.

merce among the states is the power to make such commerce regular; it is not the power to prohibit commerce any more than the power to make regular the flow of water entails the power to shut off the flow. According to this distinction between regulation and prohibition, it is not a violation of the rights retained by the people for government to provide for genuinely necessary regulations of the exercise of liberty.[96] But the power to regulate does not include the power to prohibit the rightful exercise of liberty.[97]

Thus for a law to be both "necessary and proper" to effectuate the Commerce Power, it must be a regulation that is truly *necessary*, but it must also be *proper* insofar as it is a regulation of commerce and not a prohibition. A genuine regulation that is unnecessary violates this clause, and a law that purports to regulate, but is really intended as a prohibition also violates the clause. Whereas the Ninth Amendment argues against a latitudinarian interpretation of a measure's necessity, both the Ninth and Tenth Amendments argue against a latitudinarian interpretation of whether a measure falls within the enumeration of powers and is proper. In this manner, even had no Bill of Rights ever been enacted, the Necessary and Proper Clause would give the judiciary the power to protect the rights retained by the people.

II. Effectuating the Necessary And Proper Clause

We are now in a position to see how the Necessary and Proper Clause may be made effectual. The only doctrine preventing mean-

[96] Of course a regulation will of necessity "prohibit" all actions that do not conform to its requirements and this will unavoidably lead to hard cases where it is difficult to discern whether the real purpose of a law is to regulate as opposed to being a pretext for a prohibition. But easy cases of unconstitutional prohibitions of liberty will exist as well and the ability to address them is well worth making the effort to distinguish regulation from prohibition.

[97] By a "rightful" exercise of liberty I mean an action which does not violate the rights of others. So, for example, the (enumerated) natural right of freedom of speech does not prevent the legal prohibition of fraud. As natural rights theorist John Locke argued,

But though this be a *State of Liberty*, yet it is *not a State of Licence*. . . . The *State of Nature* has a Law of Nature to govern it, which obliges every one: And Reason, which is that Law, teaches all Mankind, who will but consult it, that being all equal and independent, no one ought to harm another in his Life, Health, Liberty, or Possessions.

John Locke, *Two Treatises of Government* (1690), ed. Peter Laslett, rev. ed. (New York: New American Library, 1963), 311. Though more needs to be said about this than can be said here, comparatively few of all governmental interferences with liberty can reasonably be justified as the prohibition of rights-violating or "wrongful" behavior, and few such justifications on their behalf are even offered.

ingful scrutiny of the necessity and propriety of legislation infringing upon personal or economic liberties (whether or not these liberties are enumerated in the Constitution) is the setting of the background interpretive presumption. There are at least four distinguishable approaches towards legislation that one may take: First is the *laissez-faire* approach of complete judicial deference: adopt a general presumption of constitutionality towards *all* legislation affecting the liberties of the people. Second is the original *Carolene Products* approach: adopt a presumption of constitutionality to legislation that does not infringe upon only those liberties that are specified in the Bill of Rights. Third is the current approach: adopt the *Carolene Products* approach, but add protection for the right of privacy and perhaps other selected unenumerated rights deemed to be fundamental. We may call this approach *Carolene Products-plus*. Fourth is my proposal: adopt a *general presumption of liberty* which places the burden on the government to establish the necessity and propriety of any infringement on individual or associational freedom.

To adopt the *laissez-faire* approach would be to make Congress the sole judge of its own powers in every dispute between it and a citizen concerning the necessity and propriety of a legislative interference with the citizen's rightful exercise of liberty. Essentially it would eliminate judicial review of legislation infringing on constitutional liberties, including those enumerated in the Bill of Rights. Consequently, few advocate this position and it has never been accepted as the correct approach to judicial review.

Adopting the original *Carolene Products* approach is also deeply problematic. First, it flies in the face of the many unenumerated rights that have received protection from the Supreme Court for well over a hundred years—such as the right to travel (which had been enumerated in the Articles of Confederation), and the right to provide one's children with religious education or education on one's native language.[98] This approach directly conflicts as well with the unenumerated right to privacy that has been explicitly protected for over thirty years.[99] Finally, the *Carolene Products* approach is undercut by the text of the Ninth and Fourteenth Amendments.

The present *Carolene Products-plus* approach is also objectionable. With it judges now find themselves in the uneasy position of having to pick and choose among the unenumerated liberties of the people

[98] See Walter F. Murphy, James E. Fleming, & William F. Harris, *American Constitutional Interpretation* (Mineola, NY: Foundation Press, 1986), 1083–84 (listing unenumerated rights that have been recognized by the Supreme Court).

[99] See, e.g., *Griswold v. Connecticut*, 381 U.S. 479 (1965).

to find those that justify switching the presumption and those that do not. This places courts in the uncomfortable position of making essentially moral assessments of different exercises of liberty. A liberty to take birth control pills is protected, but a liberty to take marijuana is not. The business of performing abortions is protected, the business of providing transportation is not. What "protected" means is in this context is that a particular exercise of liberty is sufficient to rebut the presumption of constitutionality and then the government must establish that such legislation is both necessary and proper.

With the 1992 decision in *Planned Parenthood v. Casey*,[100] there is virtually no chance that this Supreme Court will retreat all the way back to a purified *Carolene Products* approach in the near future. In *Casey*, the Court strongly asserted that "[i]t is a promise of the Constitution that there is a realm of personal liberty which the government may not enter. We have vindicated this principle before."[101] In support of this assertion the court cited several cases including the two surviving *Lochner* era cases of *Pierce v. Society of Sisters*[102] and *Meyer v. Nebraska*,[103] each of which scrutinized legislation infringing upon unenumerated rights. The Court in *Casey* explicitly relied upon the Ninth Amendment to justify the protection of unenumerated liberties under the Fourteenth Amendment. As Justices Kennedy, O'Connor, and Souter wrote:

> Neither the Bill of Rights nor the specific practices of States at the time of the adoption of the Fourteenth Amendment marks the outer limits of the substantive sphere of liberty which the Fourteenth Amendment protects. See U. S. Const., Amend. 9.[104]

The principled alternative to a consistent presumption of constitutionality or an ad hoc *Carolene Products*-plus approach is to shift the presumption of constitutionality when legislation affects *any* exercise of liberty. Such a *presumption of liberty* would place the burden on the government to show why its interference with liberty is both necessary and proper rather than, as now, imposing a burden on the citizen to show why the exercise of a particular liberty is a fundamental right. No where does the constitution speak of fundamental (as distinct

[100] 112 S.Ct. 2791 (1992).
[101] Id. at 2805.
[102] 268 U.S. 510 (1925).
[103] 262 U.S. 390 (1923).
[104] 112 S.Ct. at 2805.

from nonfundamental) rights,[105] but it does speak of all laws being necessary *and* proper.

As I have explained at greater length elsewhere,[106] whenever government interferes with a rightful exercise of a citizen's liberty, it should have to bear the burden of showing (a) that its objectives are proper and (b) that it cannot accomplish these objectives by means that do not restrict the liberties of the people and, for this reason, its actions are also necessary. If a particular interference with liberty is truly necessary and proper, then this is not too much to ask of government officials. A "rightful exercise of liberty" is one that does not violate the rights of any other citizen. It roughly corresponds to what courts refer to as a "liberty interest," except that, at present, liberty interests are not protected unless they are also deemed to be fundamental rights. No court today would find an action that violated the rights of others to be a "liberty interest."

Would this not mean, however, that unelected federal judges with lifetime tenure would be asked to speculate about "the rights of man"? What qualifies them to determine what learned philosophers disagree about? Where in their legal education or experience did they gain expertise in distinguishing rightful from wrongful conduct? A moment's reflection should dissipate such concerns. I would not expect federal judges assessing the necessity and propriety of legislation to distinguish *ab initio* between those actions that are rightful exercises of liberty and those that are not. Rather, in our legal order, distinguishing rightful from wrongful conduct is generally made every working day at the state level—or in federal courts operating in diversity cases in which they try to follow state law. Indeed, at least a quarter of a law student's legal education is devoted to this subject in courses such as contracts, torts, property, agency and partnership, secured transactions, commercial paper, portions of criminal law, etc. Ever since the forms of action were abolished, the concepts provided in these subject areas have been used to assess the merits of claims that one person has violated the rights of another.

I am not suggesting that I agree with all the current rules and principles that currently define a person's rights—that is why I teach and write about contract law—or even the exact process by which such decisions are currently made. Rather, I am only providing an

[105] Except to note that the enumeration of certain rights "shall not be construed to deny or disparage others retained by the people." See U.S. Constitution, amend. 9.
[106] See Barnett, "Getting Normative," 113–21.

answer to the question of how, as a practical matter, decisions about rightful and wrongful conduct are to be made. My answer: Such decisions should be made for better or worse, the way these distinctions are made at present. There is today a healthy division of labor between state court processes and federal diversity cases assessing the rights of the people against each other, and federal constitutional adjudication that protects the rights of the people from infringement by government. It is only when federal judges are asked to distinguish protected fundamental rights from unprotected "liberty interests," as they must do under the current *Carolene Products*-plus approach, that they arguably exceed the boundaries of their competence.

When assessing the practicality of this proposal, one must keep in mind two facts. First, very little legislation at the federal or state level even purports to be defining and prohibiting wrongful behavior—that is, behavior by one person that violates the rights of another. Rather, legislation is typically claiming to "regulate" the exercise of rightful conduct or to prohibit rightful conduct altogether so as to achieve some "compelling state interest" or social policy. To use the distinction made popular by Ronald Dworkin,[107] legislation rarely concerns matters of principle, and usually concerns matters of policy. Moreover, it simply is not the case that every claim of government power can plausibly be recast in terms of vindicating some individual's rights.

Second, not all laws restrict the liberties of the people. The many laws that regulate the internal operation of government agencies or the dispensation of government funds, for example, would be unaffected by a presumption of liberty. When the post office sets its hours of operation or the price of its postage stamps, it is not restricting the rightful liberties of the citizenry any more than a private organization that does the same. If heightened scrutiny of the necessity and propriety of such laws is warranted,[108] as it may very well be, it would have

[107] Dworkin, *Taking Rights Seriously*, 22, 90–94.

[108] I do not address in this essay the issue of when, if ever, conditioning the receipt of government benefits or employment on the waiver of one's background rights should be protected by a presumption of liberty. See generally Richard A. Epstein, *Bargaining with the State* (1993) (discussing the appropriate limits on the power of government to bargain with its citizens). Whether or not such so-called "unconstitutional conditions" violate the rights retained by the people, however, they may be insidious or "improper" enough in their own right to justify shifting the presumption of constitutionality, thereby placing the burden on the government to show that such conditions are both necessary and proper. So too with laws that unnecessarily or improperly infringe upon principles of federalism or separation of powers, though it is not clear that states or branches of the federal government require the same degree of protection as do individuals.

to be justified on grounds other than that the laws in question potentially infringe upon the rights retained by the people.[109]

On the other hand, when Congress asserts that to effectuate its power "to establish post offices,"[110] it is necessary and proper to grant a legal monopoly to its post office, those companies who wish to carry first class mail are entitled to demand that Congress or the executive demonstrate the necessity and propriety of such a restriction on liberty. As Madison argued with respect to the national bank, "It is a monopoly, which affects the equal rights of every citizen."[111] Similarly when Congress asserts that to effectuate its power "to raise and support Armies,"[112] it is necessary and proper to draft young men or women to serve in the military, those who are subject to this form of involuntary servitude are entitled to demand that Congress or the executive demonstrate to the satisfaction of an independent tribunal of justice that armies cannot be raised by using volunteers.

Perhaps there are times when post offices cannot be provided without granting a monopoly, or when an all-volunteer army is insufficient for the defense of the United States. When it seeks to put competitors out of business or draft young men or women, however, a presumption of liberty would put the onus on Congress to demonstrate that this is one of those times. In my view, when pressed with cases of genuine necessity, courts would not hesitate to uphold legislation as necessary. Indeed, even were a presumption of liberty to be adopted, I think government-employed judges are far more likely to uphold unnecessary restrictions on liberty than to strike down a law that is truly necessary.

Using a general presumption of liberty to effectuate the Necessary and Proper Clause can be justified, not only on the grounds that it gets the court out of the business of picking and choosing among the liberties of the people, and not only on the grounds that it is more harmonious with the text (and original meaning) of the Ninth and Fourteenth Amendments. It can also be justified as a more realistic presumption in light of what we know of legislative behavior. After

---

Perhaps it is enough to recognize that such laws may be stricken as unnecessary or improper without shifting the presumption of constitutionality. I take no position on these matters here.

[109] For example, heightened scrutiny of the necessity of laws that tell state government how they are to behave might be justified as infringing the powers reserved to the states or to the people mentioned by the Tenth Amendment. Heightened scrutiny of laws might also be warranted when laws appear to violate the Equal Protection Clauses of the Fifth and Fourteenth Amendments.

[110] U.S. Constitution, art. 1, sec. 8.

[111] *Annals of Congress*, 1:1900 (statement of Rep. Madison).

[112] U.S. Constitution, art. 1, sec. 10.

all, the original justification of the presumption of constitutionality rested, in part, on a belief that legislatures will consider carefully, accurately, and in good faith the constitutional protections of liberty before infringing it. It assumes that legislatures really do assess the necessity and propriety of legislation before enacting it. In recent decades, however, we have remembered the problem of faction that at least some of the framers never forgot.[113] We now understand much better (or are more willing to admit) than our post-New Deal predecessors on the left and on the right that both minorities and majorities can successfully assert their interests in the legislative process to gain enactments that serve their own interests rather then being necessary and proper.

In short, our understanding of the facts on which the presumption of constitutionality rests has changed. And, with this change in its factual underpinnings, the presumption—*which appears nowhere in the constitutional text*—must fall. Statutes that emerge from the legislative process are not entitled to the deference they now receive unless there is some reason to think that they are a product of necessity, rather than mere interest. And a statutory *prohibition* of liberty will not be presumed to be an appropriate *regulation*. Statutes do not create a duty of obedience in the citizenry simply because they are enacted. Without some meaningful assurance of necessity and propriety, statutes are to be obeyed merely because the consequences of disobedience are onerous. This is an insidious view of statutes that undermines respect for all law.

The only way that statutes may create a *prima facie* duty of obedience in the citizenry is if some agency not affected by interest will scrutinize them to ensure that they are both necessary and proper. However imperfect they may be, only courts are available to perform this function. Without judicial review, statutes are mere exercises of will, and are not entitled to the same presumption of respect that attaches to statutes surviving meaningful scrutiny.[114]

This is not to say that scrutiny must be strict. A standard of review that no statute can pass is as hypocritical as a standard of review that every statute can pass. Rather, some form of intermediate means-ends fit indicating *necessity*, and an assessment of a measure's *propriety* to see if its intention is really to regulate rather than prohibit an exercise of liberty, would be an important step towards both restoring legitimacy to legislation and protecting the liberties of the people.

[113] See note 3 above.
[114] See Barnett, "Getting Normative" (arguing that for laws to bind in conscience, they must not violate the background natural rights retained by the people).

I have previously recommended the presumption of liberty as a means of implementing the Ninth Amendment's protection of unenumerated rights retained by the people.[115] This symmetry is no coincidence. For the Necessary and Proper Clause can and should be viewed as creating a textual limit on congressional power that served to protect these unenumerated rights from infringement. Recall that, when this clause was enacted, the Bill of Rights had yet to be proposed or ratified.[116] For two years *all* of the natural rights retained by the people were unenumerated rights. The only legal standard protecting them from infringement was that "all Laws . . . for carrying into Execution the . . . powers" of the national government shall be "necessary and proper."[117]

Further, as Madison argued, the Ninth Amendment can be viewed as precluding a latitudinarian interpretation of the Necessary and Proper Clause.[118] Gary Lawson and Patricia Granger have concluded: "The Ninth Amendment potentially does refer to unenumerated rights, but the [Necessary and Proper] Clause's requirement that laws be 'proper' means that Congress never had the delegated power to violate those rights in the first place."[119] Thus it is should come as no surprise that both the Ninth Amendment and the Necessary and Proper Clause can be effectuated at the same time and in the same manner.

CONCLUSION

When establishing government, the people retained the natural rights that protect their liberties. This much is established textually by the Ninth Amendment. When enacted statutes receive the benefit of an extratextual presumption of constitutionality, however, the people have no reason to be confident that their rights have been respected, and therefore the legitimacy of legislation—that is, its ability to bind the citizenry in conscience—is severely undermined. A presumption of liberty, on the other hand, protects these rights from the administrative state by giving effect to the Necessary and Proper

[115] See Barnett, "Introduction: Implementing the Ninth Amendment," 10–19; and Barnett,"Getting Normative," 113–121.

[116] See Lawson and Granger, "The 'Proper' Scope," 267–70 (discussing whether the Constitution prohibited takings without just compensation prior to the ratification of the Fifth Amendment and suggesting that, because of the Necessary and Proper Clause, it did).

[117] U.S. Constitution, art. 1, sec. 8.

[118] See note 25 above.

[119] Lawson and Granger, "The 'Proper' Scope," 273.

Clause in a manner that is consistent with the powers that are granted to the national government. With this presumption in effect, as citizens we can have increased confidence that because a particular enactment has been shown to be both necessary and proper, it does not constitute an unjust infringement on our liberties, and we owe it at least a prima facie duty of obedience.

OUTER LIMITS: THE COMMERCE CLAUSE AND JUDICIAL REVIEW

Robert P. George and Gerard V. Bradley

THE DEFINING FEATURE of judicial review since the New Deal has been the vindication of claims of individual and minority group rights over against the "collective interests" of "majorities."[1] Footnote 4 of the *Carolene Products* case is the kerygmatic statement: the rule of judicial deference to legislative choices is suspended where Bill of Rights freedoms or the interests of "discrete and insular minorities" are affected.[2] This approach to judicial review has been defended in its most expansive form by Ronald Dworkin.[3] Its purest judicial expression is probably in church-state cases, where the solitary atheist enjoys a "trump" right to still the religious expression in public space, including schools, of, in principle, the united voices of everyone else in the community.[4]

Judges since the New Deal have focused upon the limits of *all* public authority—national, state, local. A corollary development has been judicial quiescence where litigants' claims are rooted in the structure of our national government (separation of powers) or in state freedom from federal regulation (federalism). Most notably, judicial review of Congress's Article I, §8 power over interstate commerce reached the near-vanishing point in the 1986 *Garcia* decision.[5]

[1] See Robert P. George, *Making Men Moral: Civil Liberties and Public Morality* (Oxford: Clarendon Press, 1993), chap. 3.

[2] *United States v. Carolene Products*, 304 U.S. 144 (1938).

[3] See, e.g., Ronald Dworkin, *A Matter of Principle* (Cambridge: Harvard University Press, 1986); see also critical discussion in George, *Making Men Moral*, 83–109.

[4] See Gerard V. Bradley, "Religion and the Common Good," in *The Family, Civil Society and the State*, ed. Christopher Wolfe (forthcoming).

[5] *Garcia v. San Antonio Metropolitan Transit Authority*, 469 U.S. 528 (1985).

Interestingly, the champions of expansive judicial power in defense of putative individual rights—William Brennan, Thurgood Marshall, Harry Blackmun—have led the judicial retreat in federalism cases.

The leading criticism of the recent rights-oriented judicial activism has been methodological. Under the broad banner of "originalism," conservatives including Robert Bork, Antonin Scalia, and, now, Clarence Thomas have charged the Warren and Burger Courts with an unwarranted, even an unconstitutional, use of judicial power. Their criticism is that, all too often, judges have invalidated legislation as violative of alleged rights which cannot be discovered in the text of the Constitution or inferred from its logic, structure, or original understanding. Their charge is that the judges' largely undefended and, in any case, misguided philosophical predilections—and nothing more—have been the source of these putative rights.

We think that this charge is fair. We do not in this essay, however, offer a global defense of its accuracy. Our goal is the limited one of defending the recent revival of Commerce Clause jurisprudence in *United States v. Lopez*,[6] the Gun-Free School Zones Act case from 1995, against the allegation that its proponents—Rehnquist, Scalia, Thomas among them—are phony originalists. We aim to defend the "New Federalism" as instantiated in *Lopez* against the *Lopez* dissenters' claim that it is "judicial activism" of the sort the *Lopez* majority ordinarily criticizes as an unconstitutional usurpation.

Justice Souter claimed in his *Lopez* dissent that the Court held an "untenably expansive conception of judicial review,"[7] and that the *Lopez* holding was "an exercise in judicial activism."[8] Dissenting Justice Breyer said that the *Lopez* result was against the tradition of judicial interpretation of the Commerce Clause, save "one wrong turn subsequently corrected,"[9] and contrary to the great opinion of Chief Justice Marshall in the first Commerce Clause case, *Gibbons v. Ogden*.[10] Justice Souter likened the *Lopez* Court's protection of state autonomy to the discredited *Lochner* turn-of-the-century laissez faire jurisprudence,[11] a charge he repeated in the subsequent *Seminole Tribe* Eleventh Amendment case.[12] Souter there made the "phony originalism" charge most plainly: the *Seminole* majority, identical to the *Lopez* majority, was guilty of "subordinating" the "plain text" of the Constitu-

[6] *United States v. Lopez*, 115 S.Ct. 1624 (1995).
[7] Id. at 1652.
[8] Id. at 1655.
[9] Id. at 1665.
[10] *Gibbons v. Ogden*, 9 Wheat. 1 (1824).
[11] *Lopez*, 115 S.Ct. at 1652.
[12] *Seminole Tribe of Florida v. Florida*, 116 S.Ct. 1114 (1996).

tion to "principles untethered to any written provision."[13] Souter played, as had Breyer in *Lopez*, the *Lochner* card: "It is, in fact, remarkable that as we near the end of this century the Court should choose to open a new constitutional chapter in confining legislative judgments by resort to textually unwarranted common-law rules, for it was just this practice in the century's early decades that brought this Court to the nadir of competence that we identify with *Lochner v. New York*."[14]

I.

We aim to defend the result in *Lopez*—meaningful judicial limitation of Congress's power over interstate commerce—on originalist grounds. Our argument differs in some important respects from the originalist concurrence of Justice Thomas, and more so from the *Lopez* majority opinion (which was, in any event, more a rationalization of decided cases than an originalist argument). We shall defend, more exactly, an autonomous state police power against congressional usurpations under the authority allegedly granted to Congress by the interstate Commerce Clause.

We think that argument must be originalist because we believe that originalism is the soundest method for judicial construction of the Constitution. We have elsewhere explained and defended at length our general commitment to originalism.[15] We note here only that if we succeed in defending *Lopez* on originalist grounds, we will have met, in significant part, the leading criticism of originalism. Professor Henry Monaghan, who is sympathetic to originalism, put the criticism succinctly: insisting "upon original intent as the only legitimate standard for judicial decision making entails a massive repudiation of the present constitutional order."[16] The constitutional theorist must, in other words, make sense of an irrevocably nonoriginalist universe. We aim to show that the result in *Lopez* is both solidly grounded in an originalist jurisprudence *and* not an untenable resurrection of the past.

II.

In *Lopez* the Supreme Court for the first time since the New Deal invalidated a congressional regulation of private activity on the

[13] Id. at 1176–78.
[14] Id. at 1176.
[15] See, e.g., Gerard V. Bradley, "The Bill of Rights and Originalism," *University of Illinois Law Review* (1992): 417–43.
[16] Henry Monaghan, "Stare Decisis and Constitutional Adjudication," *Columbia Law Review* 88 (1988): 727.

ground that it was beyond the scope of Congress's power to regulate commerce among the states. The law struck down the Gun-Free School Zones Act, which made it a federal crime to possess a firearm near a school. The law did not, as federal criminal laws typically do, contain a jurisdictional rider: neither the firearm nor the act of possessing it near a school had to affect interstate commerce in order to allow for federal prosecution.

The *Lopez* majority identified "three broad categories of activity that Congress may regulate under its commerce power," the first two of which appear to be beyond judicial limitation. The majority allowed that with regard to 1) "the channels of interstate commerce" and 2) "intrastate activities" which "threat[en]" the "persons or things *in* interstate commerce," Congress may exercise a plenary police power.[17]

Let us call these two categories simply "interstate commerce." A clear case of (1) is interstate rail transportation. A clear case of (2) would be interruption of a budding conspiracy to hijack an airliner. They possess in common an obvious *purpose* to do something *about, for,* or *with* precisely that over which Congress has jurisdiction— interstate commerce.

That Congress enjoys "plenary police power" means not that Congress was, or is likely to, regulate exhaustively. In fact, Congress might exercise its plenary police power by abstention, by leaving, say, interstate trucking to be regulated by market forces. Or, Congress might authorize some regulation by states exercising a kind of concurrent jurisdiction. "Plenary police power" means that Congress possesses in principle *all* governmental power that *may* be exercised under the Constitution. The *Lopez* Court thus invites one to imagine "interstate commerce" as a module of national authority twisting its way through the states, a kind of District of Columbia in motion.

What then is the constitutional distinction between that "police power" denied to Congress because reserved to the states, and the limited, enumerated power of Congress over interstate commerce? The *Lopez* majority distinguished the limited congressional power both qualitatively and quantitatively. *All* "noneconomic" or "noncommercial" *intra*state activities are beyond the reach of Congress. Only those "commercial" or "economic" intrastate activities that "substantially affect" interstate commerce may be reached by Congress.[18] *Accord* Justice Thomas, concurring: Congress can regulate

---

[17] *Lopez*, 115 S.Ct. at 1629 (emphasis added).
[18] Id. at 1629–31.

only "intrastate commerce" that "substantially affects" interstate commerce.[19]

The *Lopez* majority defended this two-part limitation as the distillate of precedent. It was, the Court said, "consistent with the great weight of our case law."[20] Apart from this appeal to authority, the *Lopez* majority argued for its holding only by a *reductio*: accepting the government's position in *Lopez*—that Congress may regulate anything that "affects" interstate commerce—would leave the Justices "hard-pressed to posit any activity by an individual that Congress is without power to regulate."[21] Such a "general" or "plenary" "police power" could not be squared with the Constitution's enumeration of powers.[22]

Justice Thomas used the *reductio* argument, too. The dissent's view seemed to him to grant Congress a "police power over the Nation."[23] Any interpretation which would, as the dissent's did, authorize the federal government "to regulate marriage, littering, or cruelty to animals, throughout the 50 states," was in need of reexamination.[24]

Justice Thomas argued that the majority's "substantial effects" test implicitly gave Congress a prohibited "police" power. For this reason and because, in Justice Thomas's view, the original understanding of the commerce power and its interpretation up until the New Deal did *not* cede to Congress power over whatever "substantially affected" interstate commerce, he called for a modification of that test "in an appropriate case." Then a "coherent test" which preserves the distinction between local and national might be developed.[25]

Justice Thomas saw no need in *Lopez* to draft such a test. He agreed with the majority that either because the regulated activity—gun possession near a school—was wholly separate from business, or because it did not, whatever its intrinsic character, substantially affect interstate commerce, Congress could not reach it.[26]

What degree of deference would the majority accord explicit congressional findings of "substantial" effect? There were no such findings in *Lopez*. But the Court said that it would "of course consider" such findings "as part of our independent evaluation of consti-

[19] Id. at 1647.
[20] Id. at 1630.
[21] Id. at 1632.
[22] Id. at 1634.
[23] Id. at 1649.
[24] Id. at 1642.
[25] Id. at 1642–43.
[26] Id.

tutionality."[27] Congressional findings "would enable us to evaluate the legislative judgment" of "substantial" effect.[28] This does not sound like deference, but rather like a judicial determination to hear and consider all the relevant evidence. Besides, the *Lopez* Court treated the "effects" question logically, not empirically: If gun possession near schools *did* "substantially affect" commerce, the "implication" would be that Congress had unlimited power.[29] Therefore it would be *deemed* local by the Court—the *reductio* argument again.

III.

In the principal *Lopez* dissent, Justice Breyer said that an intrastate activity must merely have a "significant," not a "substantial," effect upon interstate commerce in order to be within Congress's reach. He rejected entirely the Court's qualitative limitation to "commercial" or "economic" activity. Breyer also maintained that except for one anomalous state victory (the 1918 case of *Hammer v. Dagenhart*,[30] involving a federal regulation of child labor), Commerce Clause doctrine since *Gibbons v. Ogden* in 1824 tracked what he called "economic reality." Congress, according to Justice Breyer, possessed a power commensurate with the needs of the national economy.[31] The measure of Congress's power depended entirely on "empirical judgment[s]," questions of "degree" or "size" of the effect upon interstate commerce of any intrastate activity.

"The Commerce Clause does not operate," Justice Breyer said, "so as to render the nation powerless to defend itself against economic forces that Congress decrees inimical to or destructive of the national economy."[32] Given the solely "quantitative" nature of Justice Breyer's limit upon Congress, it is not surprising that he retained a highly deferential "rational basis" test: "We must ask whether Congress could have had a *rational basis* for finding a significant (or substantial) connection between gun-related school violence and interstate commerce."[33]

And there is an end to it. Justice Breyer did not advance a "political safeguards" argument, as the *Garcia* majority did, to the effect that while there are considerable limits upon congressional power,

[27] Id. at 1631.
[28] Id. at 1631–32.
[29] Id.
[30] 247 U.S. 251 (1918).
[31] *Lopez*, 115 S.Ct. at 1658.
[32] Id. at 1662.
[33] Id. at 1657, emphasis original.

the Justices must, for various reasons, treat them as matters for congressional self-restraint. Breyer denied that his opinion implied or entailed that Congress may regulate *whatever* it pleases. It is hard, however, to see how it does not entail precisely that. Breyer was convinced that some aspects of education and family life are (empirically? logically?) reserved to the states. He would no doubt enforce some limits upon national regulation of the family in the name of individual rights. But he affirms, it seems to us, no limit on grounds of federalism. State authority begins where an unimpeded Congress decides not to regulate or forbid regulation. The nation's writ runs as far as "economic realities," declared conclusively by Congress itself, carry it.

IV.

The *Lopez* majority affirmed some "outer limit[]" to congressional commerce power.[34] We do too. The majority sought that limit in what we call Congress's "horizontal" reach—the nation's writ runs out at the edge of some "individual acts" which are, permanently, just over the horizon from the commerce power. The Court seemed to want some act, some chunk of raw behavior or area of law (marriage, family law, criminal law, education), which could be said to be, a priori, immune from congressional regulation. The *Lopez* Court wanted to prove by this mode of argument the proposition that the national government does not enjoy the plenary "police power" that the states possess. The proposition is true. And all the members of the *Lopez* majority affirm it. But what does the proposition mean? The *reductio* argument of the *Lopez* majority suggests that "police" means exhaustive, complete, encompassing. But there is no practical prospect of Congress legislating exhaustively, of so exercising a "general police power." The states will always be practically important centers of public decision making and administration, much as cities, countries, villages and towns are practically significant features of state government. In this view of it, the *reductio* argument does not prove anything that could reasonably be denied. There will always be, as a matter of fact, some acts that Congress does not regulate.

V.

Our argument begins by placing the burden of strict construction upon defenders of congressional power. Federalism—or the con-

---

[34] Id. at 1628.

cept of dual sovereignty—is indeed, in Justice Kennedy's term, "our Nation's own discovery."[35] The Framers could not call upon a tradition, or any close example, for guidance. No developing theory of federalism—nor any common law inheritance—could serve to illumine the arrangement specified in the constitutional text. (This was not the case, for example, with separation of powers.) Federalism is not about the substantive justice of particular laws. No principle of natural justice that might shape interpretation is nearby. Federalism is about *jurisdiction*, which is the authority to make and apply laws for the common good of a politically organized community. Because no one (apart from heads of households and assuming no divine right of kings) has a natural right to exercise political authority, we think that the scope of our federalism is acutely a matter of positive law— the Constitution. We think that the Framers understood that theirs was not a finished work at Philadelphia. We think the Framers and ratifiers anticipated that the contours of our federalism would take shape as the practice of it unfolded, and that its shape would be authoritatively specified by the "umpire" of the federal system, the Supreme Court. We think, in sum, that federalism *is* a proper subject for the legitimate development of doctrine by the Supreme Court.

We do not find in *Gibbons* the broad "affecting" commerce test that Justice Breyer finds there. We think, that is, that Justice Thomas has the better of that argument. We think that "commerce", as understood by the Constitution's ratifiers and, for that matter, by Americans for well over a hundred years after ratification, *was* buying and selling, plus the transportation incident thereto. We agree with the dissenters, though, that the Constitution yields something like an "affecting commerce" test when the "necessary and proper" clause is brought into view. At least according to the *McCulloch* doctrine on "necessary and proper", Congress would be empowered, at least prima facie, to regulate appropriate activities in order to execute its commerce power. More strictly, we think that Congress may, prima facie, regulate intrastate activities where such regulation is "necessary and proper" to effectuate a congressional scheme of regulating interstate buying, selling, bartering and transportation.

Congress might regulate, for example, the location of playgrounds—say, forbidding them within 500 feet of an interstate rail line—as "necessary and proper" to interstate commerce. But a child's play is not "commercial" activity, as the *Lopez* majority Court would have to say it is if it would uphold the regulation. We concede as well that whether Congress has, at least prima facie, commerce power

[35] *U.S. Term Limits, Inc. v. Thornton*, 115 S.Ct. 1872 (1995).

(supplemented by the "necessary and proper" clause) over a particular intrastate activity is basically an "empirical" matter. A congressional judgment to that effect deserves great deference from the Court. So, we do not affirm much more than a formal judicial limitation upon Congress' horizontal reach under the Commerce Clause.

VI.

We think the fundamental distinction between Congress's limited power over "commerce" and the states' general "police power," as originally understood and as a free-standing philosophical matter, concerns *not*, as the *Lopez* Court thought, the horizontal reach of Congress, but the end (purpose, object) for which Congress regulates. As Chief Justice John Marshall suggested in *McCulloch*, let the end be legitimate—and not a "pretext"—and appropriate means will be upheld.[36] Breyer's account (and, to some extent, other twentieth-century Commerce Clause decisions) reverses this original understanding. Breyer's view is, let the *means* be legitimate—that is, let there be a minimum nexus with interstate commerce—and Congress may pursue whatever ends it pleases.

We characterize our alternative focus as "vertical." It is not concerned to identify what Congress may, and may never, reach; rather, its premise is that whatever Congress reaches must be reached for a proper (i.e., limited) purpose. What it means—and has historically meant—to say that Congress has no general "police power" is that Congress may *not* regulate to secure all those ends of political society—public health, safety, morality, welfare—which constitute the police power.

Justice Breyer mentions 100 statutes which contain an "affecting commerce" jurisdictional element, including at least 25 criminal statutes.[37] Simply put, the Gun-Free School Zone Act (which did not even make *that* nexus an explicit requirement) is unconstitutional because Congress tried to regulate an *intra*state activity *for public safety reasons*, for the security not of interstate commerce but of schools. Congress may not use an interstate commerce nexus to legislate for *any* purpose save to regulate interstate buying, selling and transportation incident thereto. We suspect, though we have not investigated the matter, that most of Breyer's 100 statutes would not pass muster.

VII.

The distinction among ends (purposes, objects) was central to Commerce Clause decisions from *Gibbons* up to the New Deal. There

[36] *McCulloch v. Maryland*, 4 Wheat. 316 (1819).
[37] *Lopez*, 115 S.Ct. at 1664.

are many examples, beginning at least with *McCulloch*, of concern
about illicit congressional "motives," "purposes," or "pretextual"
"ends." Here, too, is the ground of the reservation expressed by such
liberal constitutionalists as Gerald Gunther about the Civil Rights Act
of 1964.[38] Congress invoked its "commercial" power to eradicate the
moral evil of Jim Crow.[39] A laudable end, to be sure, but *not* a commercial purpose. As a very general matter, the distinction captures
the heart of federalism: while Congress has great leeway to do whatever "interstate commerce" requires, state authorities—and *not* Congress—have care of health, safety and morals of citizens.

The *E. C. Knight* opinion[40] limiting the reach of the Sherman
Antitrust Act trafficked in this same distinction. That opinion is often
cited (by Justice Thomas in *Lopez*,[41] for example) for the proposition
that "manufacturing" simply is not "commerce," that manufacturing
is a "local" as opposed to an interstate activity. But *Knight* is a better
illustration of the distinction between regulations whose purposes are
"commercial," as that term was originally understood, and "police"
regulations. The *Knight* opinion does indeed say that "[c]ommerce
succeeds to manufacture and is not a part of it."[42] But there the Court
had in view the objective ends of the entrepreneurs who sought to
establish the sugar monopoly. They, according to *E. C. Knight*, aimed
to control the manufacture of sugar, and only in a "secondary," "incidental," or "indirect" way could they be said to monopolize
interstate trade. The infamous quotation is not a statement that a
monopoly of manufacture is, as such, beyond congressional control.
Consistent with the opinion in *E. C. Knight*, Congress might break
up a combination which aimed to monopolize rail transportation by
buying up all available rolling stock.

The *Knight* Court distinguished the "police power" as the power
to protect the "lives, health, and property of its citizens, and to preserve good order and the public morals."[43] The power to relieve citizens of the distress caused by monopolies—basically, the threat, if not
the reality, of necessaries being priced at the pleasure of another—

[38] Gerald Gunther, *Constitutional Law*, 11th ed. (Mineola: Foundation 1985), 163.
[39] Please note that we are not claiming that the Civil Rights Act of 1964 was unconstitutional. Our claim is merely that Congress improperly invoked as the constitutional basis of the act its authority under the Commerce Clause. In our view, it should rather have invoked its authority under the post-Civil War amend-ments, especially its authority under sec. 2 of the 13th Amendment.
[40] *United States v. E. C. Knight Co.*, 156 U.S. 1 (1895).
[41] See *Lopez*, 115 S.Ct. at 1649.
[42] See *E. C. Knight*, 156 U.S. at 11–13.
[43] Id. at 11.

was part of this police power. But "[t]he power to regulate commerce is the power to prescribe the rule by which commerce shall be governed, and is a power independent of the power to suppress monopoly."[44] According to the *Knight* Court, Congress did not assert in the Sherman Act the "power to deal with monopoly directly as such."[45] It is clear, however, that had Congress targeted this monopoly of manufacture, the *Knight* Court would have nullified it.

VIII.

The *Knight* Court had the right concern about the scope of a contrary holding, the concern of Madison and the *Lopez* Court and so many in between: "The result would be that Congress would be invested, to the exclusion of the States, with the power to regulate, not only manufacturers . . . but every branch of human industry. For is there one of them that does not contemplate, more or less clearly, an interstate or foreign market?"[46] This fear is perfectly valid, but it is no longer operative. The *Knight* Court assumed (with good reason, in light of precedent) that Congress's power over interstate commerce was exclusive. If the power argued for (all that "affects" commerce) was vested in Congress, then it was denied to the States.[47] On this assumption the *Knight* Court opted for the lesser evil. A holding that only Congress could legislate on "every branch of human industry" would have been truly unappealing. Once we appreciate that Congress and the states enjoy a concurrent jurisdiction over "human industry," the central concern of the *Knight* Court disappears. And, to the extent the *Knight* Court needed but could not imagine some stopping point once "affecting commerce" was loosened, we propose an answer: judicial review of the ends of regulation.

We think the *Knight* Court could have concluded that a suitably drawn congressional enactment, if not the Sherman Act itself, could have regulated intrastate manufacturing as the "necessary and proper" means of protecting against predatory (i.e. monopolistic) pricing on the interstate market. The crucial distinction is that intrastate conditions would be regulated for the purpose of alleviating some undesirable effect upon interstate commerce, and not for ameliorating the condition itself.

Indeed, the *Knight* Court allowed that Congress might suppress

[44] Id. at 12.
[45] Id. at 16.
[46] Id. at 14.
[47] Id.

monopolies as such "whenever the transaction is itself a monopoly of commerce."[48] This corresponds, roughly, to the *Lopez* majority's first two categories where Congress may regulate the health, safety and morals of, so to speak, "interstate commerce" itself.[49]

IX.

This distinction is further illustrated in *Champion v. Ames*.[50] The attorney general argued in what were then novel terms:

> Steam and electricity have woven the American people into a close-ness of life of which the Framers of the Constitution never dreamed, and the necessity for federal police regulations as to any matter within the Federal sphere of power becomes increasingly apparent. Obviously it [a police power over matters within Federal power] does not exist in the States; therefore it must exist in the Federal government, and there is nothing in the legislative or judicial history of the country that in any manner gainsays this conclusion.[51]

A bare majority of the Court seemed to embrace a genuinely national police power:

> As a state may, for the purpose of guarding the morals of its own people forbid all sales of lottery tickets within its limits, so Congress, for the purpose of guarding the people of the United States against the "widespread pestilence of lotteries" and to protect the commerce which concerns all the States, may prohibit the carrying of lottery tickets from one State to another.[52]

A dissenting quartet, comprised of Chief Justice Fuller and Justices Shiras, Peckham, and Brewer, responded:

> It is urged, however, that because Congress is empowered to regulate commerce between the several States, it, therefore, may suppress lotteries by prohibiting the carriage of lottery matter. Congress may indeed make all laws necessary and proper for carrying the powers granted to it into execution, and doubtless an act prohibiting the carriage of lottery matter would be necessary and

[48] Id.
[49] See *Lopez*, 115 S.Ct. at 1629.
[50] 188 U.S. 321 (1903).
[51] Id. at 344.
[52] Id. at 357.

proper to the execution of a power to suppress lotteries; but that power belongs to the States and not to Congress. To hold that Congress has general police power would be to hold that it may accomplish objects not entrusted to the General Government, and to defeat the operation of the Tenth Amendment, declaring that: "The powers not delegated to the United States by the Constitution, nor prohibited by it to the States, are reserved to the States respectively, or to the people."[53]

The underlying vision of the *Champion* majority is made clearer in *Hoke v. United States*,[54] upholding the White Slave Traffic (Mann) Act of 1910. Speaking for a *unanimous* Court, Justice McKenna wrote:

Our dual form of government has its perplexities, State and Nation having different spheres of jurisdiction, as we have said, but it must be kept in mind that we are one people; and the powers reserved to the States and those conferred on the Nation are adapted to be exercised, whether independently or concurrently, to promote the general welfare, material and moral. This is the effect of the decisions, and surely if the facility of interstate transportation can be taken away from the demoralization of lotteries, the debasement of obscene literature, the contagion of diseased cattle or persons, the impurity of food and drugs, the like facility can be taken away from the systematic enticement to and the enslavement in prostitution and debauchery of women, and, more insistently, of girls.[55]

Here is the vision of Justice Breyer's *Lopez* dissent: We are one people, united by a desire to promote our general welfare. This undifferentiated people carves up in the U.S. Constitution a concurrent jurisdiction, national and state, to promote that broad end. In this view, the national and state governments would operate as senior partner and junior associate, much as the state governments coordinate and direct the activities of their subdivisions.

The McKenna vision, it seems to us, soon took hold even of those *resisting* the spread of congressional commerce power. The dissenting Justices in *Jones & Laughlin*[56] (a group often treated as constitutional reactionaries) had a horizontal perspective: "Almost anything— marriage, birth, death—may in some fashion affect commerce."[57] The *Jones & Laughlin* dissenters took the conceptual distinction be-

[53] Id. at 365.
[54] *Hoke and Economides v. United States*, 227 U.S. 308 (1913).
[55] Id. at 322.
[56] *NLRB v. Jones & Laughlin Steel Corp.*, 301 U.S. 1 (1937).
[57] Id. at 99.

tween "direct" and "indirect" in *E. C. Knight*—where an "indirect" effect upon interstate commerce might be massive but still not strictly the object or end—to be a statement about proximity/immediacy and remoteness, indicating inner and outer locations in a widening circle of causation. Their notion of judicial limitations was a second look at the empirical magnitude of the effects.

Within a perspective like the *Jones & Laughlin* dissents, it is virtually impossible not to think of America as a single people united in pursuit of a *national* general welfare. For all we know, that *is* what they thought. Since the nation can only engage in coordinated action through the Congress, conceptualizing the states as junior partners in a congressionally directed enterprise is then inevitable. That Congress, whatever its own direct regulatory reach, may not exercise a superintending vision over the national public health, safety, and morals is then almost unthinkable.

X.

We can now see that the originalist must perform more radical surgery than worked by the *Lopez* majority. Justice Thomas's dissenting opinion in *Thornton* is the necessary corrective. He squarely rejected the notion that, in his words, "the undifferentiated people of the Nation as a whole" are the ultimate source of the Constitution's authority.[58] This was the view of the more ardent nationalists of the founding era (e.g., Hamilton), and of some in succeeding generations (e.g., Webster and Story). In their view, an American nation preceded and brought forth the Constitution. Thus, "We the people of the United States. . . ."[59]

Justice Thomas argued in the term limits case that the people of the individual states gave the Constitution life. In this view, the Constitution effectively begins, "We, the people(s) of the (several) United States. . . ." Though this is hardly the occasion to attempt a thorough examination of this long-standing debate about the social basis of the Constitution, it is worth noting that, on its own terms, the Constitution would take effect only when the people(s) of nine states consented, and then *only* in those states. So, North Carolinians, who fought in the Revolution, participated in the Confederation, sat in Philadelphia through the summer of 1787, and so would be part of an undifferentiated national people if there were one, were *not* bound by the Constitution until they accepted it.[60]

[58] *Thornton*, 115 S.Ct. at 1875.
[59] U.S. Constitution, Preamble.
[60] See *Lopez*, 115 S.Ct. at 1842.

Combined with the deeply positivistic quality of national power (see Part IV), Justice Thomas's concern allows the new federalism's judicial proponents to avoid the judicial activism charge. For the Justices *are* supposed to take an active role in policing the federal system along a line which was *not* clearly drawn by the Framers. To repeat: "federalism" was not—and was not intended to be—a finished product at Philadelphia so that judicial enforcement of it might consist of applying a norm definite enough to eliminate all, or even most, judicial discretion in its development. In this case at least, "originalism" simply does not generate strict judicial restraint.

What the Founders bequeathed us was a vertical axis of distinctions which, we submit, is not only *not* outdated, but is more serviceable as a *judicial* inquiry than a second guess at the economic interpretation of *inter*state and *intra*state activity. We affirm that Congress went too far in the Gun-Free School Zones Act, and that the Court rightly invalidated it. We believe, however, that the Court's intuition—roughly, that the regulated activity was, in no recondite sense, remote from interstate commerce—is better expressed as revealing an illicit purpose.

"Merely Judgment": The Supreme Court and the Administrative State

David K. Nichols

THE RISE OF THE administrative state is often seen as inseparable from the rise of the welfare state or of "big government." The reasons for this assumption are obvious. The government's administrative activities and reach exploded with the New Deal in connection with the growth of the national government's role as a provider of social welfare programs as well as its role as a regulator of business and the economy. The administrative state would not be what it is today if the government had not assumed the responsibility for social and economic welfare following the Depression. Moreover, much of the debate about the problems and possibilities of the administrative state would not have taken place if the state had not extended its reach into so many areas of our lives.

There is also another sense in which the administrative state is associated with big government. The idea of an "administrative state" is based, in part, on the Progressive belief that the problems of government are no longer primarily political. As Woodrow Wilson said, the most important political issues have been decided, "monarchy no longer rides tilt against democracy."[1] The questions that remain are not about the form or ends of government but about the means, the administration of government. But once we see the problem of government as a problem of means or administration, the doctrine of limited government loses its relevance. We have nothing to fear from government, and no reason to limit government if we can't really lose on any of the big issues. Government is merely there to help us to get what we all agree we want.

[1] Woodrow Wilson, "The Study of Administration," *Political Science Quarterly* 2 (June 1887): 209.

It is true but ironic that the goal of Progressivism was, in the words of Herbert Croly, "to free democracy from the bondage of law."[2] It is true because the Progressives believed that law, particularly the law of the Constitution, prevented government from recognizing its potential for good; law and politics got in the way of "good government." It is ironic because the alternative to "the bondage of law" was the growth of the rules and restrictions of a regulatory state. At least in the minds of the Progressives the administrative state and big government were inevitably linked.

The Progressive movement's immediate impact on the politics of its day was limited, but it is almost impossible to overstate the long term impact of the rhetoric of the Progressives on political debate in the United States. In the war of ideas, the Progressives succeeded on several fronts. They shaped the terms of the political debate for much of the twentieth century. Because of the Progressives we tend to believe that our choice is between an activist administrative state or a limited constitutional government.

The tendency to frame the debate in these terms is nowhere more evident than in a number of recent Supreme Court decisions involving the separation of powers and the powers of the national government vis-a-vis the states. Moreover, the problems with framing the debate in these terms is also nowhere more evident than in these recent Court opinions. The Court speaks for the Constitution, but what can the Court say when faced with the reality of the modern administrative state? If the administrative state and limited government represent opposing sides of the debate, then the Court is in the rather uncomfortable position of having to deny the legitimacy of the administrative state within the context of limited constitutional government, a position that however attractive in principle, would create havoc in practice; or the Court must admit it has little to say about the size and scope of the administrative state, and hence conclude that the idea of limited constitutional government has little relevance to contemporary political practice.

An example of this dilemma can be found in the rise and fall of the non-delegation doctrine, the doctrine that says that the legislature cannot delegate its lawmaking powers to the executive. From the case of *Fields v. Clark* in 1892 to the cases of *Panama Refining Co. v. Ryan* and *Schechter Poultry Corp. v. United States* in 1935 and *Carter v. Carter Coal Co.* in 1936, the non-delegation doctrine was used as a roadblock to increased regulation of business and the economy.[3] The

---

[2] Herbert Croly, *Progressive Democracy* (New York: MacMillan Co., 1915).

[3] *Fields v. Clark*, 143 U.S. 649; *Panama Refining Co. v. Ryan*, 293 U.S. 388; *Schechter Poultry Corp. v. United States*, 295 U.S. 495; and *Carter v. Carter Coal Co.*, 298 U.S. 238.

message from the Court was that the administrative state could not be reconciled with a constitutional government of laws. If forced to choose between the two, the Court would support constitutional government.

The Court, however, has not invoked the non-delegation doctrine since 1937; it has simply allowed all delegations of legislative power to stand. The Court's failure to find even one instance of unconstitutional delegation in the last sixty years suggests that the Court believes that the doctrine no longer has any practical relevance. Why hasn't a majority on the Court been willing to relegate the non-delegation doctrine to the dustbin of history? I am convinced that the reason the Court has not taken this step is that it has understood on some level that to do so would be to undermine its own role in the constitutional framework. The power of judicial review rests on the principle that each branch must operate within the limits established by the Constitution.

Since the turn of the century the Court has often been divided between "activists" and "restraintists." The restraintists believe that the Court should defer to the more political branches and the activists believe that the Court and the Constitution have a decisive role to play in shaping the policies of government. The restraintists were originally the liberals who wanted to leave as much room as possible for the political branches to create a more active government. It was the conservatives at the turn of the century who wished to use the Court to thwart the policies of legislatures. In one sense the liberal position has not changed. The liberals on the Court still believe in a *laissez-faire* policy when it comes to allowing the legislative and executive branches maximum leeway in regulating the economy and society. The conservatives, on the other hand, have largely given up on using the Court to restrain the welfare state or the regulatory state.[4]

At the same time the liberals have generally become the new activists on the Court.[5] The liberals have argued that the Court must adapt the Constitution to rapidly changing times and circumstances. In addition the Court is to protect the rights of minorities from tyranny of the majority, and protect the rights of the individual against the overwhelming power of government. Liberal activists have even been led to conclude that the Court must force the government to

[4]The main exception here is the renewed interest in the use of the takings clause.
[5]There have been an increasing number of complaints about "conservative activism" in the last few years. I would contend, however, that the self-understanding of most conservatives has remained restraintist.

use its considerable power to promote the rights of individuals and minorities, because such support is not likely to come from political branches whose members serve at the pleasure of the majority.

The problem with the liberal defense of activism is that the doctrine of activism itself calls into question the authority and legitimacy of the Court. First, if the primary problem of constitutional government is to find ways to adapt to change, then the Court is the branch least suited institutionally to perform that function. It is the political branches, elected by the people for limited terms, who can best reflect changing circumstances and problems, not a group of unelected judges with lifetime tenure. Second, the role of the Court as a defender of minority and individual rights against majority tyranny can only be legitimized by the Court's distinctive role as the defender of the Constitution. When the Court acts to protect the rights of minorities or individuals against the more political branches, it does so in the name of the higher law of the Constitution. But if the Constitution is at best ambiguous and at worst anachronistic, then the Court's claim to legitimacy is itself ambiguous or irrelevant in the world of today. In spite of Justice Hughes' dictum,[6] the authority of the Court could not be maintained for long if the people believed that when the judges speak of the Constitution, they are speaking only of their own policy preferences. The people would not tolerate and the Constitution did not create a government under the control of such "philosopher kings."

Contemporary conservatives believe that judicial activism has been a major force in expanding the scope of the national government beyond the boundaries established by the Constitution. Thus, by adopting a policy of judicial restraint one could restore some sense of the limits inherent in constitutional government. According to the doctrine of judicial restraint, the Constitution established a government based on the principle of majority rule. The majority is to govern through its chosen representatives. Judges are to thwart the will of the majority only when it specifically violates an unambiguous constitutional requirement. To act with less restraint is to substitute the will of the judges for the will of the majority, and that is not acceptable in a democracy.

Although the doctrine of judicial restraint does force us to con-

---

[6] In a 1907 speech before the Elmira Chamber of Commerce Hughes said "We are under a Constitution, but the Constitution is what the judges say it is." For Chief Justice Hughes's subsequent qualification of these remarks, see *The Autobiographical Notes of Charles Evans Hughes*, eds. David J. Danielski and J. S. Tulshin (Cambridge, Mass.: Harvard University Press, 1973), 143.

front the problems of legitimacy inherent in the doctrine of judicial activism, the doctrine of judicial restraint is not always supportive of limited government. The reason for constitutional government is the belief that in the short run majorities may pass laws that are foolish or dangerous to individual rights. The restraintists are correct when they say that the judiciary was not created to solve all the problems of government or to usurp the place of popular rule, even when foolish. It is, however, the business of judges to protect the balance of power between the political branches, to enforce the limits on government created by the Constitution (which are in effect limits on the short term will of the majority), and to maintain the relationship between the national government and the states created by the Constitution.

If the Court merely defers to the more political branches, there is no one who is likely to stand up for the limits established by the Constitution. The political branches are by their very nature dominated by the will of the majority. They cannot therefore be expected to serve as the bulwarks of the Constitution against the will of the majority. It is the judges who are insulated from immediate political pressure by lifetime tenure. It is also the judges whose interests are most directly tied to a defense of the rule of law. As defenders of the rule of law, the judges are the most likely defenders of the higher law of the Constitution against the dangers of majority tyranny.

Judges have a peculiar responsibility to recognize the limits of their own powers in the constitutional scheme of government; judges are not lawmakers or executives. But if judicial restraint becomes an excuse for abdicating the role of the Court as the primary spokesman for the Constitution, then the doctrine of restraint itself becomes the primary threat to the idea of limited constitutional government.

If both the doctrine of restraint and the doctrine of activism are inadequate, then what is the alternative? We can see an alternative emerging when we recognize a problem common to both activists and restraintists, and that is that both ultimately fail to understand the role of the judge. In Hamilton's famous phrase, the Court is to exercise "neither force nor will, but merely judgment."[7] Hamilton was attempting to assuage fears that the Court would become too powerful, by emphasizing the limits of its power. That is why he said "merely judgment." But in many important respects it is precisely the element of judgment that is missing from contemporary jurisprudence.

What I intend to show is that in interpreting the constitutional

[7] Alexander Hamilton, James Madison, and John Jay, *The Federalist*, ed. Jacob E. Cooke (Cleveland: Meridian Books, 1961), no. 78, 523.

powers and limits of the national government, both conservatives and
liberals too often retreat to standards that require no judgment. The
language of the Court is frequently used to obscure this fact. When
the Court speaks of a "rational basis" test or of "strict scrutiny" it
sounds as though it is exercising judgment based on careful examination of the facts and a logical application of the law. But in reality
the opposite is true. The rational basis test is synonymous with the
acceptance of any action on the part of the government, just as strict
scrutiny means in practice that a particular action will never stand up
to examination by the Court.

The use of such tests is offered as an alternative to judgment.
They supply a rule which takes the place of judgment. But we can
apply such rules only when we believe there are no competing claims
to be reconciled and only when we believe that there is no ambiguity
in the character of law or in its application to particular circumstances. We turn to such rules only when we fail to recognize that the
role of the judge is based not just on the principle of the rule of law
but also on the recognition of the limits of the rule of law. Judges
would not be necessary if laws could simply rule, if laws could cover
all imaginable circumstances for all time. We need judges, however,
because the rule of law is always incomplete. Laws may limit the scope
of judgment, but they cannot eliminate the need for judgment. When
we try to deny this need, we end up either with the unchecked will of
the majority as expressed in the laws passed by the legislature, or with
the unfettered will of the judges who substitute their understanding
of individual rights for constitutional principles.

But what has all of this to do with the administrative state? First,
it is necessary to come to grips with the Court's understanding of its
role in the constitutional system if we are to discover what if any role
the Court has or should play in encouraging or limiting the administrative state. Second, there is a parallel between our difficulties in
understanding the role of the Court in relation to the Constitution
and the idea of an administrative state in the context of constitutional
government. We are uncomfortable with the idea of unaccountable
bureaucrats directing the operations of government, just as we are
uncomfortable with idea of unelected and unaccountable judges substituting their will for the will of the people. Our democratic prejudices quickly alert us to the elitism inherent in such practices. On the
other hand, we do understand that some decisions are better made
away from the immediate pressure of the political arena. The potential for corruption in a politically accountable bureaucracy has been
amply demonstrated throughout our history, and the dangers of
undue political influence in the application of the law as opposed to

the creation of law was one of the primary reasons for the creation of an independent judiciary. Perhaps of even greater importance, however, is the recognition that in certain institutional settings, individuals insulated from political pressure may best be able to see what is required by the law and what is required by the circumstances and how those two considerations fit together. Indeed it is to such individuals that we often owe our appreciation of the powers and limits of constitutional government.

Two cases from the Court's 1994 term demonstrate both the tendency to deny a role for judgment in defining the powers of the national government under the Constitution, as well as a growing recognition of the need for such judgment by the Court. In *United States v. Lopez*,[8] the Court held that the Gun Free School Zones Act of 1990 exceeds the powers delegated to Congress under the commerce clause. *U.S. Term Limits, Inc. v. Thornton*[9] struck down an amendment to the Arkansas Constitution prohibiting a candidate for Congress from appearing on the ballot if that candidate has already served three terms in the House of Representatives or two terms in the Senate.

The implications of *United States v. Lopez* for defining the scope of the administrative state are obvious. By addressing the power and limits of the national government under the commerce clause, the Court takes up the central constitutional provision legitimizing the activities of an expansive administrative state. The relevance of the case of *U.S. Term Limits, Inc., v. Thornton* to the issue of the administrative state is less obvious. But I hope to show that the question of who controls congressional elections, the national government or the states, raises many of the same issues of judicial interpretation and constitutional principles found in *Lopez*.

UNITED STATES V. LOPEZ: DEFINING THE COMMERCE POWER

The Court's decision in *Lopez*, a 5–4 decision that pitted the conservative judges against the liberals, represents a significant break with judicial interpretations of the commerce clause since the New Deal. In his dissenting opinion Justice Souter writes:

> [I]t seems fair to ask whether the step taken by the Court today does anything but portend a return to the untenable jurisprudence from which the Court extricated itself almost 60 years ago.[10]

[8] 115 S.Ct. 1624 (1995).
[9] 115 S.Ct. 1842 (1995).
[10] *Lopez*, 115 S.Ct. at 1654.

According to Souter, beginning with the 1937 case of *NLRB v. Jones and Laughlin Steel Corp.*,[11] the Court had adopted a rational basis test when examining legislation under the commerce clause. If the Court could find any rational basis that legislation addressed a subject that had a substantial effect on interstate commerce, then the Court would defer to the wisdom of the legislature. "[A]doption of rational basis review expressed the recognition that the Court had no sustainable basis for subjecting economic regulation as such to judicial policy judgments."[12]

Souter believes that, in rejecting this principle, the majority in *Lopez* ignores one of the "most chastening experiences" in the history of the Court—the period from the turn of the century to 1937, when the Court applied "highly formalistic notions of 'commerce' to invalidate federal social and economic legislation." It was also during this period that "the Court routinely invalidated state social and economic legislation under an expansive conception of Fourteenth Amendment substantive due process."[13] Both of these practices ultimately proved untenable and were replaced by the rational basis standard. Deviating from past applications of that standard, the majority in *Lopez*, according to Souter, now "treats deference under the rationality rule as subject to gradation according to the commercial or noncommercial nature of the immediate subject of the challenged regulation."[14] But, Souter says, the Court will have as much difficulty distinguishing between what is patently commercial and what is not as it had in the past in distinguishing between what directly affected commerce or only indirectly affected commerce. In all likelihood the return to such a standard would result in the Court invalidating a major portion of contemporary commercial legislation. Souter concludes that if the majority opinion is seen as anything other than a short term aberration, we risk relegating the national government to its pre-New Deal status.

One need look no further than Justice Thomas's concurring opinion to find reason for Justice Souter's concerns. Justice Thomas finds nothing to criticize in the pre-1937 commerce cases. He cites approvingly the distinction between manufacturing and commerce found in *United States v. E.C. Knight Co.*,[15] a distinction that barred any effort on the part of the government to regulate nationwide manufac-

[11] 301 U.S. 1.
[12] *Lopez*, 115 S.Ct. at 1653.
[13] Id. at 1652.
[14] Id. at 1653.
[15] 156 U.S. 1 (1895).

turing enterprises. Justice Thomas claims that the understanding of "commerce" in *E. C. Knight* is far closer to the Founder's understanding than we find in the Court opinions of the last sixty years. For the Founders "the term 'commerce' was used in contradistinction to productive activities such as manufacturing and agriculture."[16] Thomas also argues that the commerce clause is not substantially broadened by the necessary and proper clause. If that were the case than many of the Court's enumerated powers, e.g., the powers to enact bankruptcy laws, coin money, or fix standards of weights and measures, would be wholly superfluous. Congress would already have those powers under the elastic definition of commerce.

Thomas concludes that if the Founders had wished to give Congress the power to regulate manufacturing they would have done so. The Founders were well aware of the differences between commerce, agriculture and manufacturing. They chose to delegate to Congress only the authority to regulate commerce. In *Federalist* 17, Hamilton explicitly states that "the supervision of agriculture and other concerns of a similar nature . . . can never be desirable cares of a general jurisdiction."[17] Justice Thomas contends that agriculture and manufacturing are similar in that they involve the production of goods, an activity that must occur in one place. It is only in the area of commerce, the traffic in the goods produced, that the issue of interstate relations can arise. At this point we might conclude, as does Souter, that Thomas would return us to a pre-New Deal understanding of the regulatory powers of the national government, but Thomas closes with a qualification.

> This extended discussion of the original understanding and our first century and a half of case law does not necessarily require a wholesale abandonment of our more recent opinions. It simply reveals that our substantial effects test is far removed from both the Constitution and our early case law. . . . The analysis also suggests that we ought to temper our Commerce Clause jurisprudence.[18]

In a footnote Thomas explains that he makes this concession primarily because of his recognition of the principle of *stare decisis*.[19] Thomas

[16] *Lopez*, 115 S.Ct. at 1643.

[17] *Federalist* no. 17, 106.

[18] *Lopez*, 115 S.Ct. at 1650.

[19] In footnote 8 Thomas says: "Although I may be willing to return to the original understanding, I recognize that many believe that it is too late in the day to undertake a fundamental reexamination of the past 60 years. Consideration of *stare decisis* and reliance interests may convince us that we cannot wipe the slate clean." Ibid.

offers no principled basis on which one could reconcile the opinions in the post-New Deal commerce cases with the understanding of the Constitution found in *E.C. Knight.* He does, however, appear to accept the statement of alternatives adopted by the dissenters—either everything is allowable under the commerce clause or most of the national economic regulation passed since the New Deal is at odds with the principles of the Constitution. Ultimately Thomas's opinion does not provide an alternative to these two extremes.

But Thomas has focused on the limitations inherent in the meaning of "commerce" for a reason. He says that by adopting a rational basis test the Court has allowed Congress to regulate in any area that has a substantial effect on commerce. The Court has in effect said that "everything may be regulated under the guise of the Commerce Clause."[20] Carried to its logical conclusion, the substantial effects test "would give Congress a police power over all aspects of American life."[21] Thomas's opinion reminds the dissenters that the word "commerce" has some finite meaning. Thomas tries to balance the scales of interpretation, by giving due weight to the limits as opposed to the possibilities of judicial interpretation. In large part, Thomas's opinion is a response to the definition of commerce offered by Justice Breyer.

Justice Breyer believes that there is a rational basis for the claim that guns in or near schools have an impact on interstate commerce:

> Could Congress rationally have found that "violent crime in school zones," through its effect on the "quality of education," significantly (or substantially) affects "interstate" or "foreign commerce"? . . . As long as one views the commerce connection, not as a "technical legal conception," but as "a practical one," the answer to this question must be yes.[22]

Much of Breyer's opinion is devoted to showing that in today's world, violence in schools has a negative impact on education, and that education is essential to a healthy economy. Breyer contends that if these two propositions are accepted, then one must accept as fact that the right to regulate interstate commerce comprehends the regulation of guns in local schools. To do otherwise would be to deny the practical realities of modern America. That is why since the 1930s the Court has consistently deferred to the right of Congress to determine where in practice commercial regulation was necessary.

[20] Ibid.
[21] Id. at 1642.
[22] Id. at 1659.

[A] holding that the particular statute before us falls within the commerce power would not expand the scope of that Clause. Rather, it simply would apply pre-existing law to changing economic circumstances.[23]

Breyer also strikes a note of moderation in his opinion. He agrees with Rehnquist's claim in *Hodel v. Virginia Surface Mining and Reclamation Association, Inc.* that "simply because Congress may conclude that a particular activity substantially affects interstate commerce does not necessarily make it so."[24] Nor does it mean that Congress would be free to regulate "any activity that it found was related to the economic productivity of individual citizens."[25] Marriage, child custody, divorce and certain aspects of education would not be covered by even a broad reading of the commerce clause.

We are left to wonder, however, by what principle Breyer would exclude such activities. All of these activities and more could be understood to have a substantial effect on commerce. One can construct a logical argument that virtually anything is related to commerce. In doing so, however, one is reminded of the Platonic dialogues. One dialogue begins by asking what is justice, another what is piety, and the list goes on and on, but whatever the question, Socrates always manages to lead us to philosophy as the answer. The problem is, what becomes of all the other virtues? Is there any way to prevent these virtues from being consumed by philosophy? Have they no principle of integrity that can be maintained in the face of philosophy? Interstate commerce may pervade life in modern America, much as philosophy does the Platonic corpus, but just as Plato showed the dangers as well as the virtues of philosophy, it may be also desirable to articulate the limits and scope of the commerce clause.

Breyer, however, rejects this task. He denies the possibility of judging whether or not a particular activity is sufficiently related to commerce: "[T]he question of degree (how much effect) requires an estimate of the 'size' of the effect that no verbal formulation can capture with precision."[26] If we cannot articulate a precise standard of judgment, then, Breyer implies, we should not judge at all. As Justice Thomas said: "The one advantage of the dissent's standard is certainty: it is certain that under its analysis everything may be regulated under the guise of the Commerce Clause."[27] But this is a standard

[23] Id. at 1662.

[24] *Hodel v. Virginia Surface Mining and Reclamation Association, Inc.*, 452 U.S. 264 (1981), as cited in *Lopez*, 115 S.Ct. at 1658.

[25] *Lopez*, 115 S.Ct. at 1661.

[26] Id. at 1657.

[27] Id. at 1650.

that avoids rather than supports judgment. Just as Thomas fails to suggest how the language of the Constitution is open to the accommodation of changing circumstances, Breyer fails to provide any basis on which to distinguish between commerce and any other human activity. Thus we are left with the following question: Can we find room for judgment within the language of the Constitution, while avoiding the temptation of judicial willfulness?

In his majority opinion, Chief Justice Rehnquist suggests that we can. Rehnquist captures the principles at issue in the debate between Breyer and Thomas, by returning to *Gibbons v. Ogden*.[28] He quotes two passages from Justice Marshall's opinion:

> [The commerce power] is the power to regulate; that is, to prescribe the rule by which commerce is to be governed. This power, like all others vested in Congress, is complete in itself, may be exercised to its utmost extent, and acknowledges no limitations, other than are prescribed in the constitution.
>
> It is not intended to say that these words comprehend that commerce, which is completely internal, which is carried on between man and man in a State, or between different parts of the same State, and which does not extend to or affect other States. Such a power would be inconvenient, and is certainly unnecessary.
>
> Comprehensive as the word 'among' is, it may very properly be restricted to that commerce which concerns more States than one. . . . The enumeration presupposes something not enumerated; and that something, if we regard the language or the subject of the sentence, must be the exclusively internal commerce of a State.[29]

On the one hand Marshall says the commerce power is "complete" and "may be exercised to its utmost extent," on the other he says that the commerce clause is "restricted to that commerce that concerns more states than one." Breyer is right about the potential elasticity of the commerce power, but Thomas is correct that there are limits to that elasticity. And in the *Lopez* case, Rehnquist agrees with Thomas that the limits of the commerce clause take precedence. Rehnquist declares that "[t]he Act neither regulates a commercial activity nor contains a requirement that the possession be connected in any way to interstate commerce."[30]

Rehnquist, however, stops short of accepting Thomas's criticisms of the line of commerce cases stretching back to *Jones and Laughlin*

[28] 9 Wheat. 1 (1824).
[29] As cited in *Lopez*, 115 S.Ct. at 1627.
[30] Id. at 1626.

Steel. He recognizes that *Jones and Laughlin, United States v. Darby Lumber Co.,*[31] and *Wickard v. Filburn*[32] "ushered in an era of Commerce Clause jurisprudence that greatly expanded the previously defined authority of Congress under that Clause."[33] He even suggests that this was a legitimate response to the "great changes that had occurred in the way business was carried out in this country."[34] But Rehnquist believes that one can accept this expansion of the commerce power, and still find a principled basis for restraining that power. Rehnquist points out that even in *Jones and Laughlin* the Court balanced its expansion of the commerce power with a recognition of its necessary limits. He quotes from *Jones and Laughlin* the following warning:

> [The commerce power] must be considered in the light of our dual system of government and may not be extended so as to embrace effects upon interstate commerce so indirect and remote that to embrace them, in view of our complex society, would effectually obliterate the distinction between what is national and what is local and create a completely centralized government.[35]

Changing circumstances may create some elasticity in the commerce clause, but to allow the Gun-Free School Zones Act to stand would clearly violate those constitutional limits. The Court could only uphold the government's contentions if it was willing to "pile inference upon inference" to the point that it would "convert Congressional authority under the Commerce Clause to a general police power of the sort retained by the States."[36] According to Rehnquist this is precisely the road we would take if we were to follow the principles articulated by Justice Breyer.

Rehnquist admits that Breyer is correct when he points to the difficulty in determining "whether an activity is commercial or noncommercial." But he contends that "[a]ny possible benefit from eliminating this 'legal uncertainty' would be at the expense of the Constitution's system of enumerated powers."[37] Legal uncertainty is the reason we need judges. As Rehnquist concludes, "[T]hese are not precise formulations, and in the nature of things they cannot be. But we think they point the way to a correct decision in the case."[38] Thus Rehnquist suggests that judgment is legitimate and possible.

[31] 322 U.S. 100 (1941).
[32] 317 U.S. 111 (1942).
[33] *Lopez,* 115 S.Ct. at 1627.
[34] Id. at 1628.
[35] Ibid., quoting *Jones and Laughlin Steel,* 301 U.S. at 37.
[36] *Lopez,* 115 S.Ct. at 1634.
[37] Id. at 1633.
[38] Id. at 1634.

SWITCHING SIDES: THE CASE OF *U.S. TERM LIMITS, INC. V. THORNTON*

The more liberal justices, Breyer, Ginsburg, Souter, and Stevens were all dissenters in the *Lopez* case, but they found themselves in the majority in *U.S. Term Limits, Inc., v. Thornton.* Conversely, the more conservative justices, O'Connor, Rehnquist, Scalia and Thomas were in the majority in *Lopez*, but found themselves dissenting in *Thornton.* If we look at the cases from the perspective of states rights v. national power, the alignment in these cases makes perfect sense. The liberals defended the power of the national government to regulate commerce in *Lopez* and the right of the national government to strike down a state constitutional amendment in *Thornton.* The conservatives, on the other hand, defended the right of the states in both cases.

However, if we look at these cases from the standpoint of the role of the Court in constitutional interpretation, we find an interesting inconsistency. In *Lopez* the liberals wanted the Court to exercise restraint, whereas the conservatives were willing to use the power of the Court to strike down a congressional statute. In *Thornton* the conservatives held up the banner of judicial restraint, whereas the liberals supported activism to strike down an amendment to a state constitution. One should not be shocked to find liberals or conservatives adopting principles of interpretation on the basis of political convenience, but we also should not be reluctant to explore the problems with such a practice.

As in his concurring opinion in *Lopez*, Justice Thomas uses his dissenting opinion in *Thornton* to point out the importance of constitutional principles that have often been neglected by the Court in recent years. In particular he tries to show that the states still have an important role to play in our constitutional system. He claims that

> [n]othing in the Constitution deprives the people of each State of the power to prescribe eligibility requirements for the candidates who seek to represent them in Congress. The Constitution is simply silent on this question. And where the Constitution is silent, it raises no bar to action by the States or the people.[39]

Moreover he explains that the 10th amendment makes "clear that powers reside at the state level except where the Constitution removes them from that level. All powers that the Constitution neither delegates to the Federal Government nor prohibits to the States are

[39] *Thornton,* 115 S.Ct. at 1875.

controlled by the people of each State."[40] Although the Constitution does create some qualifications for congressional office, it nowhere says that the states are forbidden from adding additional qualifications. The grants of power to the national government are explicitly limited, but the powers of the people and the states are open-ended.

Thomas's primary objection to the majority position is that it fails to appreciate the right of the people to choose whomever they see fit to represent them in Congress. The people are free to pass a constitutional amendment limiting access to the ballot in their individual states, even in national elections. There need be no uniform voting standards in national elections. The Constitution recognizes that whenever the people act they act through their states. Members of Congress are elected from each state, just as members of the Senate represent the states; and even the qualifications of members of the electoral college are left to the discretion of the state governments. The Constitution itself was ratified by the people in their states, and its amendment process requires the approval of the states. "The Constitution simply does not recognize any mechanism for action by the undifferentiated people of the Nation." "The selection of representatives in Congress is indisputably an act of the people of each state, not some abstract people of the nation as a whole."[41]

In providing a justification for the evolution of state power, however, Thomas neglects the principles of the Constitution that might justify the exercise of national authority in this area. He presents the relationship between the national government and the states almost as if the Constitution had never replaced the Articles of Confederation. As Justice Stevens points out in his majority opinion, "[T]he Framers envisioned a uniform national system, rejecting the notion that the Nation was a collection of States, and instead creating a direct link between the National Government and the people of the United States."[42] This fact has important implications for how we understand the relationship among the national government, the states, and the people.

Both Stevens and Thomas agree that the source of all government authority is the people. In fact they both claim that their opinions defend popular choice. They differ, not on this fact, but on the proper mechanism of popular choice. Thomas claims that the proper mechanism is through the states, whereas Stevens contends that popular choice is to be implemented through the mechanisms provided

[40] Id. at 1876.
[41] Id. at 1877.
[42] Id. at 1855.

by the Constitution. In many cases there would be no conflict. The
Constitution does specify a role for the states even in matters related
to the national government, as Thomas has reported. But it is also
noteworthy that the list of those activities is a part of the Constitution.

What of Thomas's contention that the Constitution itself was a
creature of the states? In the first place, the Framers explicitly rejected ratification by the state governments. They argued that this was
to be a government of the people, and should therefore be ratified
by the people. Thomas admits that there is some legitimacy to this
point:

> [O]ne could plausibly maintain that qualification requirements
> imposed by state legislatures violate the constitutional provisions
> entrusting the selection of Members of Congress to the people of
> the States, even while one acknowledges that qualification require-
> ments imposed by the people themselves are perfectly constitu-
> tional. The majority never justifies its conclusion that "democratic
> principles" require it to reject even this intermediate position.[43]

But if Thomas is willing to admit that the state legislatures may not
have the authority to restrict ballot access in congressional elections,
then he may be forced to admit more.

Thomas implies that a distinction should be made between the
state legislatures and the people. But why should we speak of state
legislatures as opposed to state governments? The point of creating a
direct connection between the people and the national government
was to insure that the national government was a government of the
people rather than a league of state governments as was the case
under the Articles. The people were to have a relation with the national government that was not filtered through state government.
An amendment to a state constitution violates this principle as much
as any law passed by the state legislature. In amending a state constitution, the people are altering the form of their state government. Thus
the right of the people to establish term limits for national officials
by law or by state constitutional amendment rests on the assumption
that the people speak to the national government through the state
governments, an assumption that was decisively rejected by the Constitutional Convention.

The examples Thomas gives of widely accepted roles for the
states in national elections actually support the assumption of national supremacy. The state governments play a role in the national

[43] Id. at 1893.

government only to the extent specifically provided for by the Constitution. The Senate was originally created to represent the state governments, a role that was drastically altered by the 17th Amendment. The states were given the right to determine the qualifications of members of the electoral college, a right they still possess, but that right was part of a broader right to determine the method of choosing electors, a right that was explicitly granted to the state governments under the Constitution. Even the ratification procedure for the Constitution was spelled out in the Constitution itself, not left to the discretion of the state governments.

The people have a right to determine who will represent them in Congress, and they are to exercise that right by means of an electoral process created by the Constitution. If we were to accept Thomas's reading, it would be difficult to see why the people of a state could not pass a state constitutional amendment allowing only those candidates approved by the state legislature to be permitted on the ballot for the House, a provision that would blur the distinction between the House and Senate, and in some respects make the House more like the original Senate than the Senate we have today. In principle why could not the people pass an amendment allowing only the names of incumbents to appear on the ballot, in effect insuring lifetime tenure? Neither of these possibilities is explicitly forbidden by the U.S. Constitution, and would therefore be part of the reserve powers of the states, according to Thomas's argument.

The reason the states could not adopt such amendments is that election to national office is clearly a matter to be governed by the U.S. Constitution. If the Constitution does not control the election of national officers, then it can in no way be said to create a government of the people. The people can amend the U.S. Constitution through the means established in that document, or the people can refuse to elect a member of Congress for more than three terms. But the people cannot be required by a state law, a state constitutional amendment, or any other mechanism of a state government, to limit a member of the U.S. Congress to three terms.

In deferring to the power of the states, Thomas seeks to defend federalism and judicial restraint. But in this case, his deference leads him to sacrifice the principle of constitutional restraint. If one is to defend the idea of limited government, one must be willing to recognize what is essential to the national government under the Constitution as well as what is essential to the state governments. Too much deference to Congress or the states undermines the Court's role as the defender of constitutional government. The conservatives in the *Thornton* case are as guilty of this failing as the liberals are in *Lopez*.

PRAGMATISM OR PRINCIPLES: THE CASE OF JUSTICE KENNEDY

The only justice to vote with the majority in both of these cases is Justice Kennedy. This fact may not be surprising to those who have identified Kennedy as a swing vote on the Court. He is often described as a moderate, one whose vote is in the pocket of neither liberals or conservatives. There is also a more negative version of this characterization, however. Kennedy has also been described as an unprincipled pragmatist, one who is constantly seeking the middle, seeking not to offend anyone. According to this view Kennedy is less concerned with constitutional principles than with immediate political problems and perceptions.

In the *Lopez* case Kennedy at times is almost apologetic about siding with the conservative justices. He begins his opinion by reminding us that our economic system has undergone a radical transformation and that the Court must give great deference to Congress to address these changes. He claims that the history of the commerce clause cases has not been marked by either "a coherent or consistent course of interpretation."[44] When the Court did try to apply rigid principles at the turn of the century, it was largely a failure. At the beginning of the century the Court succeeded only in those cases, such as the railroad rate cases, where it took a "more practical approach."[45] Kennedy even applauds more recent Court decisions such as *Heart of Atlanta Motel*,[46] *Katzenbach v. McClung*,[47] and *Perez v. United States*[48] for their "practical conception of commercial regulation."[49] It is these recent cases that form a stable foundation for interpretation of the commerce clause, according to Kennedy, and "the Court as an institution and the legal system as a whole have an immense stake in the stability of our Commerce Clause jurisprudence as it has evolved to this point."[50]

Kennedy's opinion might appear as a model of pragmatic jurisprudence, going so far as to appeal to both stare decisis and the idea of a Constitution that changes to keep pace with the times. But Kennedy rejects both "stare decisis" and the "living Constitution" as the standards for decision in the *Lopez* case. He votes with the majority because

[44] *Lopez,* 115 S.Ct. at 1634.
[45] Id. at 1636.
[46] *Heart of Atlanta Motel,* 379 U.S. 241 (1964).
[47] *Katzenbach v. McClung,* 379 U.S. 294 (1964).
[48] *Perez v. United States,* 402 U.S. 146 (1971).
[49] *Lopez,* 115 S.Ct. at 1637.
[50] Ibid.

[t]he statute before us upsets the federal balance to a degree that renders it an unconstitutional assertion of the commerce power, and our intervention is required. As the Chief Justice explains, unlike the earlier cases to come before the Court here neither the actors nor their conduct have a commercial character, and neither the purposes nor the design of the statute have an evident commercial nexus.[51]

However adaptable the Constitution may be, there must ultimately be some limits. This case, according to Kennedy, takes us beyond those limits. It requires the justices "to consider [their] place in the design of the government and to appreciate the significance of federalism in the whole structure of the Constitution."[52]

According to Kennedy federalism is a key component of our constitutional system. But if federalism is to be preserved we "must know which of the two governments to hold accountable for the failure to perform a given task."[53] It is too much to expect that either the national or the state legislatures will always find it in their interest to exercise due vigilance. The Court must be able to intervene "when one or the other level of government has tipped the scales too far."[54]

Kennedy does not take this task lightly. But he claims the Court is "often called upon to resolve questions of constitutional law not susceptible to the mechanical application of bright and clear lines."[55] By trying to balance the competing claims of constitutional authority, Kennedy may be open to the charge of pragmatism, but he is also following the only course open to one who wishes to maintain allegiance to complex, even competing, constitutional principles. I think that is why we also find Kennedy in the majority in the *Thornton* case.

Following Justice Marshall's argument in *McCulloch v. Maryland*, Kennedy says in *Thornton* that the people did not create a Constitution in which the national government would be dependent on the state governments. The people may act in their states, "[b]ut the measures they adopt do not, on that account, cease to be the measures of the people themselves, or become the measures of the State governments."[56] According to Kennedy, there is "a relationship between the people of the Nation and the National Government with which the states may not interfere."[57]

[51] Id. at 1640.
[52] Id. at 1637.
[53] Id. at 1638.
[54] Id. at 1639.
[55] Id. at 1640.
[56] *McCulloch v. Maryland*, 4 Wheat. 403 (1819), as cited in *Thornton*, 115 S.Ct. at 1873.
[57] *Thornton*, 115 S.Ct. at 1875.

Kennedy is therefore consistent in defending the states against federal intrusion in *Lopez* and national authority against state interference in *Thornton*. He is a simple advocate neither of state's rights nor of the powers of the national government. As he explains:

> That the States may not invade the sphere of federal sovereignty is as incontestable, in my view, as the corollary proposition that the Federal Government must be held within the boundaries of its own power when it intrudes upon matters reserved to the States.[58]

The Constitution is the mechanism by which the people define the spheres of state and national authority. Partisans of both the national government and the states must understand that each must remain within its constitutional boundaries, if either is to be secure in its powers.

In spite of his voting to overturn both national and state actions in *Lopez* and *Thornton*, Kennedy is a champion of judicial restraint. But as we see from these cases, he is not dogmatic in his commitment to that principle. The Court does have a role to play in defending the Constitution, although that role is itself subject to constitutional limits. The Court should have neither force nor will, but it cannot relinquish the power of judgment. A judge makes a determination based upon an examination of competing claims. Therefore, it is difficult at times to distinguish between pragmatism and judgment. The virtue of our legal system may in fact be that if a judge actually looks at the competing claims presented in practice, he will often be led to take into account the competing principles inherent in the Constitution. We ignore this possibility when we assume that there is a radical dichotomy in our legal system between theory and practice. The distance between theory and practice may actually be less than we often assume. The more important disjunctions may be those between a theory that takes into account the complexity of the world and dogmatism, or between the practical appreciation of competing political claims and partisanship.

THE SUPREME COURT AND THE ADMINISTRATIVE STATE

Only when the Court appreciates the complexity and possibility of judgment can it comprehend the place of the administrative state within the context of limited constitutional government. The idea of an administrative state goes back much further than the New Deal or

[58] Id. at 1873.

the Progressives. It goes back at least to Alexander Hamilton who said "the true test of a good government is its aptitude and tendency to produce a good administration."[59] Hamilton understood that the heart of modern liberal government was to be found in administration. But unlike the Progressives, Hamilton appreciated that administration was not all there was to modern politics. The problems of politics would never be solved to everyone's satisfaction. That is why administrators must ultimately serve the will of the people as it is expressed through the political branches. Hamilton also recognized the importance of constitutional government. Only in such a government would the rights of the people be secure, because only in such a government would even popular will be limited, at least in the short run, by the Constitution. Administration must find its field of action within the limits established by popular will and the Constitution.

The growth of the administrative state is a result of the recognition of the possibilities for administrative action within the boundaries of popular will and the Constitution. However, supporters of the administrative state may have discovered so much room to roam within those boundaries that they came to forget there were any boundaries at all. In response, supporters of limited government have concluded that the administrative state must be securely tethered if republican government is to remain safe. But this approach may rob government of its energy and adaptability. Republican government at its best recognizes the need for both energy and restraint. To define the administrative state is to understand both its power and limits, to know what it is and what it isn't. If we look only at what it is, we will begin to assume that it is everything. If we look only at what it isn't, we will assume that it does not exist at all. All too often the Court has vacillated between these two extremes. It has assumed that the meaning of administration can be expanded to cover all of the tasks of government, or it has concluded that there is no room left for administrative discretion within a government committed to the rule of law.

If there is no room for administrative discretion, there also is no room for judicial judgment within the Constitution. We must choose between the popular will and the Constitution, or between competing rules of interpretation. The essence of judgment, however, is the ability to comprehend the complex character of the meaning of the Constitution. The powers and limits of the administrative state can only be defined in terms of the interplay of constitutional principles. They can never be articulated by means of a precise application of rules.

[59] *Federalist* no. 68, 461.

Judicial Management of the Separation of Powers: Recent Trends

Nelson Lund

I. Introduction

What is federal law? Most people would probably think first of the statutes passed by Congress and signed by the president (or enacted over his veto). Lawyers would also think of decisions by the federal courts, and many of them would think of these decisions first of all. Almost everyone, if reminded of the Constitution, would agree that it, too, is a part of federal law. Some people might also mention regulations promulgated by federal agencies, and a few might point to treaties or to the executive orders issued from time to time by the president.

With so many sources of law, conflict is bound to arise. Some conflicts arise from inconsistencies between various expressions of the law. Sometimes, for example, different provisions within a statute seem to contradict each other. Or an agency may issue a regulation pursuant to one statute that seems to conflict with a regulation issued by a different agency under another statute. Or different courts may resolve an ambiguity in a statute differently. What then is *truly* the law? Our legal system has mechanisms for ameliorating these kinds of uncertainty. Judicial review, along with the hierarchical structure of the court system, is the most well-known device, and probably the most important.

Another kind of conflict arises when different institutions struggle to assert preeminence in determining what the law shall be. Congress, for example, sometimes passes legislation ordering the president to act or refrain from acting on matters that the president considers to be within his own constitutional discretion. Similarly, the federal government sometimes enacts legislation that a state govern-

233

ment believes is an invasion of the state's prerogatives. Or a state may enact a law that a federal agency believes incompatible with the federal statute the agency is charged with enforcing. Here, too, the conflict is often resolved by judicial review. In these cases, however, the courts are doing more than removing uncertainty, for they must also resolve competing claims to power.

This essay examines recent developments in the Supreme Court's separation of powers jurisprudence—the collection of decisions and doctrines by which it seeks to police the Constitution's allocation of authority among the major institutional components of our federal system. I suggest that the Court perceives Congress as the most dangerous threat to the system's proper balance, and that the Court does not regard the constitutional rules directly allocating authority as an adequate check on congressional ambition. Accordingly, the Court has begun to develop a series of auxiliary doctrines that are aimed at strengthening the Constitution's protections against congressional self-aggrandizement.

II. The Most Dangerous Branch

Few would deny that the federal courts have an important role to play in the preservation of our liberties. This role is played out most strikingly when a court tells another governmental institution that the Constitution forbids it to take an action that infringes what we usually think of as individual rights. There are countless cases, many quite famous, protecting rights such as those involving the freedom of speech, the free exercise of religion, due process of law, and the equal protection of the laws.[1] Cases like these attest to the strong popular and judicial interest in the most obvious arena for governmental overreaching.

For its Framers, however, the Constitution's role in the direct protection of such individual rights was distinctly secondary.[2] The

---

[1] In some contexts, it would be misleading to distinguish "individual rights" or "civil liberties" like these from other rights that may be vindicated by the courts, such as the right not to pay a duty of tonnage that a state has imposed without congressional authorization. There is nonetheless a rough and useful common sense distinction between constitutional rules that wall off specified spheres of personal conduct from government interference and rules that determine which powers may be exercised in which ways by which governmental institutions.

[2] The original Constitution specifically forbade the federal government from infringing a few personal liberties, though the principle of enumerated powers could reasonably have been expected to protect many others. With respect to the state governments, however, the original Constitution created clear protections for only three kinds of individual rights: the states were forbidden to enact ex

main task, and the hardest, was to find a way to preserve liberty by preventing the undue accumulation of power in any one institution of government. And the greatest source of concern was the legislature. As James Madison wrote in the *Federalist*:

> It will not be denied that power is of an encroaching nature and that it ought to be effectually restrained from passing the limits assigned to it. After discriminating, therefore, in theory the several classes of power, as they may in their nature be legislative, executive, or judiciary, the next and most difficult task is to provide some practical security for each, against the invasion of the others. What this security ought to be, is the great problem to be solved. . . .
>
> . . . [I]n a representative republic . . . where the legislative power is exercised by an assembly, which is inspired, by a supposed influence over the people with an intrepid confidence in its own strength; which is sufficiently numerous to feel all the passions which actuate a multitude, yet not so numerous as to be incapable of pursuing the objects of its passions, by means which reason prescribes; it is against the enterprising ambition of this department that the people ought to indulge all their jealousy and exhaust all their precautions.[3]

The Constitution's principal formal device for inhibiting congressional imperialism is the principle of limited and enumerated powers. Unlike the federal courts, which are granted the entire "judicial Power of the United States,"[4] and unlike the president, who is granted the entire "executive Power,"[5] Congress is supposed by the Constitution to possess only those "legislative Powers herein granted."[6] The Constitution contains an enumeration of those powers, which includes such matters as levying taxes and borrowing money, establishing post offices and post roads, raising armies and declaring war, and enacting uniform laws on naturalization and bankruptcy.[7] Congress was also given the power to make all laws "necessary

post facto laws and bills of attainder; they were forbidden to impair the obligation of contracts; and citizens who traveled from one state to another were guaranteed the same privileges and immunities enjoyed by citizens of the states that they visited. Freedom from ex post facto laws and from bills of attainder were the only individual rights that our original Constitution expressly made good against both the federal and state governments.

[3] Alexander Hamilton, James Madison and John Jay, *The Federalist Papers*, ed. Clinton Rossiter (New York: Mentor, 1961), no. 48, 308–10.

[4] U.S. Constitution, art. 3, § 1.

[5] Ibid., art. 2, § 1.

[6] Ibid., art. 1, § 1.

[7] See ibid., art. 1, § 8.

and proper" for carrying the federal government's other powers into execution, but this grant of implied powers was not meant to convey a generalized authority to make any law "necessary and proper" for the welfare of the nation. As the Tenth Amendment emphasized: "The powers not delegated to the United States by the Constitution, nor prohibited by it to the States, are reserved to the States respectively, or to the people."[8]

The Framers, of course, are famous for their distrust of parchment barriers.[9] Madison in particular emphasized that the real key to preventing Congress from dominating the other departments of government lay in an economy of incentives: "Ambition must be made to counteract ambition. The interest of the man must be connected with the constitutional rights of the place."[10] Some recent examples will illustrate how the economy of incentives has worked—and how it has failed to work—in the context of executive-congressional relations and in the context of federal-state relations.

A. *Congress and the President*

The Constitution specifies in Article 1, § 7 how Congress may see its wishes enacted into law. After a bill passes one house of Congress by majority vote, the identical bill must then pass the other house by majority vote, and be presented to the president. The president may either complete the enactment process (affirmatively by signing the legislation or passively by doing nothing for ten days) or he may veto the bill by returning it to Congress with the reasons for his disapproval.[11] A presidential veto may be overridden only by a two-thirds vote of both houses of Congress.

As the Framers had reason to expect, this elaborate process has proved frustrating to Congress, in large part because the president can use his veto to block legislation that majorities of both houses desire to have enacted.[12] But the Constitution is tolerably clear about the procedures for enacting legislation, and legislators have had to accept the president's formal role in the legislative process.[13] A re-

---

[8] Ibid., amend. 10.

[9] See, e.g., *Federalist* no. 29, 183 (Hamilton), no. 47, 307–08 (Madison), no. 48, 308–09 (Madison); no. 73, 442–43 (Hamilton).

[10] Ibid., no. 51, 322. Hamilton reiterated the point in no. 73.

[11] In the special case where Congress adjourns within ten days of presenting a bill to the president, such inaction has the opposite effect. This is the "pocket veto" (which is not subject to congressional override).

[12] See, e.g., *Federalist* no. 73, 442–46 (Hamilton).

[13] One point on which the Constitution is not quite clear involves the scope of the pocket veto, which is available to the president only when "the Congress by

lated frustration has arisen from the president's constitutional power to administer or "execute" the laws. It would be quite impracticable for Congress to spell out in legislation all the legal details needed for the operation of many programs Congress wishes to establish. Statutes therefore frequently delegate to the president (or to agencies that the president controls[14]) the authority to make additional law in the course of implementing the statute. Because presidents can and do have policy agendas of their own that are quite different from those of Congress, this delegated authority is sometimes exercised in a manner quite displeasing to congressional majorities. But if Congress wishes to correct such deviations from its wishes, it encounters the president's constitutional authority to block corrective legislation through the veto power.

The problems, described above, which Congress sometimes faces in trying to get its general goals carried out by delegating a portion of its own legislative authority to the president or his subordinates illustrate what economists call "agency costs." These costs arise from the conflict of interest that ordinarily exists between principal and agent, and the resulting tendency of agents not to act in a manner that maximizes the welfare of the principal. We are all familiar with countless examples such as expensive and unnecessary repairs by automobile mechanics and shirking by tenured professors. Generally speaking, agency costs may be defined as the sum of a) the resources used by the principal to control the behavior of the agent; b) the

their Adjournment prevent [a bill's] Return." Disputes between presidents and Congress have arisen as to which congressional adjournments prevent a bill's return within the meaning of the Constitution, and these disputes have not yet been resolved by the Supreme Court.

[14] The president's control over executive agencies stems from two main sources. First, the president appoints the top officials at these agencies. This power, however, is qualified in the most important cases by the need to obtain the Senate's approval of the nominees. Second, and more important, the president has the unrestricted power to remove most top officials from their posts.

For the sake of simplicity, this essay will not address in detail the constitutional questions raised by the so-called "independent agencies," which resemble other executive agencies except that those who head them are statutorily insulated to one degree or another from removal by the president. The Supreme Court has upheld such efforts, though without any serious analysis of the constitutional issues they raised. See *Humphrey's Executor v. United States*, 295 U.S. 602 (1935); *Wiener v. United States*, 357 U.S. 349 (1958). More recently, the Court rejected the theory apparently underlying these early decisions, and replaced it with a new rule that may place new limits on congressional discretion in this area. The new rule, however, is extremely amorphous, and it was issued without any meaningful explanation. See *Morrison v. Olson*, 487 U.S. 654, 687–91 (1988). It is therefore unclear whether we can expect to see significant new judicial constraints on Congress' ability to employ this device in the future.

resources used by the agent to assure the principal that he will forego certain actions harmful to the principal; and c) any residual divergence between the agent's actual decisions and the decisions that would have maximized the principal's welfare.[15]

In modern times, Congress has experimented with two especially interesting devices for reducing the agency costs entailed in delegating legislative authority to the president. One of these devices is the "legislative veto," through which legislative authority is delegated by law to the president or those whom he controls while at the same time authorizing Congress (or some subset of Congress such as a single house or even a congressional committee) to nullify particular exercises of that legislative authority without the enactment of a new law. The other approach is to delegate legislative authority to agencies that are under the control of Congress rather than the president. In a series of recent cases, the Supreme Court declared certain manifestations of these congressional efforts unconstitutional.

1. *INS v. Chadha*

The legislative veto first came to prominence in the 1930s, when Congress and the president were in the process of erecting an administrative apparatus far larger and more complex than anything the nation had seen before. Because this project necessarily involved a great deal of experimentation, the president was given enhanced authority to reorganize the government. In an effort to minimize the diminution of its own authority over the structure of government, however, Congress retained the right to review and nullify the president's reorganization plans before they went into effect. In the early 1970s, following another explosion in government programs and faced with an ideologically hostile president, Congress began to use the legislative veto device very frequently.

Because they favored the underlying delegation of legislative power to themselves, presidents routinely signed legislation that incorporated the legislative veto. Nonetheless, they were quite hostile to this device. Indeed, Franklin Roosevelt went so far as to overrule his own attorney general by executing a legal opinion declaring the legislative veto unconstitutional.[16] And President Carter, despite being of the same party as the congressional majority, undertook a

---

[15] See Michael C. Jensen and William H. Meckling, "Theory of the Firm: Managerial Behavior, Agency Costs and Ownership Structure," *Journal of Financial Economics* 3 (1976), 308.

[16] See Robert H. Jackson, "A Presidential Legal Opinion," *Harvard Law Review* 66 (1953), 1353–61.

major initiative to develop a test case through which the constitutional question could be tested in the courts. Carter's project was continued during the Reagan administration, and it came to fruition with the Supreme Court's decision in *INS v. Chadha*.[17]

Chadha held the legislative veto unconstitutional. Under the statute at issue in the case, the attorney general had been delegated the authority to suspend the deportation of certain resident aliens whose visas had expired. This authority had been exercised by the attorney general's delegate in the Immigration and Naturalization Service (INS) to allow Chadha to remain in the United States. The attorney general's authority, however, had been made subject to a one-house legislative veto, and the House of Representatives exercised this veto on the ground that Chadha did not meet the statutory requirements allowing deportation to be suspended.

Chief Justice Burger's opinion for the Court stressed the importance of maintaining the separation of powers by adhering strictly to the formalities of the Constitution. Congress, he said, could exercise its lawmaking powers *only* through bills passed by both houses and presented to the president. And the one-house veto was an exercise of the power to make law. It "had the purpose and effect of altering the legal rights, duties, and relations of persons, including the Attorney General, Executive Branch officials and Chadha, all outside the Legislative Branch."[18] The legislative character of the veto exercised in this case was confirmed by the fact that it was a substitute for the "clumsy, time-consuming private bill procedure" that had previously been used to allow selected deportable aliens to remain in this country.[19] In exchange for the efficiency made possible by delegating the suspension authority to the attorney general (which in turn was delegated to low-ranking officials in the INS), Congress had necessarily relinquished the authority it had previously exercised through its absolute discretion to refrain from passing private bills. "Congress must abide by its delegation of authority until that delegation is legislatively altered or revoked."[20]

The ruling in *Chadha* was vigorously sought by two presidents who in many other ways could not have been more different. And *Chadha* is widely regarded as the most important judicial victory in modern times for the office of the presidency. The extent of its actual

[17] 462 U.S. 919 (1983). For a detailed study of the development of the government's litigation strategy in this case, see Barbara Hinkson Craig, *Chadha: The Story of an Epic Constitutional Struggle* (New York: Oxford University Press, 1988).
[18] 462 U.S. at 952.
[19] Id. at 954.
[20] Id. at 955 (footnote omitted).

effects, however, is open to serious question. Political scientists have failed to detect any real shift of power between Congress and the president that could be attributed to the rise of the legislative veto or to its subsequent demise.[21] More strikingly, Congress has continued to enact legislative vetoes and presidents have continued to honor them. During the Bush administration, for example, the president issued an annual denunciation of the countless legislative vetoes he had signed into law, and declared that he would treat them all as legal nullities.[22] So far as I am aware, however, there is no evidence that the Bush administration ever sought to test this claim by provoking a legislative veto which it could then disregard.

Chadha made it clear that Congress lacks the *legal* power to enforce legislative vetoes. But its informal powers to accomplish the same result were unaffected by the Supreme Court's decision, and those powers are enormous. Thus, for example, statutory "report and wait" provisions are perfectly constitutional. This device requires an executive agency to report to Congress before taking certain actions, and then wait for a fixed period of time before implementing the contemplated action. If, during this time, the agency is urged to refrain from going forward by the agency's oversight committee or by the appropriations subcommittee that controls the agency's budget, that will almost always be enough to stop the action from occurring. Similarly, if an appropriations law contains a *Chadha*-violative legislative veto provision, the president may denounce it, but he is extremely unlikely to require the affected agency to test the will of those who inserted the provision into the bill.[23]

[21] See Jessica Korn, *The Power of Separation: American Constitutionalism and the Myth of the Legislative Veto* (Princeton: Princeton University Press, 1996).

[22] See Statement on Signing the Treasury, Postal Service, and General Government Appropriations Act, 1993, 28 *Weekly Compilation of Presidential Documents* 1873 (Oct. 6, 1992); Statement on Signing the District of Columbia Mental Health Program Assistance Act of 1991, 27 *Weekly Comp. Pres. Doc.* 1575 (Oct. 31, 1991); Statement on Signing the Department of the Interior and Related Agencies Appropriations Act, 1991, 26 *Weekly Comp. Pres. Doc.* 1768 (Nov. 5, 1990); Statement on Signing the Treasury, Postal Service and General Government Appropriations Act, 1990, 25 *Weekly Comp. Pres. Doc.* 1669 (Nov. 3, 1989).

[23] Since *Chadha*, formal legislative vetoes have usually been included in appropriations bills rather than in substantive legislation. Because the power of the purse gives the appropriations committees extremely powerful tools for exercising *informal* legislative vetoes, this pattern may simply reflect a disdain by these committees for the notion that anyone should tell them how to communicate their commands to the agencies whose funding they control. Thus, the principal effect of *Chadha*, to the extent it has had any at all, may have been a slight increase in the relative power of congressional appropriations committees in comparison with authorizing committees and with those members who lack influence in the committee process.

2. *Bowsher v. Synar*

After *Chadha*, attention turned to another device for reducing the agency costs created by the president's independent constitutional powers. If Congress may not formally review and reject administrative actions taken by an agency that the president controls, one alternative might be to place the administration of the law in an agency that answers to Congress rather than to the president.

This approach was adopted in the Gramm-Rudman-Hollings Act, which tried to control the federal government's deficit spending by requiring automatic spending cuts under certain conditions. The cuts were required to take place when projected spending and projected revenues were sufficiently out of balance that deficits exceeding certain limits could otherwise be expected to occur. The implementation of this law required some agency to make estimates of projected spending and revenues, and then to calculate what reductions in which programs would be needed to keep the deficit within the statutory limits.

Gramm-Rudman-Hollings assigned final authority to make these estimates and calculations to the comptroller general, whose decision the president was required to carry out. The comptroller general is appointed by the president from a list of three candidates submitted by the congressional leadership, but he serves a fixed term and can be removed from office before the expiration of the term only at the initiative of Congress. In recognition of the constitutional questions raised by the comptroller general's role, Gramm-Rudman-Hollings included a fallback provision under which Congress, in case the comptroller general's role was declared unconstitutional, would follow expedited procedures to consider ordinary legislation making the requisite spending cuts.

The Supreme Court, again speaking through Chief Justice Burger, held that the comptroller general arrangement was unconstitutional, thus triggering the fallback provision.[24] Because the tasks assigned to the comptroller general were executive in nature, and because authority over removal from office is central to the power of controlling an administrator, the statute had in effect given Congress powers assigned by the Constitution to the president. For the Court, the connection with *Chadha* was clear:

> To permit an officer controlled by Congress to execute the laws would be, in essence, to permit a congressional veto. Congress could simply remove, or threaten to remove, an officer for execut-

[24] *Bowsher v. Synar*, 478 U.S. 714 (1986).

ing the laws in any fashion found to be unsatisfactory to Congress. This kind of congressional control over the execution of the laws, *Chadha* makes clear, is constitutionally impermissible.[25]

As a matter of logic and doctrine, it is not quite so clear as the Court suggests that *Bowsher* follows from *Chadha*, or indeed that either of them follows from the Constitution. In *Chadha*, for example, why should the same action (ordering Chadha's deportation) be considered "legislative" if it resulted from a one-house veto, but "executive" if it resulted from a decision by an INS employee? Similarly, in *Bowsher*, the decisions assigned to the comptroller general were characterized as "executive" when performed by him, but the Court assumed that the same decision would be properly "legislative" if enacted under the fallback provision.

Justice Stevens raised some of these questions in a concurring opinion.[26] He rejected the notion that the case should turn on whether the authority assigned by the statute to the comptroller general was "executive" or "legislative." Such labels are unhelpful, according to Stevens, because "a particular function, like a chameleon, will often take on the aspect of the office to which it is assigned."[27] Stevens agreed with the majority that the comptroller general was an agent of Congress, and he thus believed that the real question in the case was this: "If the delegation [of the authority to make policy decisions having the force of law] to a stranger is permissible, why may not Congress delegate the same responsibilities to one of its own agents?"[28]

The answer, according to Stevens, is provided by *Chadha*: the Framers made a decision, whether rightly or wrongly, to prevent Congress from making policy decisions with the force of law except through the "single, finely wrought and exhaustively considered, procedure" involving bicameral approval and presentment to the president. But there is a problem with this answer, which one can see by reversing Stevens' question: If Congress may not delegate the responsibility for making law to one of its own agents, why may it delegate the same responsibility to the president or to the courts?

As a legal matter, the permissibility of delegating legislative authority to other departments of government had been settled a long time ago, and such delegation is crucially involved in many of the

[25] Id. at 726–27.
[26] See id. at 736–60 (Stevens, J., concurring in the judgment). This opinion was joined by Justice Marshall.
[27] Id. at 749.
[28] Id. at 753.

statutes through which the federal government now undertakes its most significant activities. It would have been odd, and maybe irresponsible, to re-open the question in *Chadha* or *Bowsher*. But Stevens' opinion calls attention to a real problem in the *Chadha/Bowsher* approach to the separation of powers. The results in these cases were explained largely on the basis of an appealingly formalistic reading of the Constitution, according to which one should strictly follow the letter of our fundamental law simply because it is the law. But because the relevant provisions of the Constitution contain ambiguous, undefined terms like "executive" and "legislative," it turns out to be impossible to be perfectly formalistic in one's approach. Unlike the *Bowsher* majority, Stevens freely acknowledged that he must therefore fall back in the end on a belief that the "finely wrought" procedures in the Constitution were meant primarily to prevent Congress from accumulating too much power. That is no doubt true, but it does not tell us how much is too much. Nor does it tell us whether the real constitutional problems in *Chadha* and *Bowsher* arose from the amount of power Congress was trying to exercise, or from the forms through which it tried to exercise that power.

3. The *Airports Case*

The Supreme Court got a chance to clarify these issues after Congress began probing the limits of the *Chadha/Bowsher* constraints on its lawmaking authority. As we shall see, when Congress sought to get around *Chadha* and *Bowsher*, it teamed up with the very institutional actors that had the most to lose: the Reagan administration, which had obtained the victory in *Chadha*, and the Bush administration, which was even more committed than its predecessor to resisting congressional encroachments on the presidency. In this case, executive ambition did not counteract congressional ambition. In the *Airports Case*,[29] the Supreme Court refused to go along, but it had to abandon the formalistic pretensions of *Chadha* and *Bowsher*.[30]

The *Airports Case* arose from a congressional effort to create an ingenious substitute for the legislative veto. For our purposes, the story begins in 1984, when a consensus developed that capital improvements at Washington National and Dulles Airports could best be carried out if operating control and financial responsibility for the

[29] *Metropolitan Wash. Airports Auth. v. Citizens for the Abatement of Aircraft Noise,* 501 U.S. 252 (1991).

[30] The following discussion is drawn in part from a more detailed analysis in Nelson Lund, "Lawyers and the Defense of the Presidency," 1995 *Brigham Young University Law Review,* 70–79.

airports were transferred from the federal Department of Transportation to some sort of newly created state, local, or interstate entity.[31] In 1986, after an elaborate series of consultations, President Reagan approved legislation under which Virginia and the District of Columbia would be permitted to create a new operating authority for the airports. As a condition of taking over the airports, however, the new operating authority would be required to establish a "board of review" with the power to veto the operating authority's most important decisions. The board of review would comprise members of Congress appointed by the operating authority from a list, submitted by Congress, of members sitting on transportation-related congressional committees. Although the legislation purported to require that the members of the board of review serve in their "personal capacities," the board was manifestly intended to exercise a power in the nature of a legislative veto.

Once Virginia and the District of Columbia enacted the required enabling legislation, and the Secretary of Transportation entered into long-term leases with the new operating authority, the board of review was appointed from lists provided by the congressional leadership. In 1988, a citizens' suit was brought, challenging the new arrangement on the ground that the veto power granted to the board of review was unconstitutional.

After George Bush became president, the Department of Justice (DOJ) intervened in the litigation to *defend* the constitutionality of the statute. The case eventually came before the Supreme Court, where DOJ filed a startlingly ambivalent brief. The government began by attacking the significance of the fact that the board of review was created pursuant to state law. That fact, according to DOJ, did not preclude the board from being characterized as an agent of Congress, and therefore invalid under *Chadha* (which forbids legislative vetoes) or under *Bowsher* (which forbids agents of Congress from exercising executive authority). The government's brief observed that treating the board of review as a mere creature of state law would open "a massive loophole in the separation of powers." To permit such influence-laundering would allow Congress to require the states, as a condition of receiving federal financial assistance, to appoint members of Congress to state offices controlling the administration of virtually all roads, schools, housing, and health care, thereby completely supplanting the federal agencies through which the president performs his central function of executing the federal laws.

In a stunning effort to evade the logic of this argument, however,

[31] These two were the only civilian airports operated by the federal government.

the president's lawyers then claimed that the statute at issue in the *Airports Case* was constitutionally valid. Noting that congressmen on the board of review were supposed to serve in their "personal capacities," DOJ contended that such individuals were especially well suited to represent the interests of all other users of the airports because members of Congress must make frequent trips between Washington and their home districts. The Court was asked to imagine that members of Congress would somehow be appropriate representatives of airport users because they use the airports heavily, while they would not be appropriate representatives of those who use roads, schools, and hospitals because they partake in those programs to the same extent as other citizens.

By a vote of 6–3, the Supreme Court invalidated the board of review, observing that the facts of the case "belie the ipse dixit that the Board members will act 'in their individual capacities.' "[32] Rather than accept this "individual capacity" fiction, the Court held that the board-of-review device, although difficult to characterize, logically must be either an effort to exercise legislative power in violation of *Chadha* or an attempt to exercise executive power in violation of *Bowsher*.[33] Repudiating DOJ's suggestion that the Court uphold the statute while essentially confining the case to its facts, Justice Stevens forcefully argued that such ad hoc constitutional decisionmaking would be a dereliction of the Court's responsibilities:

> [T]he statutory scheme challenged today provides a blueprint for extensive expansion of the legislative power beyond its constitutionally-confined role. Given the scope of the federal power to dispense benefits to the States in a variety of forms and subject to a host of statutory conditions, Congress could, if this Board of Review were valid, use similar expedients to enable its Members or its agents to retain control, outside the ordinary legislative process, of the activities of state grant recipients charged with executing virtually every aspect of national policy. As James Madison presciently observed, the legislature "can with greater facility, mask under complicated and indirect measures, the encroachments which it makes on the co-ordinate departments." Heeding his warning that legislative "power is of an encroaching nature," we conclude that the Board of Review is an impermissible encroachment.[34]

As this passage suggests, DOJ's brief supplied the Supreme Court with the key argument for the unconstitutionality of the board-of-

---

[32] 501 U.S. at 267.
[33] Id. at 275–76.
[34] Id. at 276–77 (footnote and citation omitted).

review device. By rejecting the applicability of the argument to this case, however, the president's lawyers invited the Court to overlook any threat to the separation of powers. The three dissenting justices, indeed, accepted this invitation, for they stressed how odd it was that the Court was reaching out to protect the president's authority from a threat that the president's own lawyers denied was real.[35]

The dissenters also explained, in terms evoking the Framers' economy of incentives, why they saw little cause for alarm: "Should Congress ever undertake such improbable projects as transferring national parklands to the States on the condition that its agents control their oversight, there is little doubt that the president would be equal to the task of safeguarding his or her interests."[36] Because there is no obvious distinction between national parklands and national airports, one might dismiss the dissenters' approach as an unprincipled appeal to practical realities. But this would overlook their *formalist* argument. The airports authority and the board of review, the dissent emphasized, were both creatures of state, rather than federal, law. While it is true that Virginia and the District of Columbia may have been responding to incentives created by federal law when they created the board of review, "[c]ongressional suggestion does not render subsequent independent state actions federal ones."[37] If the board is understood simply as a state creation, however, it clearly could not violate *Chadha* or the constitutional separation of executive and legislative powers. The majority could not point to anything that is actually in the Constitution to answer this objection, and therefore had to rest its case on the importance of resisting the "encroaching nature" of congressional power.

Reasonable minds can disagree about the magnitude of the danger posed by the board of review device, and whether that danger was serious enough to justify rejecting the dissent's formalist argument. For our purposes here, the important points to note are how relentless Congress has been in challenging what are at most rather modest restrictions on its legislative power, and how ready presidents have been to go along with congressional wishes.[38]

---

[35] "[N]ever before has the Court struck down a body on separation-of-powers grounds that neither Congress nor the Executive oppose." Id. at 286 (White, J., dissenting). White's dissent was joined by Chief Justice Rehnquist and Justice Marshall.

[36] Id. at 293 (White, J., dissenting) (citation omitted).

[37] Id. at 281 (White, J., dissenting).

[38] In this case, the probable explanation for what has been happening is that Congress wanted to divest itself of responsibility for raising the money to carry out capital improvements at the airports, but feared that a state-controlled operating authority would shift flights from Washington National (which is very near the

This congressional reluctance to relinquish control over Washington National and Dulles is especially striking in light of the fact that Congress could recover the use of its extremely effective *informal* legislative-veto powers simply by putting operation of the airports back in the hands of the federal Department of Transportation. This suggests that the underlying phenomenon about which the *Airports Case* majority was concerned—the congressional appetite for exercising power outside the constitutionally prescribed procedures for enacting legislation—is something that the Court's separation of powers doctrine will be able to affect only at the margins. But the passivity of two presidents also suggests that the courts may be about the only thing standing in Congress' way.

B. *Congress and the States*

Ordinarily, when we talk about the "separation of powers" we mean the constitutional division of authority among the legislature, the executive, and the judiciary. Properly understood, however, the separation of powers also includes an even more fundamental aspect: the division of sovereignty between the federal and state governments.

Like the separation of powers among the three great departments of government, dual sovereignty serves the purpose of ob-

---

Capitol) to the more remote facility at Dulles. Such a shift would cause some *personal* inconvenience to members of Congress who must frequently fly home to their districts.

Congress responded to the *Airports Case* decision with a new bill that provided for a new board of review that differed only superficially from the one that had been invalidated. Although membership on the new board was not in terms restricted to members of Congress, the board's members had to meet specified qualifications that few people outside Congress would possess, and the congressional leadership was given complete control over choosing candidates for the board. The new board also lacked an absolute veto over the operating authority's decisions, but it was given the power to delay (for up to six months) important actions with which it disagreed. President Bush signed the bill, again acquiescing in Congress' wishes, though he now said that he considered the board-of-review gambit unconstitutional. See Statement on Signing the Intermodal Surface Transportation Efficiency Act of 1991, 27 *Weekly Comp. Pres. Doc.* 1861 (Dec. 18, 1991). The courts eventually agreed, invalidating the device as a violation of the separation of powers. *Hechinger v. Metropolitan Washington Airports Auth.*, 36 F.3d 97 (D.C. Cir. 1994), *cert. denied* 115 S. Ct. 934 (1995). It is not clear, however, that this saga is over. Within days of this judicial decision becoming final, the chairman and ranking member of the House transportation committee introduced legislation to replace the invalidated board-of-review device with an "advisory commission" that might exercise something like a legislative veto while surviving scrutiny under the *Airports Case*. See H.R. 1036 (introduced Feb. 24, 1995).

structing the accumulation of power in any one person or institution. But it also has other purposes. In discussing the appropriate size of political jurisdictions, Madison offered the following analysis:

> It must be confessed that in this, as in most other cases, there is a mean, on both sides of which inconveniences will be found to lie. By enlarging too much the number of electors, you render the representative too little acquainted with all their local circumstances and lesser interests; as by reducing it too much, you render him unduly attached to these, and too little fit to comprehend and pursue great national objects. The federal Constitution forms a happy combination in this respect; the great and aggregate interests being referred to the national, the local and particular to the State legislatures.[39]

Madison might have added that this "happy combination" was something easier to describe in words than to maintain in practice. Writing about half a century later, Alexis de Tocqueville was impressed with how stable the combination had remained. That stability he attributed in large measure (though by no means exclusively) to what he saw as a genuinely novel device in our Constitution. When the thirteen original states created our federal system, they gave the new government the power not only to make laws but to administer them directly, without intermediation by the constitutive states. This idea, which seems obvious to us today, was actually so remarkable that Tocqueville was able to say that there was still no word for the resulting form of government, even several decades after it was put into place. He himself described what we have here in the United States, not as a federal government, but as an "incomplete national government."[40]

Unlike many of his contemporaries, Tocqueville believed that the greatest threat to our constitutional arrangements then lay in a weakening of the federal government that might lead to a dismemberment of the union.[41] As we now know, the War Between the States proved him right. But in the longer term, Tocqueville thought that the greater danger lay in the inherent tendency of democratic nations to concentrate power at the center.[42] And he has proved right about that, too, as our federal government has become less and less "incomplete." It is worth pausing to recall part of Tocqueville's explanation for the fragility of decentralized governmental forms:

[39] *Federalist* no. 10, 83.
[40] Alexis de Tocqueville, *Democracy in America*, ed. J. P. Mayer, trans. George Lawrence (Garden City, N.Y.: Doubleday, 1969), 157.
[41] Ibid., 363–95.
[42] Ibid., 671–74.

> Not only is a democratic people led by its own tastes to cen-
> tralize government, but the passions of all its rulers constantly urge
> it in the same direction.
>
> It may easily be foreseen that almost all the able and ambi-
> tious men in a democratic country will labor constantly to increase
> the scope of social power, for they all hope sooner or later to con-
> trol it themselves. It is a waste of time to demonstrate to such men
> that extreme centralization may be harmful to the state, for they
> are centralizing in their own interests.
>
> The only public men in democracies who favor decentraliza-
> tion are, almost invariably, either very disinterested or extremely
> mediocre; the former are scarce and the latter powerless.[43]

If Tocqueville is right, the Supreme Court may be the most important
instrument for preserving the "incompleteness" of the federal government. Although the justices cannot be assumed to be "very disinterested," they may have somewhat more incentive than presidents
to resist congressional expansionism (as the *Airports Case* suggests).
And, though some justices may be "extremely mediocre," such medi-
ocrity is for them not nearly the obstacle to power that it is in most
other contexts.

Although the Court may be the principal bulwark against centralization, it has never proved to be much of one for long. The principal legal constraint on the centralizing forces of democracy was
supposed to be the principle of limited and enumerated legislative
powers, a principle that was reinforced by the Tenth Amendment.
The courts, however, have interpreted one of those powers—the authority to regulate commerce among the states—so broadly that it
has became a license to regulate virtually anything. The emblematic
Commerce Clause decision is *Wickard v. Filburn*,[44] which upheld a law
forbidding a farmer to grow wheat on his own farm for his own con-
sumption. The rationale was that if lots of farmers did the same thing,
the price of wheat moving in interstate commerce could be affected.
It is easy to see that this rationale really has no limits.[45]

[43] Ibid., 735.

[44] 317 U.S. 111 (1942).

[45] The Court recently concluded, for the first time since the New Deal era, that
there must be *some* kind of limit and that Congress had finally exceeded its authority under the Commerce Clause. *United States v. Lopez*, 115 S. Ct. 1624 (1995). It
is too soon to know whether this case will prove to have anything more than
academic significance, but there is little reason to expect the Court to enforce
anything remotely resembling the meaningful constraints that the Framers contemplated. *Lopez* was a 5–4 decision, and two members of the majority wrote
separately to emphasize that "the Court as an institution and the legal system as
a whole have an immense stake in the stability of our Commerce Clause jurispru-

Eventually recognizing that its extremely relaxed interpretation of the Commerce Clause left Congress with virtually unfettered discretion to displace the decisionmaking role of the states, the Supreme Court began trying to erect some limits on the federal government's regulatory authority over the states themselves. That process began in 1976 with *National League of Cities v. Usery*,[46] which held that the federal minimum wage and overtime laws could not constitutionally be applied to "displace the States' freedom to structure integral operations in areas of traditional governmental functions."[47] Thus, although the Court assumed that this statute was perfectly constitutional as applied to private businesses, it rejected its application with respect to at least some state employees.

For a number of reasons, this decision was extremely controversial. It was a sharp departure from prior precedent, and it required overruling a comparatively recent decision.[48] The Court's new position, moreover, was endorsed only by a bare majority of the justices, and one of them (Justice Blackmun) wrote an ambivalent concurring opinion. Perhaps most important, then-Justice Rehnquist's majority opinion provided no clear delineation of the boundaries of the states' protected functions. Examples were given—including fire prevention, police protection, sanitation, public health, and parks and recreation—but the Court did not explain how these examples were chosen or how one could identify whether particular federal regulations impermissibly interfered with the states' control over such functions.

Less than a decade later, *National League of Cities* was itself overruled. In *Garcia v. San Antonio Metropolitan Transit Authority*, the Court again reviewed the application of the federal wage and hour laws to state employees, and declared that "[a]ny rule of state immunity that looks to the 'traditional,' 'integral,' or 'necessary' nature of governmental functions inevitably invites an unelected federal judiciary to make decisions about which state policies it favors and which ones it dislikes."[49] More radically, the Court suggested that it would never be able to identify *any* conception of state sovereignty that could define

dence as it has evolved to this point." Id. at 1637 (Kennedy, J., joined by O'Connor, J., concurring). Only one member of the Court expressed any serious interest in rethinking the existing case law. See id. at 1642–51 (Thomas, J., concurring).

[46] 426 U.S. 833 (1976).
[47] Id. at 852.
[48] See id. at 853–55 (expressly overruling *Maryland v. Wirtz*, 392 U.S. 183 [1968]).
[49] 469 U.S. 528, 546 (1985).

the limits of the federal regulatory power.[50] Thus, the states' constitutional protection against federal domination was found to be entirely procedural: "The political process ensures that laws that unduly burden the States will not be promulgated."[51]

Like the case it overruled, *Garcia* was a 5–4 decision. The dissenting justices filed multiple opinions that offered elaborate critiques of the majority's abdication from "the constitutional role of judicial review."[52] And three of the dissenters went so far as to predict that *Garcia* would itself be overruled.[53] What the dissents did not do was formulate a clear and agreed-upon alternative to the majority's decision to leave the development of state-federal relations to the political process.[54]

The *Garcia* decision has not been overruled, at least not completely and not in so many words. But in the years after it was decided, the composition of the Court changed and new majorities began looking for ways to restore some judicial protection to the states. One of the most striking examples of the new approach is the 1992 decision in *New York v. United States*,[55] in which both of the remaining *Garcia* dissenters and the four new justices outvoted the three remaining members of the *Garcia* majority. This case arose from a federal statute that was designed to alleviate a national shortage of disposal sites for low level radioactive waste. As construed by the Court, the statute created a variety of incentives for state governments to provide for the disposal of waste generated within their borders. The Su-

[50] See, e.g., id. at 550 ("we have no license to employ freestanding conceptions of state sovereignty when measuring congressional authority under the Commerce Clause").

[51] Id. at 556.

[52] Id. at 579 (Powell, J., dissenting); see also id. at 581 (O'Connor, J., dissenting) (arguing that if federalism is to remain meaningful, "this Court cannot abdicate its constitutional responsibility to oversee the Federal Government's compliance with its duty to respect the legitimate interests of the States").

[53] See id. at 580 (Rehnquist, J., dissenting); id. at 589 (O'Connor, J., joined by Powell and Rehnquist, JJ., dissenting).

[54] Justice Powell defended *National League of Cities* as a decision in which the Court "weigh[ed] the respective interests of the States and Federal Government," but he offered only the most general suggestions as to how the Court should balance those interests. See id. at 562–63 (Powell, J., dissenting). Similarly, Justice O'Connor advocated that the Court "enforce affirmative limits on federal regulation of the States to complement the judicially crafted expansion of the interstate commerce power." Id. at 587 (O'Connor, J., dissenting). But she, too, refrained from trying to specify exactly what those limits should be. Chief Justice Burger joined Powell's opinion, but did not join O'Connor's. Justice Rehnquist joined both opinions, but noted some subtle differences between Powell's approach and that of *National League of Cities*. See id. at 580–81 (Rehnquist, J., dissenting).

[55] 505 U.S. 144 (1992).

preme Court upheld two of these incentive schemes: a tax on interstate commerce in radioactive waste, which is then used to provide
monetary awards to states that take specified steps to provide for
waste disposal; and a license, available only to states taking specified
waste-disposal steps, to engage in discrimination (which would otherwise be judicially invalidated) against waste produced in states that
have not taken sufficient steps of their own to provide for waste-disposal facilities.

A third set of incentives, however, was struck down. Under this
scheme, states were given a choice between either a) adopting feder-
ally prescribed waste-disposal regulations or b) taking title to radioactive waste generated within their borders and becoming liable for
damages caused by any failure to take prompt possession of the waste.
The Court concluded that the federal government lacked the constitutional authority to impose either of these requirements on the
states, and therefore could not put the states to such a choice.

Justice O'Connor's opinion for the Court attempted to distinguish *Garcia* as a case involving the application to state governments
of a generally applicable law, in contradistinction to the radioactive-
waste statute, which regulated only the states and not the private sector. *Garcia*, however, had made no mention of this distinction, and it
is less than obvious why the constitutionality of a regulation that in-
vades the sovereignty of a state should depend on whether the regulation is also applied to the private sector. Apart from some
questionable readings of certain pre-*Garcia* precedents, the Court offered no reason for focusing on this distinction, and it certainly did
not explain how its decision could be reconciled with *Garcia*'s claim
that the states were entirely dependent on the ordinary political process for protection from federal domination.[56]

More important, perhaps, than figuring out the extent of *Garcia*'s continued vitality is understanding the difference between *New
York*'s approach to federalism and that adopted in *National League of
Cities* and in the *Garcia* dissents. Whereas those opinions had offered
little more than general discussions of the importance of protecting
the states against federal overreaching and an amorphous collection
of suggestions about how to identify unconstitutional encroachments,
New York provides a clear and definite rule: "No matter how powerful
the federal interest involved, the Constitution simply does not give
Congress the authority to require the States to regulate. . . . Where a

[56] As Justice White's dissent emphasized, the state governments had played an
extraordinarily active role in framing the terms of the challenged waste-disposal
statute. See id. at 189–94 (White, J., dissenting).

federal interest is sufficiently strong to cause Congress to legislate, it must do so directly; it may not conscript state governments as its agents."[57]

Besides having the virtue of clarity, this rule was accompanied by an interesting theoretical justification. When states are forced to regulate by the federal government, the accountability of officials in both governments is diminished. As O'Connor explained, citizens adversely affected by state regulations are likely to blame the agents who promulgated them rather than those actually responsible, which creates perverse incentives for federal officials.[58] Although she did not point this out, it is also true that state officials who are prevented from regulating in accord with the wishes of their constituents are thereby encouraged to divert resources away from attending to the interests of their constituents and into efforts to shift the blame for unwelcome results onto their federal overseers. For our purposes here, these effects are important primarily because they help to illustrate why so-called "agency problems" or "agency costs" can be a good rather than a bad thing. Agency costs are almost always undesirable from the principal's point of view, but they may well be highly desirable from the point of view of the principal's principal. And in the United States, of course, the true sovereign is understood to be the people rather than any legislature or other governmental institution. To the extent that the Supreme Court's approach to the separation of powers has come to be informed by these considerations, it has at least the merit of fidelity in spirit to the deepest purposes of the Constitution itself.

III. CONCLUSION

The Constitution is in some ways quite vague about the boundaries that are meant to separate the various institutions by which it requires us to be governed. This vagueness is not the result of indifference to where those boundaries might be drawn, or of any insensitivity to the danger that the most aggressive and powerful institutions will take advantage of opportunities to expand their jurisdiction. Rather, the Framers appear to have believed, and with considerable justification, that it would be impossible to specify the boundaries with the clarity and precision that would forestall disputes about their location.

The result, as was certainly anticipated, has been a certain

[57] Id. at 178 (majority opinion).
[58] Id. at 168–69.

amount of tugging and pulling among the institutions in question. Some of these struggles have been genuinely traumatic, like the bloody conflict over slavery and the union. Others, like President Nixon's battle to conceal the contents of his notorious tapes, have turned out to be considerably less momentous. The greatest danger—that Congress would assume a completely dominant position within a domineering national government—has not come to pass, but the possibility of such a development has remained very much alive.

The absence from the Constitution of clear rules about the allocation of power has presented special problems for the courts, which are expected both to enforce constitutional limits on other institutions and to confine themselves to enforcing the limits that are actually in the Constitution. Sometimes, as in *Garcia*, the Court has been inclined to avoid the ineluctably political judgments entailed in drawing lines that the Constitution itself leaves unclear. More recently, the Court has displayed a renewed enthusiasm for asserting itself as a restraint against the natural tendencies toward congressional domination. It remains to be seen whether these many small steps will have a major effect in preventing Congress from becoming the efficient engine of government that Madison would have "pronounced the very definition of tyranny."[59]

[59] See *Federalist* no. 47, 301.

American Constitutional Sovereignty vs. International Law: Where Is the Supreme Court?

Jeremy Rabkin

I. Introduction

The defense of American sovereignty has lately become the battle cry for an unlikely coalition of political dissidents. At least in its appeal to common rhetorical phrases, the coalition seems to extend all the way from Patrick Buchanan on the right to Ralph Nader on the left, while encompassing Ross Perot, too, in some dimension of his own. It appears to be a coalition of angry outsiders. Much of what they say appears to be the stuff of demagoguery which is not taken seriously by respectable political leaders.

Mainstream conservatives, once quite concerned about national sovereignty, have in recent times learned to live with international law and international organizations—or rather, learned to disdain them as impotent and irrelevant. Can the world's only remaining superpower really be tied down by international regulations, spun out by rapporteurs at UN conferences? It is a concern that might seem to haunt only the most obsessive conspiracy theorists, those who see terrible menace in the maneuvers of the Trilateral Commission and the Council on Foreign Relations, fronting for the more sinister intrigues of the Bilderbergers and the Free Masons.

Yet those who dismiss international law as spider webs of pious intent must reckon with the spectacle of the European Union, formerly the European Community and before that, the European Common Market. In the course of a single generation, this grouping has

developed from a limited treaty system among well-established, independent states in Western Europe to a much larger and very much
tighter federation. National sovereignty is said to be "pooled" among
the members. Treaty commitments have evolved into a constitutional
or quasi-constitutional order, implemented by a supranational bureaucracy in Brussels and enforced by a free-standing European
Court of Justice in Luxembourg. Whatever else this example indicates, it certainly suggests that "national sovereignty" is by no means
so firmly rooted in modern practice as "realist" theories of international relations have assumed.

It is still very unlikely, of course, that the United States will find
itself compelled to act against the determined consensus of its own
leaders by the mere abstract requirements of international law. But
such nightmare visions are not the real threat. As in Western Europe,
the danger for the United States is not that it will be overwhelmed by
outside force, but that it will gradually lose the instinct for defending
its own sovereignty—and the sense that the Constitution prescribes
limits to the alienation of national sovereignty.

Treaties are, by the Constitution, the "supreme law of the land."
Today, even international agreements not adopted as formal treaties
(not having been ratified by two-thirds of the Senate) are regarded
as legally equivalent to treaties. Is it absurd to suppose that judicial
activists will seize on the mushrooming tangle of international treaties, conventions and "covenants" to impose new requirements on
American domestic policy? Much less inventiveness would be required than the Supreme Court displayed in *Roe v. Wade.*[1] And many
politicians might well support such ventures for the same reason that
they have acquiesced in judicial activism under other pretexts. Even
controversial rulings often have sizable constituencies. Politicians
often find it convenient to leave controversial matters to unelected
judges. In fact, many advocacy groups, long accustomed to pressing
their agendas through activist litigation in constitutional cases, have
quietly begun to urge similar ventures in the name of international
obligations.[2]

This much is certain: international commitments have much
more credibility than might have been thought possible only a few
decades ago. The U.S. Supreme Court, it is true, has tended to take
a rather cold and dismissive view of arguments grounded on interna-

[1] 410 U.S. 113 (1973).
[2] See, e.g., American Civil Liberties Union, *Human Rights Violations in the United States, A Report on Compliance with the International Covenant on Civil and Political Rights* (New York: ACLU, 1993, co-produced with Human Rights Watch).

tional law. In this area, the Rehnquist Court has been resolutely hostile to opening new arenas for judicial activism. As in other areas, however, the Rehnquist Court has tended to fall back on rather positivist notions, regarding what the relevant law (treaty law or otherwise) happens to be, without trying to articulate a secure theory of constitutional limitations on what the law ever could be. With a slight change in the Court's membership or a slight shift in the political winds in Washington, international law may indeed emerge as a major factor in American policy making. It is therefore not at all too soon to be thinking now about the necessary constitutional limits on domestic policy making through international commitments.

II. The Trend Toward International Standards

When the United Nations was organized at the end of World War II, many well-wishers hoped it would emerge as the nucleus of a world government. Many critics, also seeing the UN as an embryonic world government, denounced it for just this reason. Both the hopes and the fears of that era now seem very far in the past. Yet the empty bombast of the UN's General Assembly and the sad failure of so many UN "peace-keeping" ventures have tended to obscure some very serious and important changes in the character of international law.

One can summarize the changes succinctly. First, there is now vastly more international law than there used to be. Second, international law now reaches more deeply into the domestic affairs of nations than it used to do. Third, international law now operates in a political climate which, especially in the United States, is much more hospitable, in many ways, than it used to be. In consequence, American domestic policy is much more likely to become entangled in international legal obligations than was true at any previous time.

The sheer expansion of international law can be demonstrated statistically. In the decades since World War II, the annual output of new treaty texts has been growing at five to six times the rate as in earlier decades of this century.[3] Conventions signed by dozens of na-

---

[3] The League of Nations registered 4,834 new treaties, extending through 205 volumes in its official reporter of the texts, in the period between the world wars. In a comparable period following World War II, the United Nations registered 21,806 treaties, more than five times as many (and extending through 1,307 volumes of printed text, more than six times as many as in the League series for a comparable span of years). Treaties reported in these series are not necessarily sponsored by the League or the UN; they are simply "registered" with these organizations to make them public knowledge. Mark W. Janis, *An Introduction to International Law*, 2d ed. (Boston: Little, Brown, 1993), 11.

tions (rather than a handful of immediate parties to a particular dispute) were still unusual before World War II. Since the war, they have become commonplace.

There are not simply more treaties, but more subjects covered by international agreement. So, for example, when the United Nations General Assembly issued its Universal Declaration of Human Rights in 1948, international norms in this field were still very much a novelty. And at that, the Universal Declaration was characterized at the time as a mere statement of ideals, rather than a binding legal commitment. It took the United Nations over twenty years to hammer out detailed provisions implementing the ideals of the Universal Declaration in binding treaties—the Covenant on Civil and Political Rights and the companion Covenant on Economic and Social Rights. Since then, the UN has churned out a whole series of new human rights conventions, including special conventions on sex discrimination and the rights of children.

Similarly, trade agreements before the Second World War were limited to specialized understandings between particular countries. Over the past fifty years, generalized trade liberalization agreements, negotiated under the General Agreement on Tariffs and Trade, have become the pace setters of global trade. And whereas new "rounds" of GATT specifications used to be worked out by marathon consensus negotiations, the World Trade Organization, established by treaty in 1994, now provides for formalized adjudication of trade disputes and a specialized process for amending elements of the latest overall agreements. Prior to the 1970s, there were virtually no international agreements on environmental issues, apart from localized treaties on particular border pollution problems and a few conservation agreements on migratory animals. But in the past two decades, there has been a whole series of global agreements seeking to establish common approaches to such generalized problems as the thinning of the ozone layer due to emission of fluorocarbon compounds around the world.

The proliferation of international norms in new fields has, in turn, altered the customary reach of international agreements. The lines between international and domestic concerns have become more and more blurred. In the field of human rights, for example, the change is illustrated by the very existence of international agreements purporting to standardize how governments deal with their own citizens. In the first decades after the establishment of the United Nations, the new approach in this area was defended on the grounds that a government that can repress its own citizens will find it easier to attack its neighbors and will, in any case, likely generate fear and distrust in neighboring countries, generating dangerous threats to international peace.[4] The argument may have seemed plausible to a generation that still remembered the rise of the dictators in the 1930s. But when UN conventions attempt to standardize the obligation of governments to provide day care facilities for working mothers,[5] it is hard to take seriously that "human rights"—in this very extended sense—has any real connection with threats to international peace.

So, too, trade agreements used to focus exclusively on the treatment of goods crossing international boundaries. The latest GATT round stipulates respect for international standards regarding the protection of "intellectual property" so that governments are now concerned not only with the products crossing their borders but with the way they were produced (with proper regard to the patent or copyright holders in other countries). Environmental agreements stipulate that governments may impose trade sanctions to penalize production methods in other countries that violate agreed environmental norms.[6] Side-agreements to the North American Free Trade Agreement go a step further, binding the United States, Canada and Mexico to enforce their own regulatory standards on environmental and labor protection matters, on penalty of sanction by one (or both) of the other NAFTA partners. The theory is that a nation should not be allowed to seek economic advantage against its trade partners by under-enforcing its own regulations and so creating an artificially favorable business climate for its own exporting firms. How the United States chooses to enforce its own pollution control or worker safety laws within its own borders has thus become the subject of international legal commitments. Many voices now urge that the United States ought to go further and seek international agreements on the content of environmental and labor laws, so that other countries will

[4] See, e.g., Hersch Lauterpacht, *International Law and Human Rights* (New York: Praeger, 1950), for one of the most prestigious and well regarded statements of this argument.

[5] Convention on the Elimination of All Forms of Discrimination Against Women, Adopted by UN General Assembly, Dec. 18, 1979 (subsequently ratified by 100 states), 19 I.L.M. 33 (1980), art. 11(c).

[6] Three agreements of this sort were specifically provided for in the North American Free Trade Agreement—so that trade sanctions can be invoked to enforce them, notwithstanding the promise of the NAFTA nations not to impose trade barriers on each other: "The Convention on International Trade in Endangered Species of Wild Fauna and Flora" (March 3, 1973, TIAS 8249); "The Montreal Protocol on Substances that Deplete the Ozone Layer" (September 16, 1987, KAV 2369); "The Basel Convention on Control of Transboundary Movements of Hazardous Wastes and their Disposal" (March 22, 1989, KAV 2634).

not undercut the competitiveness of American export industries with more indulgent regulatory standards.

Perhaps the most striking change of all, however, is that, with all these other changes in the status and character of international legal commitments, the political atmosphere in the United States has become markedly more receptive to such undertakings. In the early 1950s, there was so much distrust of American submission to international human rights norms that the Eisenhower administration announced it would refrain from seeking Senate ratification of any such agreements. For more than three decades, the Senate indeed declined to ratify a single such agreement. But by the mid-1980s, even the conservative Reagan administration decided there was little risk in getting the Senate to ratify the convention against genocide. The Bush administration subsequently persuaded the Senate to ratify the Covenant on Civil and Political Rights and two lesser human rights conventions.

The Clinton administration could not so easily overcome Senate resistance when it urged ratification of further human rights agreements in the mid-1990s. But there is no longer a principled resistance to the ratification of any agreement purporting to regulate the relations between the United States government and its own citizens on matters classified as "human rights." Back in the 1950s, the American Bar Association was among the loudest critics of American adherence to international human rights agreements, on the grounds that they might prove a threat to constitutional norms in this country. In recent years, the ABA has been prominently associated with those urging that the Senate ratify yet further agreements in this area. In the 1950s, moreover, a sizable part of the opposition to American participation in human rights agreements came from representatives of southern states, fearful that these agreements might prove threatening to racial segregation. Decades later this discreditable ground of opposition is a distant memory.[7]

There has been a similar turn-around in other areas. In the late 1940s, congressional resistance killed plans for an International Trade Organization to supervise the implementation of global trade agreements. For decades, trade liberalization proceeded under the less formal auspices of the General Agreement on Tariffs and Trade. But the United States was a principal architect of the new World Trade Organization established in 1994 and American adherence to

[7]For an overview of the arguments in that era, see Natalie H. Kaufman, *Human Rights Treaties and the Senate: A History of Opposition* (Chapel Hill, NC: University of North Carolina Press, 1990).

the WTO received bi-partisan support in Congress. There was certainly a sizable contingent of doubters and critics in Congress regarding WTO, as well as NAFTA. But most criticism came from liberal forces, warning that free trade would undermine American regulatory standards and calling for international coordination of minimum wages as well as environmental and other labor standards, to protect the competitiveness of American business.

Apart from the change in the general climate, changes in particular sectors may prove especially important. As late as the 1950s, there were still prominent legal scholars raising serious questions about the constitutional character and permissible scope of international legal commitments affecting the United States. Critical voices of this kind have almost disappeared from contemporary legal scholarship. Similarly, in earlier decades, advocacy groups within the United States tended to take little notice of international norms. In recent years, there has developed a sizable network of advocacy groups which is oriented toward appealing to international standards in campaigns involving civil rights issues, environmental issues and other regulatory policies.

So the likelihood is that international norms will enter more and more into American domestic policy formulation. One may see this trend as the inevitable result of increasing international trade and increased international convergence in public policy concerns. Businessmen increasingly look to international agreements to "level the playing field" for trade across national boundaries. Policy activists similarly build ties to share and reinforce various concerns across boundaries. The trends may be seen as analogous to the growth of federal authority at the expense of states and localities within the United States, as the growth of interstate commerce stimulated demands for interstate regulation.

Yet this analogy suggests caution. Concerns about the excessive growth of federal regulation have provoked a good deal of rethinking on the proper limits of federal authority. Thus many observers have applauded recent indications that the Supreme Court, after sixty years of indiscriminate deference to federal power, is beginning to display renewed concern for preserving the constitutional balance between federal and state power. The somewhat analogous problems, however, that are posed by the expansion of international regulation have not yet received much serious attention from the Supreme Court. As with questions concerning federalism, there is a substantial constitutional tradition for the Court to draw on, if it seeks to draw some lines against the internationalization of American policy. The question is whether the Court does seek to play a line-drawing role in this area.

III. THE ORIGINAL UNDERSTANDING OBSCURED

In contrast to certain strains of contemporary conservative opinion, the American Founders were not at all contemptuous of international law. On the contrary, they treated "the law of nations," as international law was known in the eighteenth century, as a matter of most solemn importance. The provision in Article VI, ranking "treaties" as the "supreme law of the land," is only one indication of their respect for international commitments. Among the enumerated powers of Congress, the Framers expressly included the "power to define and punish . . . offenses against the Law of Nations" and the first Congress took up this task with alacrity in 1789.[8] These actions should not be dismissed as mere pious gestures. The Declaration of Independence grounds American independence on the central doctrine of the "law of nations": when the Declaration appeals to the "law of nature and of Nature's God," it is not speaking of the rights of individuals but of the claim of the United States to its "separate and equal station amongst the powers of the Earth." Individuals may be "endowed by their Creator" with "certain unalienable rights," but those rights are "secured" by governments, which "derive their just powers from the consent of the governed." The claim of sovereign states to equal status derives, as the wording of the Declaration suggests, not from "consent" but directly from the law of nature.

The doctrine of the Declaration regarding national sovereignty is related in a fundamental way to its doctrine regarding individual rights. Legitimate government must rest on the consent of the governed because there is no natural basis by which individuals could be bound to obey a government, except by their prior consent. By the same reasoning, then, a government resting on the consent of its own people cannot rightly submit to the authority of a foreign government without betraying or subverting the responsibility of the home government to its own people. The conclusion was put quite emphati-

---

[8] In 1790, to cite another example, Supreme Court Justice James Wilson, who had played a prominent role at the constitutional convention, gave a series of public lectures on American law, in which he devoted extended and highly respectful attention to the law of nations. Only a few years later, John Jay, co-author of *The Federalist* and first Chief Justice of the Supreme Court, negotiated a treaty with Britain which provided for a special international panel to adjudicate outstanding private property claims arising from the Revolution, the first such international claims tribunal in modern history.

cally by Vattel's *The Law of Nations,* the mid-eighteenth century treatise on this subject most consulted by American jurists of the founding era: It "clearly follows from the liberty and independence of Nations, that each has the right to govern itself as it thinks proper and that no one of them has the least right to interfere in the government of another. Of all the rights possessed by a nation, that of sovereignty is doubtless the most important" (II, iv, §54). Accordingly, "No foreign state may inquire into the manner in which a sovereign [government] rules, nor set itself up as a judge of [its internal] conduct, nor force [it] to make changes in [its domestic] administration" (II, iv, §55).[9]

It is easy to show that American statesmen and American courts continued to view international law in these terms until well into this century. It is equally easy to show that these conceptions have eroded almost to the vanishing point in recent decades. For ease of exposition, the erosion may be usefully described under two headings: first, the understanding of international law as limited to the rights—including the contractual rights arising from treaty—of sovereign states and second, the understanding that the treaty power in the U.S. Constitution is limited to matters of genuinely international concern.

A. *The Dignity of Sovereign States*

International law had more than an abstract prestige for the American founders. It was a body of law that American courts were expected to uphold and enforce in appropriate cases. As late as 1900, the U.S. Supreme Court affirmed that "international law is a part of our law,"[10] meaning that basic principles of international law would be recognized and enforced by American courts. Apart from the specifics of particular treaty commitments (already made a part of American law by the provision of Article VI in the Constitution), international law encompassed customary understandings, already quite old by the time of American independence, such as the right of any nation to seize and punish pirates on the high seas and the duty of every nation to assure the safety (and legal immunity) of diplomatic representatives from other nations. Beyond such specialized understandings, the main theme of international law was the duty of

[9] The Carnegie Institute of Washington published, in separate volumes (both appearing in 1916), a reproduction of the first French edition and a new English translation by Charles G. Fenwick. Divisions into books, chapters, and numbered paragraphs are the same in both versions—as (so far as I have been able to check) in the many previous editions.

[10] *The Paquete Habana,* 175 U.S. 677 (1900).

each state to respect the sovereign authority, within its own proper sphere, of every other state.

In practice, of course, stronger states often threatened or bullied weaker states. In the last resort, war could be an irresistible arbiter of disputes. But insofar as international law was conceived as a body of law to be applied by courts, it was based essentially on the reciprocal duties of sovereign states to respect each other's sovereignty. An American court would not pass judgment on the actions of sovereign states within their own territory; in return, it was assumed, other states would refrain from challenging the authority of the American government within its own territory.

As late as 1964, the Supreme Court still held to the traditional view,[11] affirmed by Chief Justice Marshall and tracing back to the doctrines of the eighteenth century,[12] when it refused to allow the expropriation policies of communist Cuba to be questioned in American courts: one sovereign state could not hold another sovereign state to account in its own courts. But Congress was so enraged by the Court's ruling that it passed a new law, insisting that even sovereign states should be answerable to American courts for violations of the property rights of Americans. In 1976, Congress enacted more general restrictions on the sovereign immunity to be accorded to foreign sovereigns in American courts.[13]

Following the trend, the Carter administration successfully persuaded a federal appeals court to allow a suit against a Paraguayan official for human rights abuses committed against Paraguayan citizens within Paraguay[14]—but ostensibly in violation of evolving international human rights standards (not at that time ratified by the United States). A similar case was launched in a federal court in California a few years later against an Argentine official involved in extreme brutality against Argentine citizens in Argentina.[15]

---

[11] *Banco Nacional de Cuba v. Sabbatino*, 376 U.S. 398 (1964).

[12] Chief Justice Marshall explained that courts of one nation may not judge the "sovereign acts" of another because of the "perfect equality and absolute independence of sovereigns" under the "law of nations." *The Schooner Exchange v. McFaddon*, 7 Cranch 116, 136 (1812) [refusing to take judicial notice of the French government's action in seizing an American ship in a French harbor]. This explanation is essentially a paraphrase of Vattel's mid-eighteenth century treatise on the "law of nations."

[13] The so-called "Sabbatino amendment" (1964) appears at 22 U.S.C. 2370-(e)(2). The Foreign Sovereign Immunities Act (1976) is found at 28 U.S.C. 1602–11.

[14] *Filartiga v. Pena-Irala*, 630 F.2d 876 (1980).

[15] *Forti v. Suarez-Mason*, 672 F.Supp. 1531 (1987).

These cases claimed jurisdiction for American courts on the basis of a 1789 statute conferring jurisdiction for offenses against the law of nations—which the courts reasoned had expanded in the twentieth century, under the impact of human rights agreements, to include acts of torture and official brutality. Congress was persuaded to give its own endorsement to the system in 1992, enacting a general statute giving jurisdiction to American courts to try any perpetrator of torture who set foot on American soil.[16] The Bush administration, which opposed this law for risking unnecessary complications in American foreign policy, nonetheless brought the captured dictator of Panama, Manuel Noriega, to trial in a federal court in Florida for conspiracy to violate American drug laws. It also insisted on capturing Mexican thugs who had tortured and killed an American Drug Enforcement Agency official in Mexico and putting these men on trial within the United States.

The aggressiveness of the United States in bringing foreign culprits to trial within the United States provoked a good deal of hostile comment in other countries. It could nonetheless be argued that the countries in which these crimes took place were simply unable to enforce justice on their own. How to ensure justice while avoiding the taint of American bullying? Many advocates insisted that the obvious solution was an international criminal court.[17] It was argued, with much force, that such a court would have special benefits in dealing with drug lords who have, through unrestrained bribery and terror, corrupted the courts of countries like Colombia. Countries struggling against powerful drug cartels might be reluctant to extradite to the United States for fear of suggesting a sort of colonial dependence. Yet they might be even more resistant to American captures of drug lords within their own territory. They might, however, be willing to send drug kingpins to an international court. So Congress gave serious attention to the idea in the early 1990s. Critics worried that the standards of due process of an international criminal court might not satisfy American standards. But almost no one raised the core princi-

---

[16]Torture Victims Protection Act, 106 Stat. 73 (1992), 28 U.S.C. 1350.

[17]For the most recent review of such arguments, see Paul D. Marquardt, "Law Without Borders: The Constitutionality of an International Criminal Court," *Columbia Journal of Transnational Law* 33 (1995): 73–148. A quarter century ago, Louis Henkin, one of the leading authorities in this field, insisted that there could be no constitutional objections to having the American government extradite American citizens for trial before an international criminal court (assuming the court followed basic standards of due process). Louis Henkin, *Foreign Affairs and the Constitution* (Mineola, NY: Foundation Press, 1972), 198–201.

ple of sovereignty—that a sovereign state has exclusive responsibility for its own citizens within its own territory. In truth, this no longer seems so clear.[18]

On the other hand, to secure agreements with more important sovereign states, Congress has been prepared to support remarkable innovations in the way the United States government itself may be called to account. In the Canada-U.S. Free Trade Agreement and then in the North American Free Trade Agreement, Congress allowed a remarkable new vehicle for formulating U.S. trade policy. Under the previous system, U.S. tariff rulings by the International Trade Commission (an American government agency) could be appealed to the American courts. The Canadians claimed, with some reason, that neither U.S. administrators nor U.S. courts would likely take an impartial view of disputes involving Canada (where the ITC sought to impose punitive duties against "dumping" of Canadian exports in the American market). So the trade pact included provisions for trade disputes to be appealed to a special panel of trade experts, chosen partly by the Canadian and partly by the American government. The same arrangement was included in the NAFTA pact with Mexico.

The system allows even American importers to challenge American duties on Canadian exports before such a bi-national panel. The ruling of the panel, though it must be enforced by American courts, cannot then be reviewed as to its correctness by American courts.[19] So, for the first time in American history, the United States has delegated to foreign courts the power to judge the propriety of its own governmental rulings involving the rights of its own citizens.[20] Perhaps it is, in the larger scheme of things, a small deviation from traditional patterns, justified by special circumstances. But it has scarcely aroused any controversy. That is probably because it is no longer clearly understood, as once it was, that the treaty power of the United States government has necessary limits under the Constitution which confers that power.

[18] For a complete set of testimonies and submissions on the subject, by the American Bar Association, the U.S. Judicial Conference and a variety of scholars and legal experts, see "International Criminal Court," Senate Committee on Foreign Relations, S. Rep. No. 71, 103d Cong., 1st Sess., 1993.

[19] The NAFTA provision is set out in Article 1904.

[20] For a sustained argument that this arrangement is actually unconstitutional, see James C. Chen, "Appointments with Disaster: The Unconstitutionality of Binational Arbitral Review Under the U.S.-Canada Free Trade Agreement," *Washington & Lee Law Review* 49 (1992): 1455–99.

B. Constitutional Limitations on the Treaty Power

The Constitution makes treaties the "supreme law of the land" and the founding generation was quite insistent on the importance of honoring treaty commitments. Precisely because they took treaty commitments very seriously, the Framers established a serious constitutional hurdle for treaties to take effect: in contrast to the system in Britain and a number of other countries, where the executive can make internationally binding commitments on its own, the American Constitution stipulates that treaties can only take effect after ratification by the Senate—and even then, the Constitution requires that the Senate ratify by a super majority of two-thirds.

This hurdle proved to be too high for President Wilson's treaty establishing the League of Nations, which might have commanded a majority (with the reservations supported by the Senate majority) but could not sustain a two-thirds majority. As Bruce Ackerman and David Golove have recently demonstrated,[21] the trauma of the Senate's rejection of the League made a lasting impact on the subsequent generation of legal commentators. Since World War II, the notion has thus come to be accepted that the United States may be committed to international agreements by a variety of mechanisms. So no serious questions were raised about the North American Free Trade Agreement or about the latest round of the General Agreement on Tariffs and Trade, the latter of which committed the United States to participation in the new World Trade Organization. These were executive agreements implemented by simple majorities in each house. Earlier generations would likely have been quite surprised to see the United States committed to such momentous undertakings without the concurrence of two-thirds of the Senate.[22]

Concern about the postwar proliferation of executive agreements, most of which were not even made subject to congressional approval, was a major contributor to the agitation behind the Bricker Amendment, the proposed constitutional amendment first presented by Senator John Bricker in 1952.[23] One of its provisions stipulated

[21] Bruce Ackerman and David Golove, "Is NAFTA Constitutional?" *Harvard Law Review* 108 (1995): 799–929.

[22] As late as 1945, the House of Representatives thought it necessary to launch a constitutional amendment to provide that treaties could take effect with no more than ordinary majorities in each house. The Senate did not endorse this proposed constitutional amendment at the time; but it ceased, in later years, to insist on its own special role in the constitutional scheme for ratifying international commitments.

[23] See George A. Finch, "The Need to Restrain the Treaty-making Power of the

that "Congress shall have the power to regulate all executive and other agreements with any foreign power or international organization." But the Bricker amendment also responded to a wider concern about the newly questionable status of international commitments. The broad scope of UN human rights treaties had alarmed many observers in the United States. Questions were raised about whether the ratification of these treaties would replace the traditional protections of the Bill of Rights with a new set of international standards (negotiated, as the critics pointed out, with representatives of communist governments as well as other dictatorships around the world).

Proponents of the Bricker Amendment sought to highlight the seriousness of these concerns by pointing at the apparent implications of the Supreme Court's ruling, decades earlier, in *Missouri v. Holland*.[24] In that case, the Supreme Court had upheld federal protective legislation dealing with migratory birds, on the ground that the legislation was necessary to implement an international treaty on the subject. Yet when Congress had earlier sought to legislate on this subject, the Court had struck down that earlier (and very similar) legislation on the ground that it exceeded the enumerated powers of Congress and interfered with the reserved powers of the states. The ruling in *Missouri v. Holland* thus implied that treaties could supersede ordinary constitutional limits on congressional power. The Bricker Amendment proposed to close this feared "loophole in the Constitution" with two very precise stipulations: "A provision of a treaty which conflicts with the Constitution shall not be of any force or effect" and "A treaty shall become effective as internal law in the United States only through legislation which would be valid in the absence of a treaty."

Opponents of the Bricker amendment scoffed at the notion that human rights treaties could pose any serious threat.[25] After all, they argued, if treaties proved to have dangerous effects, Congress could, by simple majority, enact legislation denying internal legal force to the treaties and prohibiting American participation in international enforcement of the treaties. The Supreme Court had repeatedly held that treaties ranked no higher in authority than statutes and a later statute could thus suspend the legal force (at least internally) of an

United States Within Constitutional Limits," *American Journal of International Law* 48 (1954): 57–82, for a useful overview of the arguments and concerns behind the proposal.

[24] 252 U.S. 416 (1920).

[25] See, e.g., John B. Whitton and J. Edward Fowler, "Bricker Amendment—Fallacies and Dangers," *American Journal of International Law* 48 (1954): 23–56.

earlier treaty.[26] Taking a somewhat different tack, the new Eisenhower administration, fearing the Bricker Amendment's restriction on executive agreements, assured Bricker proponents that it understood their concerns and therefore would not recommend ratification of any human rights agreements.

The Supreme Court seemed to deal a final blow to the agitation on behalf of the Bricker amendment with its 1957 ruling in *Reid v. Covert*,[27] holding that the treaty power was a power established by the Constitution which must, therefore, be restricted to exercises consistent with the Constitution. In this case, the Court overrode an agreement with Britain, whereby civilian relatives of U.S. servicemen stationed on American bases in Britain would be tried for major offenses by American military courts. The Court found this to be a denial of the due process guarantee of the Fifth Amendment. It was a particularly striking ruling since, as the dissenters pointed out, international agreements had been in place since the early nineteenth century, by which Americans living abroad were made subject to special U.S. "consular courts" (staffed by American diplomats, reputed to be none too stringent about due process).

And yet *Reid* established much less than might appear. The Court insisted that it would not allow treaty commitments to override what the Court itself viewed as constitutionally guaranteed rights. In that sense, the case stands for the proposition that the treaty power is not unlimited. But the case says very little about the actual limits on the treaty power. For the treaty power plainly is different from ordinary legislation, whether it operates in the traditional form—through ratification by two-thirds of the Senate—or in some more relaxed form.

First, there is the unavoidable fact that treaties always involve, at least in form, a commitment to other countries. Whether or not the actual subject matter of a particular treaty or agreement is important to the other signatories, an international commitment is a pledge of American reliability. If the United States treats one treaty contemptuously, it can do so with another, and perhaps more important, one. Hence the president may feel (and with reason) that the international prestige or credibility of the United States is at stake when Congress contemplates a change in policy that would conflict with a treaty commitment. The president may invoke such concerns to dissuade

[26] *Head Money Cases*, 112 U.S. 580 (1884); *Whitney v. Robertson*, 124 U.S. 190 (1888); *Chinese Exclusion Cases*, 130 U.S. 581 (1889). For an argument that these cases may have been wrongly decided and that treaties ought perhaps to have more status than mere statutes, see Louis Henkin, "The Constitution and United States Sovereignty," *Harvard Law Review* 100 (1987): 853-86.

[27] 354 U.S. 1 (1957).

Congress from enacting such a change. Even if he fails, he may invoke such concerns in vetoing the congressional action and plead his special foreign policy concerns with enough passion to win the support he needs to prevent his veto from being overridden. Such concerns will rarely apply (or rarely be seen to apply with as much force) to an ordinary statute. So it still matters whether a particular policy is undertaken as an exercise of ordinary domestic governing authority or in the context of an international commitment.

Second, treaties and international commitments have a special authority even for courts. Since the time of Chief Justice Marshall, courts have affirmed that legislation should be interpreted, if at all possible, to avoid conflict with established treaties.[28] A number of cases suggest that the Court, in fact, takes this view of the Constitution. *Missouri v. Holland* is one example and probably remains a solid precedent for taking an expansive view of federal powers (at the expense of powers otherwise reserved to the states) when this seems necessary to implement treaty commitments. Similarly, during the 1930s, even the conservative members of the old Court agreed that President Roosevelt could, pursuant to an executive agreement, assign the property claims of Russian nationals (with property held in American banks) to the Soviet government, notwithstanding established constitutional doctrines against the taking of private property.[29] In 1981, the Court held that the claims of American creditors, already pending in American courts, could be reassigned to an improvised, untested international claims commission on the say-so of the president—because President Carter had promised to take such action in the agreement settling the Iranian hostage crisis.[30] It is most unlikely that the Court would have allowed presidential initiatives of this kind in the absence of international agreement. In the one case in which the Court did draw a firm line against unilateral executive action ostensibly justified by foreign affairs concerns—President Truman's seizure of American steel mills during the Korean War[31]—it is notable that no formal international agreement was involved.

So again it matters a good deal whether policies are cast in the

---

[28] Marshall indeed affirmed the broader principle that "an act of congress ought never to be construed to violate the law of nations if any other possible construction remains," and the obligation to adhere to treaties is one of the fundamental principles of the law of nations. See *The Charming Betsy*, 2 Cranch 64, 118 (1804).

[29] *United States v. Belmont*, 301 U.S. 324 (1937); to the same effect, *United States v. Pink*, 315 U.S. 203 (1942).

[30] *Dames & Moore v. Regan*, 453 U.S. 654 (1981).

[31] *Youngstown Sheet & Tube Co. v. Sawyer*, 343 U.S. 579 (1952).

form of international commitment or mere domestic policy. Whatever else might be said of the treaty power, one condition was repeatedly reaffirmed in discussions of the founding era, as well as in subsequent court decisions and learned commentary until quite recently. That is the stipulation that the treaty power can only be exercised for subjects of proper international concern. Jefferson, in the year he entered the presidency, recorded the general consensus within Congress that a "treaty must concern the foreign nation, party to the contract, or it would be a mere nullity. . . . By the general power to make treaties, the Constitution must have intended to comprehend only those objects which are usually regulated by treaty and cannot be otherwise regulated."[32] Justice Story articulated a larger vision of necessary restrictions, which seems to rest on similar premises: "A treaty to change the organization of the Government, or to annihilate its sovereignty, to overturn its republican form, or to deprive it of its constitutional powers, would be void."[33]

Charles Evans Hughes, former Secretary of State, then Chief Justice, seconded Jefferson's vision in 1929:

> [I]f we attempted to use the treaty-making power to deal with matters which did not pertain to our external relations but to control matters which normally and appropriately were within the local jurisdictions of the States, then I again say there might be ground for implying a limitation upon the treaty-making power that it is intended for the purpose of having treaties made relating to foreign affairs and not to make laws for the people of the United States in their internal concerns through the exercise of the asserted treaty-making power.[34]

As late as 1965, the *Restatement of the Foreign Relations Law of the United States* (Second), a privately prepared, academic treatise, but one with particular prestige as a formal outline of existing doctrine, affirmed: "An international agreement of the United States must relate to the external concerns of the nation, as distinguished from

[32] Jefferson's *Manual of Parliamentary Practice*, Sec. LII. To the same effect is the statement of Chief Justice Taney: "The power to make treaties . . . was designed to include all those subjects, which in the ordinary course of nations had usually been made subjects of negotiations and treaty; and which are consistent with the nature of our institutions." *Holmes v. Jennison*, 14 Pet. 540, 569 (1840).

[33] *Commentaries on the Constitution of the United States*, vol. II, 1508.

[34] From a speech reported in *Proceedings of the American Society of International Law* 23 (1929): 196. The Hughes Court subsequently reaffirmed this outlook when it described the treaty power as limited to "subjects that properly pertain to our foreign relations." *Santovincenzo v. Egan*, 284 U.S. 30, 40 (1931).

matters of internal concern."[35] But by the mid-1980s, the third *Restatement* had dropped this restriction, explaining that no such distinctions could be made.[36] No court rulings were cited to justify the change. But the new view certainly seems to conform to the assumptions behind the practice of recent years.

IV. THE POLITICS OF DIMINISHING SOVEREIGNTY

As noted earlier, the expansion of international authority in recent years is parallel in many ways to the ongoing expansion of federal authority since the 1930s. And the parallel is sobering.

Certainly, many useful things have been accomplished by the expansion of federal power. Noxious state practices, like racial segregation and denial of voting rights, have been curbed by federal intervention. In a number of areas, federal controls have worked to free up markets from local constraints and to facilitate commerce by harmonizing standards. Nonetheless, the expansion of federal power has been associated in broad terms with a continuing expansion of government in general. Indeed, through direct and indirect means, expanding federal power even encourages the expansion of state and local government, as federal programs mandate or encourage state and local counterparts to carry forward the same general mission.

There are two general factors at work. One is that federal controls suppress competition between the states, removing incentives to be cost-conscious or sensitive to regulatory burdens. The other is that, in the federal arena, it is easier for many smaller constituencies to organize—and harder for the more fragmented legislative system to respond to distortions of particular programs. The Supreme Court seems to recognize both factors in recent decisions rebuking Congress for preempting decisions that should be made at the state level.[37]

Both of these troublesome tendencies may operate just as relentlessly—and in some ways, more so—at the international level. That is, the effect of international standards may be to encourage statist,

---

[35] §117 ("Scope of International Agreements," Comment b), p. 370.

[36] See "Comment c" and "Reporters Note 2" for §302.

[37] See, e.g., *New York v. United States*, 112 S.Ct. 2408 (1992), striking down a federal law by which Congress sought to force the states to take measures for the safe disposal of nuclear wastes, rather than undertaking this controversial task on its own; and *United States v. Lopez*, 115 S.Ct. 1624 (1995), striking down a federal law prohibiting the carrying of weapons within a thousand yards of a school, on the ground that this measure had no serious connection with interstate commerce.

bureaucratic controls, with harmful consequences for the economy. At the same time, international standards are likely to make government policies less responsive to popular opinion, with harmful consequences for the health of democracy.

Trade agreements seem at first sight to refute the first concern: the general effect of GATT standards and regional agreements like NAFTA has been to open markets to foreign competition, stimulating competitive energy even among domestic concerns. Yet fear of foreign competition has stimulated angry demands, among labor leaders, environmentalists and safety advocates, for new international standards. Bills to this effect began appearing in Congress in 1995. Proponents argue that lower regulatory standards in some countries put unfair competitive pressure on countries with higher standards, forcing the latter to reduce their own regulatory ambitions. International "harmonization" of standards is urged as the solution to this problem.[38]

But competitive pressure generally has salutary effects, forcing managers to reconsider priorities and strive for improvements in efficiency. The logic of regulatory harmonization is to safeguard governments from competitive pressures to improve their own regulatory systems. Apart from government regulators themselves, there are bound to be important constituencies demanding harmonization measures to protect the existing government standards by extending them to trade partners. Expanded trade inevitably has a dislocating effect on some domestic producers, undermining support for trade liberalization at least among some constituencies. Coalitions to support trade liberalization must therefore undertake gestures or compromises to retain their strength. The NAFTA side-accords on labor and the environment were an initial illustration of this tendency.

As noted earlier, the NAFTA side accords allow each of the NAFTA members to challenge the practices of the other members before arbitration panels, on the grounds that a country is neglecting to enforce its own labor or environmental laws. Whatever the intention of the drafters, this arrangement is not, in practice, a restriction applying only to Mexico. One of the first challenges brought to the special commission charged with overseeing the environmental accord was a complaint by American environmentalists that the United States was failing to enforce its Endangered Species Act because of a Republican-enacted measure exempting certain forest lands from the

---

[38] For a detailed and discriminating survey of such proposals, see Daniel C. Esty, *Greening the GATT: Trade, Environment and the Future* (Washington, DC: Institute for International Economics, 1994).

ESA.[39] Though this particular complaint was dismissed on technical grounds, the general principle is clear: it has now become a matter for international supervision how the United States enforces its own environmental laws. And there are many calls for expanding the principle.

So far, to be sure, little has come of such calls. Even the latest round of the GATT still generally holds to the traditional principle of trade agreements: countries adhering to the GATT are supposed to limit themselves to imposing import controls based on the character of particular goods (if they are, for example, judged dangerous to consumers under the regulatory standards of the importing country) but not to control production methods in the country of origin. But this principle is under considerable strain. It is already implicitly violated by a series of international environmental agreements that call on signatories to impose trade sanctions, in the last resort, to punish violation of these standards (on such matters as use of dangerous chemicals, trade in endangered species and so on). The World Trade Organization, now charged with enforcing the trade standards negotiated under GATT, has promised to work out formulas for reconciling contrary commitments on trade and environmental standards. When the WTO was established in 1994, both the French and American governments urged that it consider still more ambitious policies aimed at harmonizing labor protection standards and domestic environmental standards around the world. Advocates of such exclusionary policies may be restrained by international trade rules, or the rules may be adjusted to incorporate their policies and so win their support. The policy of the Clinton administration appears to be to seek both outcomes simultaneously.

And this is the point to notice: There are at present no clear limits on what promises the United States may make regarding its own domestic polices in order to win international acceptance for similar policies abroad. The bargaining is open-ended. It is also numbingly entangled and obscure, creating many opportunities for special interest deals. The potential for encouraging statist, market-clogging controls is thus reinforced by the second general tendency of international controls: their tendency to distance policymaking from normal channels of democratic accountability.

The human rights agreements, which also lean in many respects toward statist and bureaucratic controls, illustrate this tendency most

[39] "NAFTA: Environmentalists to Seek Investigation," Bureau of National Affairs, *International Environmental Reporter, Current Reports* 18, no. 16 (August 9, 1995): 607.

sharply. In one sense, this is inherent in the enterprise: instead of a consensus of American representatives, the conventions represent a consensus of representatives from around the world, where American views must be compromised and constrained for the sake of agreement. But democratic controls are even more attenuated than that. The conventions are negotiated in particular committees of the UN's Economic and Social Council—that is, in very specialized arenas—to which governments do not seem to pay much attention. The Convention on the Rights of the Child, for example, was negotiated during the 1980s. The conservative Reagan administration in the United States, while prepared to challenge Third World majorities at the UN on some issues (like the Law of the Sea Treaty) and eager to appeal to social conservatives at home, made no serious effort to challenge the final form of this treaty. Yet this convention comprises a liberal bureaucrat's wish-list, including guarantees against interference (including parental interference) with the child's correspondence and reading and viewing preferences, combined with a guarantee that government will ensure "mass media . . . material" for the "promotion of [the child's] social, spiritual and moral well-being and . . . mental health" and culminating in a general governmental guarantee to every child of a "standard of living adequate for the child's physical, mental, spiritual, moral and social development."[40] The drafting of this convention was a very low priority for the Reagan State Department so it proceeded in the context of UN euphoria about state-funded and state-mandated equalization schemes.

Such inattention by governments is, in turn, related to another fundamental feature of international standardization which may make it less accountable than normal democratic politics. In most cases, the standards agreed upon do not have the same status as domestic law. Some countries have no intention of complying with international human rights agreements, for example, and therefore cheerfully sign anything which allows them to make a good speech at the signing ceremony. International enforcement mechanisms in this field are particularly weak (at most amounting to the risk of a scolding report by an international investigating commission; and even that may be kept secret). Even trade and environmental agreements are enforced by specific complaints, leading to specific sanctions by importing nations (against the exporter). So a poor country may well violate many provisions with impunity, if it is not a major exporter to

---

[40] "Convention on the Rights of the Child," Adopted by UN General Assembly, Nov. 20, 1989, 28 I.L.M. 1448 (1989); referenced provisions from Articles 13, 16, 17, 27.

countries that care about those particular provisions—or if it has other ways of influencing the major importing countries (like the United States), to go easy on it. China, which has escaped any serious trade sanction for using slave labor (prohibited under a long established international convention), is not likely to face serious sanctions for failure to adhere to environmental agreements, either.

Log-rolling is a familiar factor in all political bargaining. But in domestic politics, those who support a measure simply to win the good will of its primary sponsors, must live with the consequences of the measure they have supported. In international politics, this is often not so. No one seriously pretends that international human rights conventions must mean the same thing in every country that subscribes to them. In 1994, for example, a UN committee charged with monitoring compliance with the Covenant on Civil and Political Rights ruled that the Australian state of Tasmania was in violation of the treaty by its maintenance of traditional laws against sodomy. Needless to say, the very vague, general formulas in that convention make no explicit mention of rights to sexual self-expression, much less to gay rights. It is, to say the least, highly doubtful that any of the diplomats who drafted that convention in the 1950s and 1960s (the drafting occupied twenty years of desultory meetings) had such guarantees in mind. At any rate, this interpretation of the treaty is most unlikely to be urged on Saudi Arabia. The Attorney General of Australia took up this interpretation with alacrity, however, declaring that the federal Parliament of Australia must now overrule the conservative state of Tasmania in order to achieve conformity with Australia's international commitments.[41]

The United States has not made its adherence to human rights conventions (nor to various trade and environmental treaties) self-executing—that is, it has not promised to make them directly enforceable in domestic courts. We can violate human rights norms and risk nothing more than a scolding. We can violate trade or environmental norms and risk nothing more than particular trade sanctions from other countries. This has no doubt made it easier to achieve Senate ratification (or congressional approval) of agreements that might be much more controversial if presented directly in domestic legislation. Again, it encourages political inattention; or, to put the same point in a different light, it encourages the delegation of policy-making to specialized political groupings, responsive to specialized

---

[41] For background, see James D. Wilets, "International Human Rights Law and Sexual Orientation," *Hastings International and Comparative Law Review* 18 (1994): 1–120, esp. 50–53.

constituencies. After all, none of the standards involved are "for real." Except that they may be real if an administration chooses to see them as such.

Agreements that are not formally binding in domestic law may indeed still influence court decisions. After all, the United States retains an obligation, in international law, to live up to its treaty commitments. Even if American courts are not empowered to enforce a particular treaty, courts have a duty to reduce conflict between American legislation and American treaty commitments whenever they can. An easy way to achieve this would be, again, to interpret legislation in light of international treaty standards—on human rights, trade or whatever it may be. It has even been argued that courts should interpret provisions of the U.S. Constitution to harmonize them, as much as possible, with international standards on human rights.[42] In fact, federal courts, including the U.S. Supreme Court, have already begun to cite international treaty norms as reference points for deliberating on the proper understanding of U.S. constitutional guarantees of basic rights.[43] No international treaty has been made the basis of decision, but litigants are already organized to urge such arguments and federal judges have shown some willingness to take note of them.

So we may soon see international standards cited more routinely to bolster the case for one or another controversial court ruling—on gay rights, for example, or the rights of children to defy parental preferences or the obligation of localities to impose drastic limits on automobile usage. Congress could probably cancel the effect of any decision that roused too much opposition. But that is true, ultimately, even of unpopular constitutional decisions. It is not easy to mobilize Congress for a confrontation with the courts and it may be especially difficult when the matter is presented as one involving international commitments. True, agreements concluded in the fantasy world of international happy talk may look quite different in congressional estimates when they are suddenly converted into real law. But it is always hard to predict how politicians will respond to the unexpected appearance of new realities. The one thing which seems unlikely at this point is that a confident legal argument will be offered to the effect that the treaty power cannot possibly commit the United States to change its policy on issues of domestic policy.

[42] See, e.g., Jordan J. Paust, "Rereading the First Amendment in Light of Treatises Proscribing Incitement to Racial Discrimination or Hostility," *Rutgers Law Review* 43 (1991): 565-73.
[43] See Richard Lillich, "International Human Rights Law in U.S. Courts," *Journal of Transnational Law & Policy* 2 (1993): 1–22.

V. Perils of Positivism

The Rehnquist Court has not been very receptive to arguments from international law. On the few occasions it has had to deal with international law, it has, in almost every case, shown a great coolness to arguments that international law should pose any serious constraint on American policy. On the other hand, the Court has shown almost no interest in articulating constitutional limits on the authority of the American government to commit itself to international norms. Nor has it shown much interest in articulating a vision of international law more compatible with the defense of American sovereignty. The Court may change direction with retirements and new appointments in the next few years. If a new Court does seek to make international law a launching pad for more activist policy directions, it will not find much precedent from the Rehnquist Court standing in its way.

There are at least three doctrines or categories of doctrine which might be used to brake the inroads of international commitments on American sovereignty. First, the Court might seek to revitalize constitutional limits on the treaty power. Second, it might seek to revitalize a vision of international law, insofar as it is enforced in American courts, as fundamentally a law regarding sovereign states. Third, the Court might seek to articulate structural norms of the Constitution that limit the delegation of governing responsibilities to foreign authorities. Thus far, however, the Rehnquist Court has done little to develop any of these approaches and has already made some decisions that may undermine them.

Perhaps the most pressing need is for a revitalization of the old doctrine that the treaty power has definite limits—that Congress cannot simply make anything at all the "supreme law of the land" (nor even an international obligation of the United States) by calling it a "treaty" or an "agreement." It might be useful to reconsider whether an agreement not endorsed by two-thirds of the Senate can ever be binding in domestic law. It certainly would be appropriate to consider whether a mere promise to be nice, without any real exchange or element of reciprocity—as in the human rights conventions—can actually have the legal status of a "treaty." It would be most appropriate to consider whether domestic policy matters with no serious or direct effect on foreign nations can properly be made the subjects of international agreements. The Rehnquist Court has made a number of decisions involving the interpretation of treaties, but has contented itself with parsing particular provisions in such cases, without addressing underlying questions about the rightful scope of the treaty power.

The Court has done somewhat better in acknowledging some implicit limits in the law of nations, but only somewhat better. This is admittedly a tricky matter. The Court has always acknowledged that Congress can overrule American obligations under international law (just as it can override a treaty commitment), if it determines to do so. There remains, however, an important question regarding presumptions. Should the Court presume that Congress has meant to stay within the bounds of international law when congressional enactments are ambiguous? It is settled doctrine (if not always scrupulously observed in practice) that legislation should be interpreted to avoid conflict with treaties. But what about conflicts with broader principles of international law? Here is an opportunity for the Court to articulate its own vision regarding the proper aims and limits of international law. But it is not an opportunity much exploited by the Rehnquist Court.

The Court gave an inkling of what might be done in the 1991 case *Equal Employment Opportunity Commission v. Arab American Oil Company.*[44] Here the question was whether the prohibitions on employment discrimination in the 1964 Civil Rights Act should be interpreted as applying to employers operating overseas. Chief Justice Rehnquist's majority opinion held that, while the legislative history was ambiguous, the reach of the law should be limited to American territory: "Without clearer evidence of congressional intent . . . we are unwilling to ascribe to that body a policy which would raise difficult issues of international law by imposing this country's employment-discrimination regime upon foreign corporations operating in foreign commerce." Yet Rehnquist's opinion did not trouble to articulate the relevant "issues of international law" nor to refute the claim of the three dissenters that international law posed no barrier to the regulation of labor practices (by American firms) in foreign countries.

In other cases, the Rehnquist Court was even more flippant about the claims of international law. In perhaps the most notable case, that of the *United States v. Alvarez-Machain*[45] in 1992, the Supreme Court overruled objections to the trial of a Mexican national, forcibly abducted from Mexico by American agents and then put on trial in the United States for the murder of an American drug enforcement agent back in Mexico. Defense lawyers argued that the United States was committed, by its extradition treaty with Mexico, to seek extradition of criminals by formal request to the Mexican government. Chief Justice Rehnquist's opinion held that while the treaty

[44] 499 U.S. 244 (1991).
[45] 112 S.Ct. 2188 (1992).

did provide for a formal system of extradition, it did not specifically prohibit the United States from bypassing this system and simply grabbing wanted criminals from Mexican territory on its own.

It was a rather strained interpretation of the treaty on its face (as three dissenting justices argued). The ruling also flew in the face of the general doctrines of international law which make such treaties necessary: sovereign states are not supposed to interfere in the internal affairs of other sovereign states, least of all by forcible abductions of the citizens of those other states. But the Rehnquist Court dismissed the point as of no relevance to the case: "Respondent and his *amici* may be correct that respondent's abduction . . . may be in violation of general international law principles" but "the decision of whether respondent should be returned to Mexico, as a matter outside the [U.S.-Mexico Extradition] Treaty, is a matter for the Executive Branch." The Court refused to let "general international law principles" guide its interpretation of the treaty.

So the Court has rather quickly tossed away what might prove to be, in another case, a quite useful safeguard of American sovereignty—the doctrine that international law requires respect for the territorial integrity of sovereign states. The most important issue is not (as the dissenters in *Alvarez-Machain* suggested) whether other countries will follow the American example in retaliation for American aggressions. Rather, the key concern should be whether the American government (absent clear and convincing congressional authorization) can trade away American sovereignty when this may seem convenient. Could the United States, for example, agree to extradite American citizens to a foreign tribunal for trial of offenses committed within the territorial limits of the United States? Could the American government allow environmental or labor or human rights cases, concerning incidents involving only Americans and occurring solely within American territory, to be decided by foreign tribunals? The Court lost an opportunity to build some limiting doctrine against such developments.

There remains a third area where the Court might seek to resist the encroachments of international commitments on American sovereignty. That would be to insist on certain implicit limitations on the delegation of constitutional authority to extra-constitutional authorities. It was once established doctrine that Congress may not delegate its legislative authority to private citizens or to private business firms.[46]

---

[46] See, e.g., *Carter v. Carter Coal Co.*, 298 U.S. 238, 311 (1936) ("delegation . . . to private persons" is "legislative delegation in its most obnoxious form"). For a more recent affirmation of the doctrine, see *Amalgamated Meat Cutters and Butcher Workmen v. Connally*, 337 F. Supp. 737, 763 (D.D.C. 1971).

Similar reasoning seems to imply that neither judicial nor executive authority can be delegated to private entities (except perhaps in some very special circumstances). It would be quite strange to think that while governmental authority cannot be delegated to private American citizens, it can be delegated to foreign governments or foreign institutions—which are, after all, even more removed from the American body politic.

Yet this sort of appeal to implicit structural principles has not found much sympathy from the Rehnquist Court. In its most important ruling on the constitutional status of executive power—the challenge to the statute providing for appointment of independent counsels by a judicial panel[47]—the Rehnquist Court held that even the core executive function of prosecuting crime may be transferred outside the executive branch, when Congress, by statute, has so provided. *Morrison* may be more than an instructive analogy. It may be an omen.

As Professors Steven Calabresi and Kevin Rhodes have recently shown,[48] the argument that allows executive authority to be splintered and displaced from presidential control lays the groundwork for a similar fracturing of judicial authority by statute. If "the executive power," which, according to Article II, Sec. 1, "shall be vested in a President of the United States," can be displaced to outside authorities, then it is difficult to give full force to the parallel phrasing of Article III, Sec. 1, stipulating, "The Judicial Power of the United States shall be vested in one supreme court and in such inferior courts as the Congress may . . . establish." If Congress may allocate executive duties to officials not accountable to the president, it would seem equally within the power of Congress to allocate judicial authority to foreign tribunals, neither appointed by the president nor accountable to the Supreme Court. As we have seen, this is precisely what Congress has already done in enacting NAFTA. It is what Congress might do on a larger scale in implementing American participation in an international criminal court. The doctrines of the Rehnquist Court place no evident constitutional barriers in the way of such developments.

This may be too pessimistic a view. It may be that the proper case would call forth a different attitude, at least regarding the authority of Congress (or the president) to delegate sovereign powers to foreign authorities. It may be argued, moreover, that the political process will

---

[47] *Morrison v. Olson*, 487 U.S. 654 (1987).

[48] Steven G. Calabresi and Kevin H. Rhodes, "The Structural Constitution: Unitary Executive, Plural Judiciary," *Harvard Law Review* 105 (1995): 1153–1216.

provide adequate checks on the degree to which Congress or the president may follow out the temptation to cede traditional sovereign powers to international authorities. We have sustained a long and vigorous debate in recent decades over the permissible scope of presidential war powers under the Constitution, even while federal courts have declined to take up any case that might have allowed them to offer more authoritative clarification on this subject. We might, in the same way, have a useful and effective debate over the constitutional limits of the treaty power, without the benefit of authoritative judicial advice.

Yet war is an extraordinary and exceptional situation. It is always difficult to weigh precedents amidst the clash of arms. By contrast, the emerging danger from abuses of the treaty power is not in the exceptional episode but precisely in the accumulation of legal precedents, building an ever more developed and dense network of connections between American policies and international standards. If courts do not have constitutional limits to invoke, they will, themselves, be drawn into the process of eroding American sovereignty.

The Supreme Court traces its ultimate authority to the Constitution which is ordained and established by "We the People." It seems, at the least, quite incongruous that the Court should assist in the gradual transfer of constitutional authority from the representatives of "the People"—this people, the American people—to some wider constellation of the "powers of the Earth."

INDEX

Aaron. See *Cooper v. Aaron*
Ableman v. Booth, 17
abortion, 130, 188
Abraham Lincoln (Charnwood), 96
Abrams v. United States, 11–12n21
academic scholarship, and constitutional criminal procedure, 115
Academics for the Second Amendment, 159
activists, vs. restraintists, 213
Adams, Abigail, 78
Adams, John, 5, 29
Adams, John Quincy, 6
Adams v. New York, 116n26
administrative state, 211–31; concept of, 175; and Supreme Court, 230–31; as welfare state, 211
affirmative action, 104
African-American citizens, and Civil Rights Act, 143, 147
Agnello v. United States, 116n26
airlines, 198
Airports Case, 243–53
Alien and Sedition Acts, 65, 78
Allwright. See *Smith v. Allwright*
Alvarez-Machain. See *United States v. Alvarez-Machain*
Amalgamated Meat Cutters and Butcher Workmen v. Connally, 280n46
Amendments, to U.S. Constitution. See *individual amendments*
American Bar Association (ABA), 260
American Civil Liberties Union (ACLU), 13, 39, 356n2
Americans United. See *Valley Forge College v. Americans United*

Ames. See *Champion v. Ames*
Amish, 39n27
Amos v. United States, 116n26
Angelou, Maya, 7
Anglo predominance, in culture, 49
Annals of Congress (Gates, ed.), 157, 160n9, 163n17, 167n30, 170n43, 172n49, 191n111
Anti-Federalists, 4, 10; vs. Federalists, 157; and trial by jury, 61
apartheid, 39
Arab American Oil Company. See *Equal Employment Opportunity Commission v. Arab American Oil Company*
Argentina, 264
Aristotle, 47, 89n55
armies, Congress's power to raise, 191
Army Air Corps, 95
Article I (of U.S. Constitution): Section 2, 81; Section 3, 81; Section 7, 236; Section 8, 57, 84, 184n90, 195; Section 10, 32, 33
Article III, 58, 60, 74
Article IV, 84
Article VI, 59, 69, 89, 262, 263
Articles of Confederation, 54, 57, 225–26
Australia, 276

Bacon Francis, 95
Baker v. Carr, 86n44, 87
Banco Nacional de Cuba v. Sabbatino, 264n11
Barnette. See *West Virginia Board of Education v. Barnette*
Barron v. Baltimore, 110

283

CONTRIBUTORS

Akhil Reed Amar is Southmayd Professor of Law at Yale Law School.

George Anastaplo is Professor of Law, Loyola University of Chicago; Lecturer in the Liberal Arts, The University of Chicago; and Professor Emeritus of Political Science and of Philosophy, Dominican University.

Hadley Arkes is Edward Ney Professor of Jurisprudence and American Institutions at Amherst College.

Randy E. Barnett is Austin B. Fletcher Professor of Law at Boston University.

Walter Berns is Resident Scholar at the American Enterprise Institute and John M. Olin University Professor Emeritus at Georgetown University.

Gerard V. Bradley is Professor of Law at Notre Dame Law School.

Stanley C. Brubaker is Professor of Political Science at Colgate University.

Robert P. George is Associate Professor of Politics at Princeton University.

Randall Kennedy is Professor of Law at Harvard Law School.

Nelson Lund is Professor of Law and Associate Dean for Academic Affairs at George Mason University School of Law.

Ken Masugi is Distinguished Visiting Professor of Political Science at the United States Air Force Academy and a Senior Fellow at the Ashbrook Center for Public Affairs and at the Claremont Institute.

David K. Nichols is Associate Professor of Political Science at Montclair State University.

Jeremy Rabkin is Associate Professor of Government at Cornell University.

James R. Stoner, Jr. is Associate Professor and Director of Graduate Studies in the Department of Political Science at Louisiana State University.

Bradford P. Wilson is Executive Director and Acting President of the National Association of Scholars in Princeton and Professor of Political Science at Ashland University.

Michael Zuckert is Dorothy and Edward Congdon Professor of Political Science at Carleton College and Visiting Professor of Political Science at Fordham University.

DATE DUE